Windows *Me* explained

by

N. Kantaris
and
P.R.M. Oliver

Bernard Babani (publishing) Ltd
The Grampians
Shepherds Bush Road
London W6 7NF
England
www.babanibooks.com

Please Note

Although every care has been taken with the production of this book to ensure that any projects, designs, modifications and/or programs, etc., contained herewith, operate in a correct and safe manner and also that any components specified are normally available in Great Britain, the Publishers and Author(s) do not accept responsibility in any way for the failure (including fault in design) of any project, design, modification or program to work correctly or to cause damage to any equipment that it may be connected to or used in conjunction with, or in respect of any other damage or injury that may be so caused, nor do the Publishers accept responsibility in any way for the failure to obtain specified components.

Notice is also given that if equipment that is still under warranty is modified in any way or used or connected with home-built equipment then that warranty may be void.

First Published - December 2000
Reprinted - February 2001
Reprinted - May 2001

British Library Cataloguing in Publication Data:

A catalogue record for this book is available from the British Library

ISBN 0 85934 493 2

Cover Design by Gregor Arthur
Printed and Bound in Great Britain by Cox & Wyman

Windows *Me* explained

Books Available

By both authors:

BP327 DOS one step at a time
BP337 A Concise User's Guide to Lotus 1-2-3 for Windows
BP341 MS-DOS explained
BP346 Programming in Visual Basic for Windows
BP352 Excel 5 explained
BP362 Access one step at a time
BP387 Windows one step at a time
BP388 Why not personalise your PC
BP400 Windows 95 explained
BP406 MS Word 95 explained
BP407 Excel 95 explained
BP408 Access 95 one step at a time
BP409 MS Office 95 one step at a time
BP415 Using Netscape on the Internet*
BP420 E-mail on the Internet*
BP426 MS-Office 97 explained
BP428 MS-Word 97 explained
BP429 MS-Excel 97 explained
BP430 MS-Access 97 one step at a time
BP433 Your own Web site on the Internet
BP448 Lotus SmartSuite 97 explained
BP456 Windows 98 explained*
BP460 Using Microsoft Explorer 4 on the Internet*
BP464 E-mail and news with Outlook Express*
BP465 Lotus SmartSuite Millennium explained
BP471 Microsoft Office 2000 explained
BP472 Microsoft Word 2000 explained
BP473 Microsoft Excel 2000 explained
BP474 Microsoft Access 2000 explained
BP478 Microsoft Works 2000 explained
BP486 Using Linux the easy way*
BP488 Internet Explorer 5 explained*
BP487 Quicken 2000 UK explained*
BP491 Windows 2000 explained*
BP493 Windows Me explained*
BP498 Using Visual Basic

By Noel Kantaris:

BP258 Learning to Program in C
BP259 A Concise Introduction to UNIX*
BP284 Programming in QuickBASIC
BP325 A Concise User's Guide to Windows 3.1

The Windows Background

Microsoft produced the first version of Windows in 1983 as a graphical extension to its Disc Operating System (MS-DOS). However, it was not a great success because, being DOS based, it was confined to the DOS memory limit of 1MB of RAM. Mind you, at that time, not many PCs had that much memory!

In 1987, an Intel 386 processor specific version of Windows was brought out that was able to run in multiple 'virtual 8086' mode, but Windows applications were still unable to use any extended memory above the 1MB. In 1990, however, Windows version 3.0 solved this problem and became a huge success.

Two years later, the much needed update, Windows 3.1, was released to fix most of the program bugs in version 3.0. The horrendous and frequent 'Unrecoverable Application Error' message became a thing of the past (well, almost!). Windows for Workgroups 3.1, followed in October 1992, and started to give the program the power to control small networked groups of computers. This was strengthened in October 1993 with the 3.11 release, which included 32-bit file management and more networking support.

Then, three year later, came Windows 95, a 32-bit operating system in its own right which made full use of the 32-bit features of the then available range of Intel processor chips. Microsoft had also put a lot of effort into this system to make it compatible with almost all existing Windows and MS-DOS based applications. This was obviously necessary, but it meant that parts of Windows 95 were still only 16-bit in operation.

June 1998 saw the launch of Windows 98, the long awaited refined upgrade to Windows 95, which ran faster, crashed less frequently, supported a host of new technologies, such as Digital Video Disc for storing digital video on PCs, improved MMX multimedia, and was year 2000 compliant. In May 1999 Windows 98 Second Edition was released.

In February 2000, Microsoft released Windows 2000 Professional, together with two additional Windows NT compatible versions of the software; Server and Advanced Server. Users of Windows 95/98 could easily upgrade (and many have) to the Windows 2000 Professional version of this Operating System (OS), while users of Windows NT could use one of the other two versions of the OS to upgrade their system according to their requirements.

Finally, in September 2000, Microsoft released Windows Me (Millennium edition), as the direct upgrade to Windows 95/98 for the home PC. At first glance, Windows Me looks nearly identical to Windows 98. The changes to the desktop icons, Start menu and the Control Panel are very subtle indeed and many are borrowed from Windows 2000. However, Windows Me has many improvements incorporated into it which fall into four general categories. These are:

- Added features that make Windows Me load faster, run more reliably, and if things go radically wrong through interference by the user, then you are allowed to return to a previous working version of the Operating System.
- Wizards that let you set up home networks a lot easier and give you the ability to share Internet connections.
- Improved support for digital cameras, video recorders, and multimedia with the introduction of the Windows Media Player 7.
- Improved features and tools in Internet Explorer 5.5 allow better printing capabilities, faster performance, and better Web communication from e-mail to instant messaging to video conferencing.

All these improvements will be introduced and discussed in due course at the appropriate section of the book.

About this Book

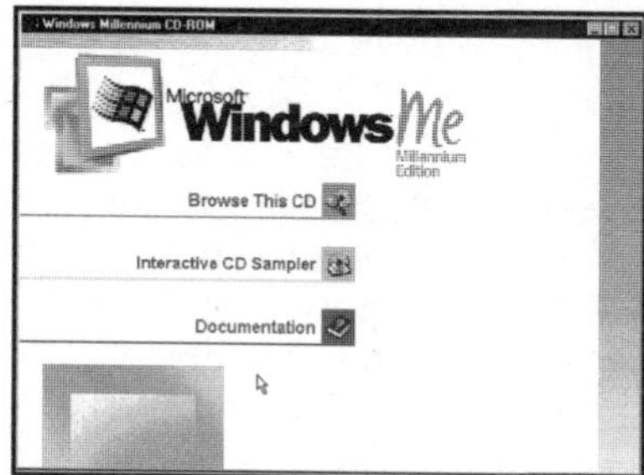

Windows Me explained was written to help both the beginner and those moving from older versions of Windows to the Windows Millennium edition. The material in the book is presented on the 'what you need to know first, appears first' basis, although you don't have to start at the beginning and go right through to the end. The more experienced user can start from any section, as they have been designed to be self-contained.

We start this book by discussing the system requirements for Windows Me, and the preparation needed prior to installing it, depending on whether you are upgrading from an earlier Windows version, or installing it on a brand new disc.

Windows Me comes with a Graphical User Interface (GUI) front end identical to that of Windows 98, and includes built-in accessories such as a text editor, a paint program and many other multimedia, networking, electronic communication, and power saving features, most of which are examined in this book. Getting to grips with Windows Me, as described, will also reduce the learning curve when it comes to using other Windows application packages. For example, once you have installed your printers and learned how to switch between them and print from them, you should never again have any difficulty printing from any Windows program. Also, learning to manipulate text and graphics in WordPad and Paint will lay very strong foundations on which to build expertise when you need to master a fully blown word processor with strong elements of desktop publishing.

The book was written with the busy person in mind. You don't need to read many hundreds of large format pages to find out most of what there is to know about the subject, when fewer pages can get you going quite adequately! It is hoped that with the help of this book, you will be able to get the most out of your computer, when using Windows Me, in terms of efficiency and productivity, and that you will be able to do it in the shortest, most effective and enjoyable way.

An attempt has been made not to use too much 'jargon', but with this subject, some is inevitable, so a fairly detailed glossary of terms is included, which should be used with the text of this book where necessary. Have fun!

If you would like to purchase a Companion Disc for any of the books, by the same author(s), in the Books Available list, **apart from this one and the ones marked with an asterisk**, containing the file/program listings which appear in them, then fill in the form at the back of the book and send it to Phil Oliver at the stipulated address.

About the Authors

Noel Kantaris graduated in Electrical Engineering at Bristol University and after spending three years in the Electronics Industry in London, took up a Tutorship in Physics at the University of Queensland. Research interests in Ionospheric Physics, led to the degrees of M.E. in Electronics and Ph.D. in Physics. On return to the UK, he took up a Post-Doctoral Research Fellowship in Radio Physics at the University of Leicester, and then in 1973 a lecturing position in Engineering at the Camborne School of Mines, Cornwall, (part of Exeter University), where between 1978 and 1997 he was also the CSM Computing Manager. At present he is IT Director of FFC Ltd.

Phil Oliver graduated in Mining Engineering at Camborne School of Mines in 1967 and since then has specialised in most aspects of surface mining technology, with a particular emphasis on computer related techniques. He has worked in Guyana, Canada, several Middle Eastern and Asian countries, South Africa and the United Kingdom, on such diverse projects as: the planning and management of bauxite, iron, gold and coal mines; rock excavation contracting in the UK; international mining equipment sales and international mine consulting. In 1988 he took up a lecturing position at Camborne School of Mines (part of Exeter University) in Surface Mining and Management. He retired from full-time lecturing in 1998, to spend more time writing, consulting and developing Web sites for clients.

Acknowledgements

We would like to thank Microsoft UK for providing the Windows Me Operating System software, also friends and colleagues for their helpful tips and suggestions which assisted us in the writing of this book.

Trademarks

HP and LaserJet are registered trademarks of Hewlett Packard Corporation.

IBM is a registered trademark of International Business Machines, Inc.

Intel is a registered trademark of Intel Corporation.

Microsoft, **MS-DOS**, **Windows**, **Windows Me**, **Windows 2000** and **Windows NT**, are either registered trademarks or trademarks of Microsoft Corporation.

PostScript is a registered trademark of Adobe Systems Incorporated.

All other brand and product names used in the book are recognised as trademarks, or registered trademarks, of their respective companies.

Contents

1

Package Overview

Windows Me (Millennium edition), Microsoft's latest desktop operating system for the home PC, is an easier to run and more efficient Operating System to install, and far more stable than previous versions of Windows. Microsoft has designed specific features in Windows Me which makes using your computer easier and more fun.

Windows Me is a 32-bit Operating System (OS), which uses a Graphical Interface identical to that of Windows 98 and, unlike Windows 2000, is just as dependant on MS-DOS (the underlining OS) as all previous versions of the program.

As with Windows 95/98, Windows Me adopts the **Start** button on the left of the **Taskbar** at the bottom of the screen. Clicking this button opens up a cascade of menus that allow you to run programs, open your documents, manage your folders and files, and maintain your system.

Windows Me comes with a number of new 'accessory' programs, but retains or upgrades most of those available under Windows 95/98, such as the word processor 'WordPad', the graphics program 'Paint', and the text editor 'Notepad'. All these accessories, new and old, as well as the new unified 'My Computer' tool, which helps you to view local, network, intranet and Internet data simultaneously, will be discussed in some detail. Of course, Windows Me caters for many new technological developments, the main ones of which (see next section) will be discussed at some length.

One of the strengths of Windows Me lies in its ability to manage all your home computing requirements and it turns your PC into a home entertainment centre, by allowing you to work with rich multimedia content such as photos, videos, and music. All of a sudden computing has become great fun!

What is New in Windows Me

Windows Me comes with a range of improvements, as described earlier. These fall within four categories, as follows:

Improved system performance and reliability - Windows Me prevents system problems before they occur by protecting critical system files. If by any chance you manage to mess up the system, then you can use the System Restore tool to return your machine back to a previously working state. This alone, merits upgrading to Windows Me.

Improved home networking - Windows Me allows several computers within a home (not so unusual these days) to be easily networked so that they can share resources, such as files, printer(s), scanner, and Internet connection. In addition, you can use this facility for home entertainment, such as playing a game with another member of the family, each using their own computer. A built-in Wizard will help you to achieve all these easily and quickly.

Improved digital media - Windows Me includes Movie Maker, a tool that allows you to transfer video from your digital or analogue camera (or even VCR) to your computer. Once this is done, you can edit your video, save it on your hard disc (stacks of videos can be saved this way, thanks to a new file format that takes hardly any disc space), and even send your favourite video to a friend via the Internet as an attachment to an e-mail. The same thing can be done with still photography. Just plug in your digital camera and Windows Me will immediately detect it. You can preview photos before downloading them on to your hard disc, edit them, arrange them in a slide show, and send them through the Internet to a friend.

Improved Internet features - Windows Me comes with the latest Web browser, Internet Explorer 5.5 which has improved printing capabilities and faster performance, particularly with its support of broad band Internet connections, such as cable modems and Digital Subscriber Lines (DSL). Internet Explorer 5.5 covers all Web communications, with tools for sending and receiving e-mail, to instant messaging to video conferencing.

Hardware Requirements

To install Windows Me according to Microsoft, you will need an IBM-compatible computer with the following specifications:

- 150 MHz or higher Pentium-compatible CPU.
- 32 MB of RAM recommended minimum; more memory generally improves the operating system's response.
- A hard disc with at least 400 MB of free space for a custom installation, 350 MB for a typical installation, or 200 MB for a compact installation.
- For each of the above installations, choosing to back up your prior version of Windows requires an additional disc space of about 150 MB.

In addition, you will also need a VGA or higher resolution monitor, a CD-ROM or DVD-ROM drive, a mouse or compatible pointing device, and for most Windows Me optional features (see below), a sound card and speakers. For Internet access you will require a modem or fax modem with a minimal speed of 28.8 Kbs and an Internet Service Provider (ISP).

If you intend to use the optional features available with Windows Me, you will also require additional hardware. For example:

To use Web TV, you will need a Pentium compatible or equivalent TV tuner card.

To use Windows Media Player, you will need a SVGA monitor, a Pentium 166 MHz processor or better, 64 MB of RAM, and 1 GB of free hard-disc space.

To use Windows Media Player with portable digital devices, you will need what is listed under Windows Media Player plus a CompactFlash or SmartMedia reader and media.

To use Windows Movie Maker, you will need a SVGA monitor, a Pentium II 300 MHz processor or better, 64 MB of RAM, 2 GB of free hard-disc space, 56.6 Kbs modem or faster, a good quality microphone, and a video capture device.

Information Required Prior to Installation

Before you start installing Windows Me, make sure you have appropriate information to hand. What you need to know, depends on the type of proposed installation. For example:

A. If you are installing Windows Me on to a brand new hard disc, then you will need the full version of Windows Me, unless you have a full product disc from a previous version of Windows, in which case the Windows Me Upgrade product will suffice. Further, if you plan to connect to the Internet, then you will need to provide the Setup program during installation with your Internet Provider's (IP) address which was assigned to you for your Internet and e-mail accounts.

   Installing Windows Me on a clean hard disc (one that has no operating system on it) requires you to make a Windows Me Start up disc. To do this, use the 3½" floppy disc that comes with the Full version of the product and follow the instructions on the disc label, or provide your own disc for the Upgrade version.

B. If you are simply upgrading an existing installation of Windows, then you only need the Windows Me Upgrade product to do so. Your existing system will be upgraded and you will not need to reinstall any of your software packages.

With either installation you will need a formatted floppy disc (3½", 1.44 MB) to hand to make a Start up disc, either as described in A above, or when prompted by the Setup program. Finally, just to be on the safe side, make a complete backup of all your vital data, and make sure you are not running any memory resident programs such as 'virus protection utilities' during installation. If you do, disable them before you start.

Installing Windows Me

To start the installation process, assuming you are upgrading, switch on your computer, start Windows, and insert the Windows Me distribution CD into the CD-ROM drive. After a few seconds the Setup program will run automatically from the CD.

If the Setup program does not run, click the **Start** button and select **Run** from the pop-up menu. Next, type E:\setup, where E is the letter that represents your CD-ROM drive, and click the **OK** button, as shown below.

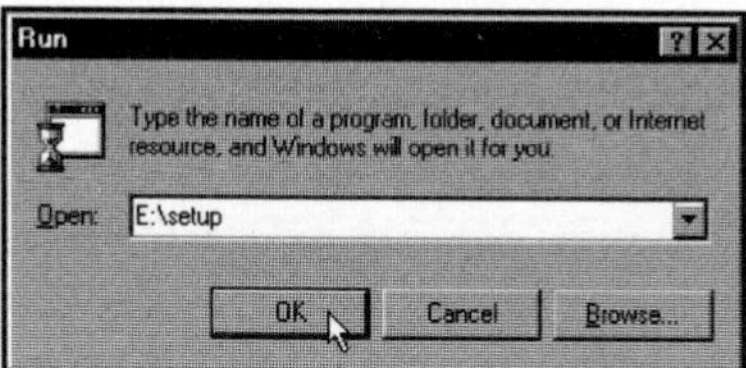

The Setup program then displays the screen shown in Fig. 1.1 below, with a 'Warning' box that states the obvious!

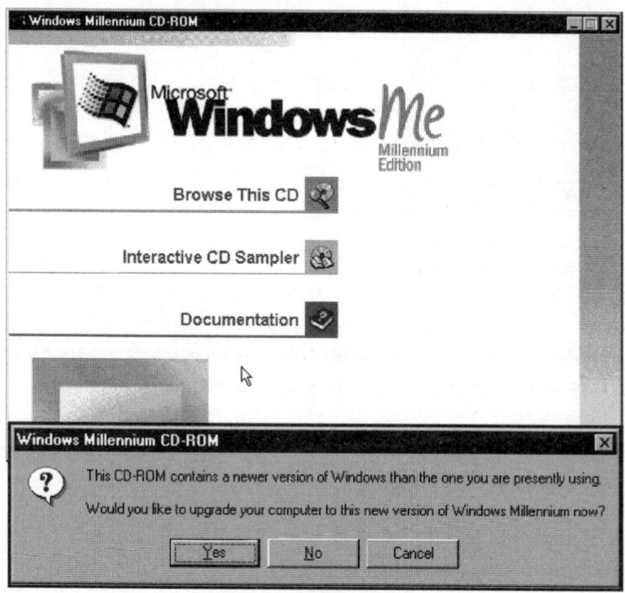

Fig. 1.1 The Windows Me CD-ROM Screen.

Left-clicking the **Yes** button causes the Setup program to check your system, as shown to the left, and prepares the Windows Me Setup Wizard.

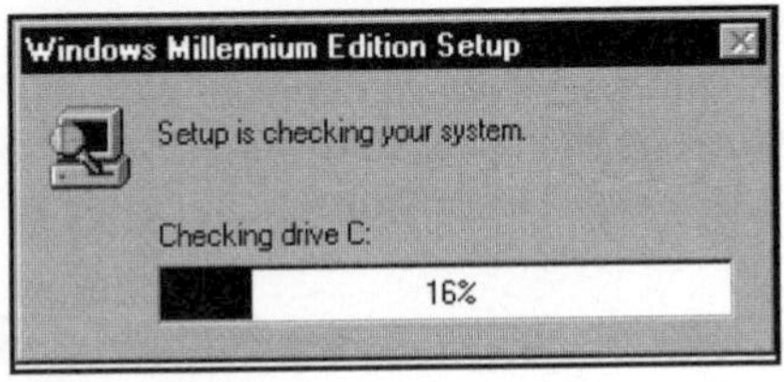

If the Setup program detects that you are running any programs on your computer at this stage a warning box is displayed recommending that you quit all Windows programs before proceeding with the upgrade. Having done this, the Welcome to Windows Me Setup screen is displayed as shown in Fig. 1.2.

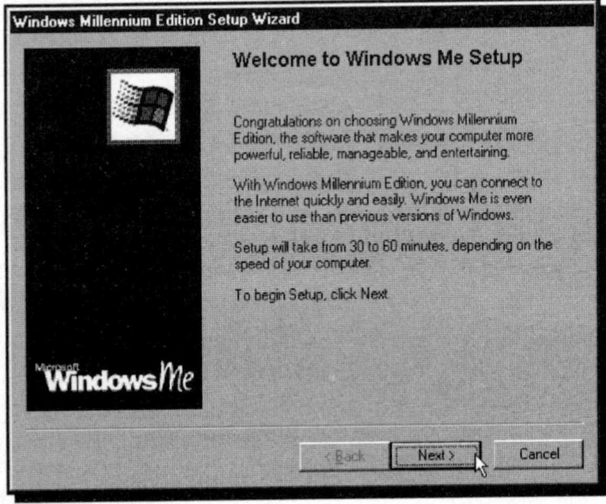

Fig. 1.2 The Welcome to Windows Me Setup Wizard Screen

Pressing the **Next** button displays the Licence Agreement screen shown in Fig. 1.3.

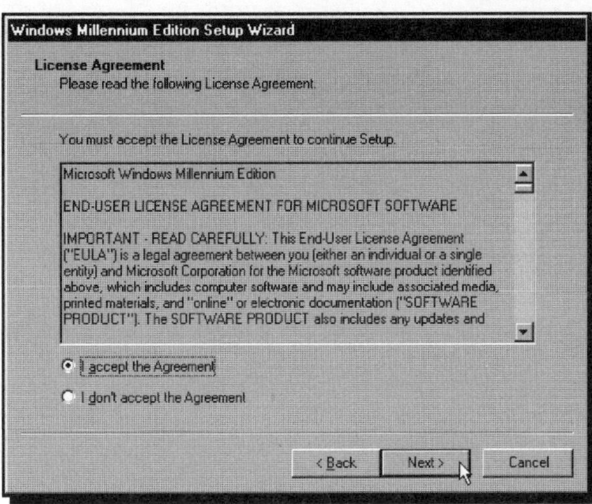

Fig. 1.3 The Windows Me Licence Agreement Screen.

Clicking the **I accept this Agreement** radio button followed by **Next**, displays the next Installation Wizard screen.

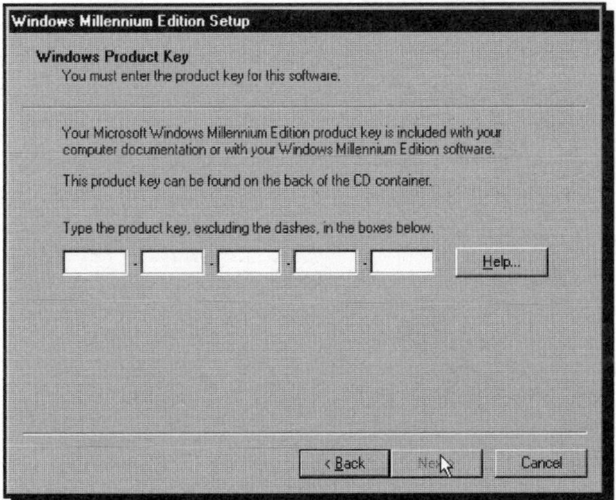

Fig. 1.4 The Product Key Screen.

Type in your Product Key, found on the back of the CD container box, then press **Next** to continue with the installation process.

Setup now performs vital checks on your computer, then checks your hard disc for any problems, and upgrades the computer's registry, followed by a check for installed components and available disc space. Throughout this process, appropriate boxes are displayed on your computer's screen to let you know what is happening.

If all is well, you are asked if you would like to save your system files, so that you can Uninstall Windows Me, and return your system to the previous version of Windows. If you choose to do so (it is recommended), you are asked to select the drive in which to save them.

Next, Setup creates a Start-up Disc, and at this point you will be asked to insert a formatted floppy in the A: drive of your computer. Once a Start-up Disc is created, label the floppy and put it in a safe place. If anything goes wrong with your Windows installation, you can use this disc to start up your computer and run a diagnostic program if need be. Finally, the Ready to Begin Copying Files box is displayed on your screen (Fig. 1.5).

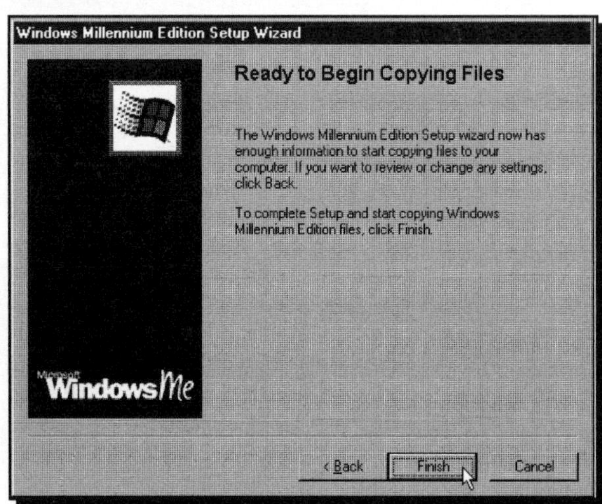

Fig. 1.5 The Ready to Begin Copying Files Screen.

Pressing the **Next** button starts the copying process, and after all the required files are copied (it takes about 30 minutes) and the Thank you screen is displayed, Setup restarts your computer. Next, Setup updates your configuration files, loads Windows Me and initialises its hardware database and sets up your hardware and any Plug and Play devices you might have attached to your system, then it restarts your computer again and continues with finalising the system's settings which takes about 20 minutes depending on your particular installation.

Finally, Setup restarts your computer once more and updates your system's settings, before displaying the Windows Me Multimedia screen which shows a short video clip of the capabilities of the new Operating System. When this fades away, the screen shown in Fig. 1.6 is displayed.

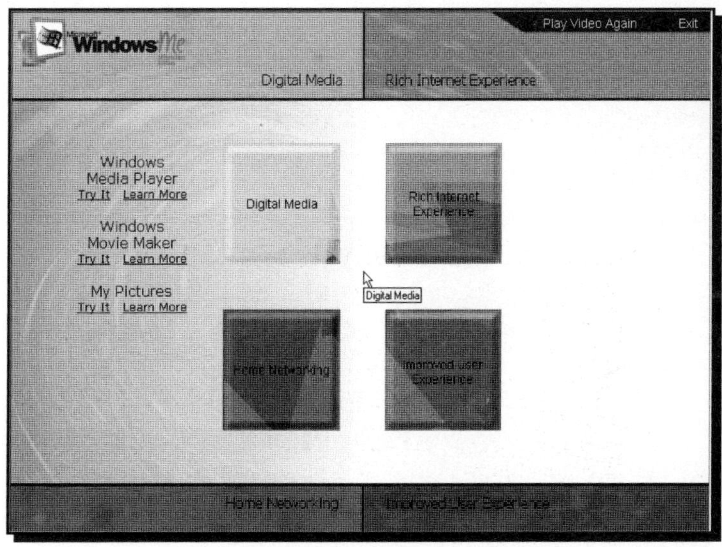

Fig. 1.6 The Windows Me Multimedia Screen.

As you move the mouse pointer across the different areas of this screen, additional information is displayed with links to a Help file.

You might like to spend some time here before clicking on **Exit** at the top right corner. To see this again, click the **Start** button, select **Help** from the pop-up menu, then click on **Tours & tutorials** on the Help and Support screen and select the Windows Millennium Preview hypertext link, as shown below.

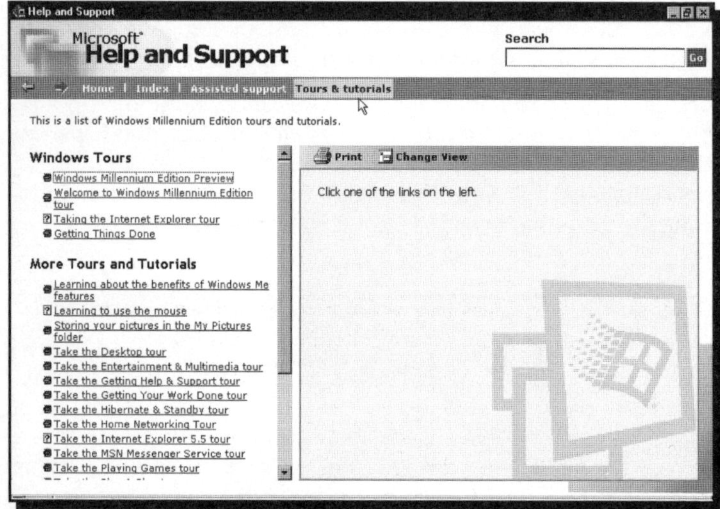

Fig. 1.7 The Help and Support Screen.

The other **Tours & tutorials** hypertext links on the **Help and Support** screen take you through a tour of four main options:

I. Welcome to Windows Millennium Edition tour
II. Taking the Internet Explorer tour
III. Getting Things Done
IV. More Tours and Tutorials

This information, apart from the second option, is read from your Windows Me installation CD which must be placed in the CD-ROM drive. To take the Internet Explorer tour, you require a connection to the Internet, as this is done online, as shown In Fig. 1.8.

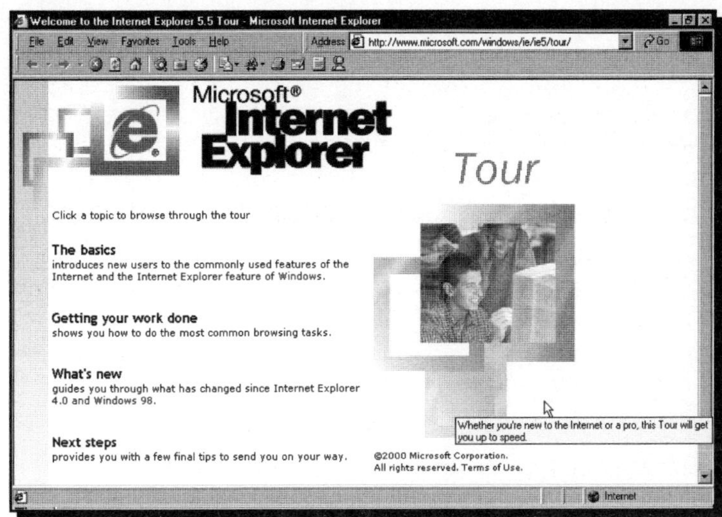

Fig. 1.8 The Internet Explorer Tour.

The four topics covered here are: The Basics, Getting your work done, What's new, and Next steps. It is a pity that you need a connection to the Internet to browse through these topics. Microsoft, of course, assumes that no one has to pay telephone bills while connected to the Internet!

The Windows Me Help system is discussed more fully at the end of Chapter 3.

2

Starting Windows Me

Once Windows Me has been installed, switching on your PC automatically loads the operating system (or displays the dual-boot option, if you have another Operating System on your hard disc).

The Windows Desktop

Below we show the Windows Me working screen, called the 'Desktop', with four items on the left of it identified as 'System icons'. In addition, the 'My Documents' item has been double-clicked with the left mouse button to open its screen.

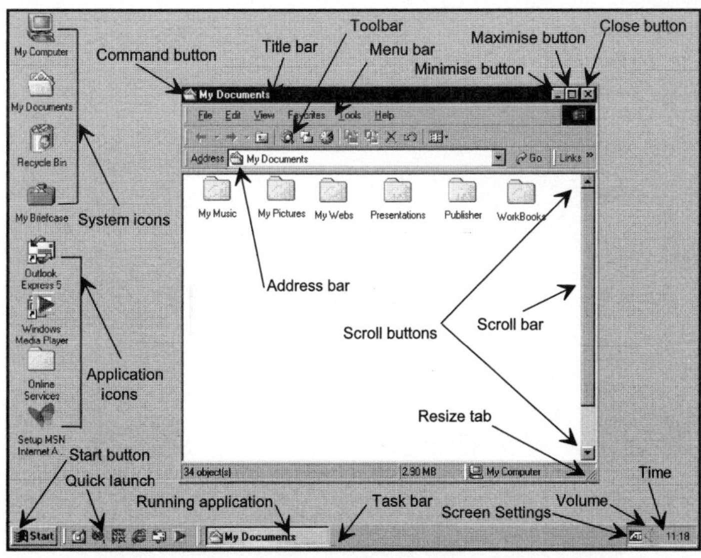

Fig. 2.1 Windows Me Desktop with Running Application.

Parts of a Window

It is worth spending some time looking at the various parts that make up the Windows screen - we use the word 'Windows' to refer to the whole environment, while the word 'windows' refers to application or document windows. Application windows contain running applications, while document windows appear with applications that can open more than one document, but share the application window's menu. Each application, and some documents you choose to work with, open and use separate windows to run in. Although every window has some common elements, not all windows use all of these elements.

An application window is easily opened by either double-clicking its icon on the Desktop, or clicking its name on one of the cascaded menus resulting from clicking the **Start** button and selecting the **Programs** option. When a program is running, an icon is placed on the Taskbar, which allows you to switch between running programs by simply left-clicking them on the Taskbar.

Although multiple application or document windows can be displayed simultaneously, only one is the active window and displays on the top of any other non-active windows. Title bars of non-active windows appear with a lighter shade than that of the active one, as shown below.

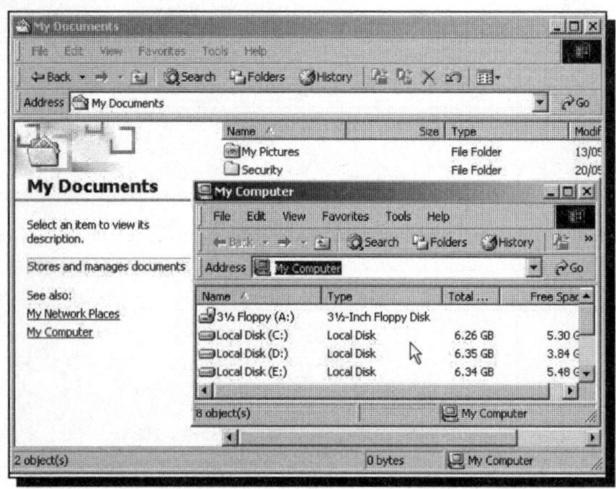

Fig. 2.2 Simultaneous Display of Running Applications.

The typical window is subdivided into several areas which have the following functions:

Area	***Function***
Command button	Clicking on the program icon (see upper-left corner of the My Computer window in Fig. 2.2), displays the pull-down Control menu which can be used to control the program window. It includes commands for restoring, moving, sizing, minimising, maximising, and closing the window.
Title bar	The bar at the top of a window which displays the application name and the name of the current document.
Minimise button	The button you point to and click to store an application as an icon on the Taskbar. Clicking on such an icon will restore the window.
Maximise button	The button you point to and click to fill the screen with the active window. When that happens, the Maximise button changes to a Restore button which can be used to restore the window to its former size.
Close button	The extreme top right button that you click to close a window.

Menu bar	The bar below the Title bar which allows you to choose from several menu options. Clicking on a menu item displays the pull-down menu associated with that item. The options listed in the Menu bar depend on the specific application.
Toolbar	A bar of icons that you click to carry out some common actions.
Address bar	Shows the location of the current folder, or the URL of the new page to go to next.
Scroll bars	The bars on the extreme right and bottom of each window that contain a scroll box. Clicking on these bars allows you to see parts of a document that might not be visible in that size window.
Scroll buttons	The arrowheads at each end of the scroll bars which you click to scroll the window contents up and down one line, or left and right one item at a time.
Resize tab	The area on a window which you drag with the mouse (hold the left mouse button depressed while moving) to resize the window.
Mouse pointer	The arrow which appears when the pointer is placed over menus, scrolling bars, buttons, and folder lists.

The Mouse Pointers

In Windows, as with all other graphical based programs, using a mouse makes many operations both easier and more fun to carry out.

Windows has many different mouse pointers, with the most common illustrated below, which it uses for its various functions. When a program is initially started up probably the first you will see is the hourglass, which turns into an upward pointing hollow arrow. Some of the other shapes, as shown below, depend on the type of work you are doing at the time.

The hourglass which displays when you are waiting while performing a function.

The arrow which appears when the pointer is placed over menus, scrolling bars, and buttons.

The I-beam which appears in normal text areas of the screen.

The large 4-headed arrow which appears after choosing the **Control, Move/Size** command(s) for moving or sizing windows.

The double arrows which appear when over the border of a window, used to drag the side and alter the size of the window.

The Help hand which appears in the help windows, and is used to access 'hypertext' type links.

Windows applications, such as word processors, spreadsheets and databases, can have additional mouse pointers which facilitate the execution of selected commands, such as highlighting text, defining areas for the appearance of charts, etc.

The Menu Bar Options

Each window's menu bar option has associated with it a pull-down sub-menu. To activate the menu of a window, either press the <Alt> key, which causes the underlining of one letter per menu option and activates (turns to a button) the first option of the menu (in this case **File**). Next, use the right and left arrow keys to activate the other options in the menu, or use the mouse to point to an option. Pressing either the <Enter> key, or the left mouse button, reveals the pull-down sub-menu of the activated option.

The sub-menu of the **View** option of the My Computer window, is shown below.

Fig. 2.3 Menu Bar Options.

Menu options can also be activated directly by pressing the <Alt> key, followed by the underlined letter of the required menu option. Thus pressing **Alt+V**, opens the pull-down sub-menu of **View**. You can use the up and down arrow keys to move the highlighted bar up and down a sub-menu, or the right and left arrow keys to move along the options in the menu bar. Pressing the <Enter> key selects the highlighted option or executes the highlighted command. Pressing the <Esc> key once, closes the pull-down sub-menu, while pressing the <Esc> key for a second time closes the menu system.

Items on the pull-down sub-menu which are marked with an arrow to their right, as shown here, open up additional options when selected, as shown on the My Computer screen dump of Fig. 2.3.

The items on the menu bar of a specific application might be different from the ones shown here. However, almost all Windows Me system applications offer the following options:

File	Produces a pull-down menu of mainly file related tasks, which allow you, amongst other options, to **open**, **print**, **send to**, **delete** or **rename** a selected file, create a **new folder** or **shortcut**, or open the **properties** of a selected item, and **close** an open window.
Edit	Gives access to the most common editing tasks which can be applied on selected items, such as **cut**, **copy** and **paste**, **copy** or **move** such items to a folder.
View	Gives you complete control over what you see on your screen. For example, selecting the **toolbars** and/or the **status bar** options checks these options and allows their display (selecting them once more removes the check mark and toggles them off). Allows you to **arrange icons** in various ways and control whether **large icons**, **small icons**, **lists** or **detailed** lists are displayed.
Favorites	Allows you to **add** and **organise** useful URL addresses, or access various pre-set **media** addresses on the Internet.
Tools	Allows you to **map** or **disconnect** network drives, and set **folder options**.
Help	Activates the help window and displays an **index** of help topics, or opens a window and displays basic system resources.

Some applications display a '?' button on the right end of their title bar, as shown here. Clicking this button changes the mouse pointer from its usual inclined arrow shape to the 'What's this?' shape. Pointing with this to an object in the window and clicking, opens a Help topic.

Shortcut Menus

To see a shortcut menu containing the most common commands applicable to an item, point with your mouse at the item and click the right mouse button. For example, right-clicking the My Computer icon reveals the options in Fig. 2.4.

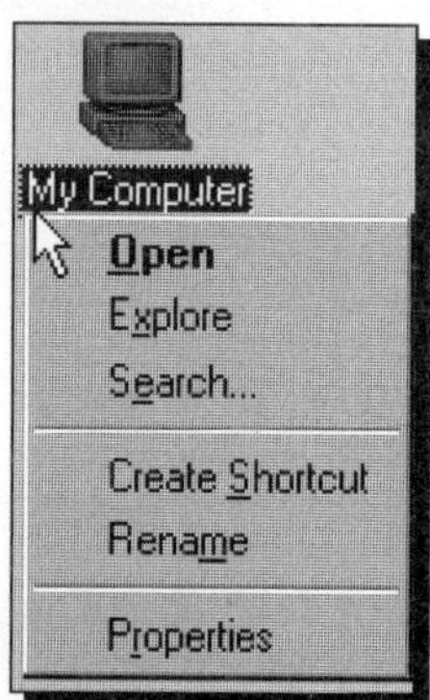

Fig. 2.4 Shortcut Menu for My Computer.

In this case we have the option to **Open** My Computer which has the same effect as double-clicking its icon, **Explore** its contents, **Search** for any file or document stored in it, **Create Shortcut** icons on the desktop, **Rename** the particular item, or see its **Properties**.

Right-clicking the desktop itself, displays the shortcut shown in Fig. 2.5. From this menu you can select how to **Arrange Icons** on your desktop, or create a **New** folder or shortcut icon on the desktop, for your favourite word processor maybe.

Fig. 2.5 Shortcut Menu for the Desktop.

It might be worth your while to right-click the rest of the icons on your desktop in turn, to find out what the differences are between their shortcut menus. For example, you will find that the My Documents icon has an additional option to delete it, while the My Computer and Recycle Bin icons do not offer such an option. You will also find out that there is no option to rename the Recycle Bin.

Note: Having activated a shortcut menu, you can close it without taking any further action by simply pressing the <Esc> key, or clicking the mouse somewhere else.

Dialogue Boxes

Three periods after a sub-menu option or command, means that a dialogue box will open when the option or command is selected. A dialogue box is used for the insertion of additional information, such as the name of a file.

To see a dialogue box, double-click the My Computer icon, select **Tools** on the menu bar of the displayed window and **Folder Options** from its sub-menu. This opens the Folder Options dialogue box shown below with its General tab selected.

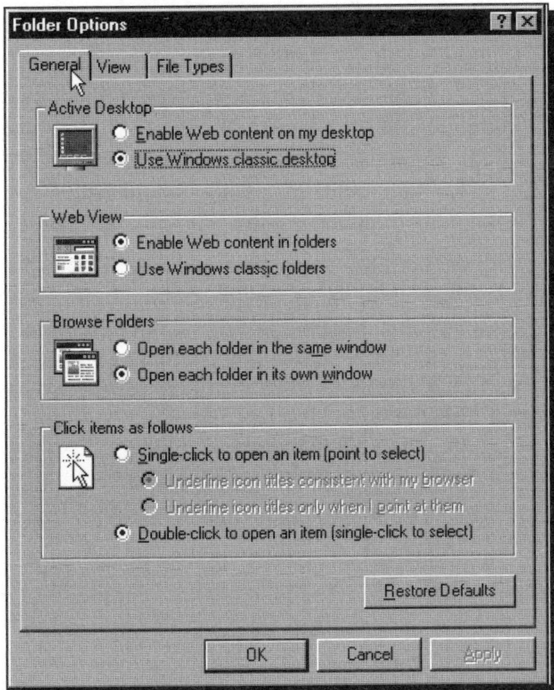

Fig. 2.6 The Folder Options Dialogue Box.

When a dialogue box opens, the <Tab> key can be used to move the dotted rectangle (known as the focus) from one field to another (<Shift+Tab> moves the focus backwards).

Alternatively you can move directly to a desired field by holding the <Alt> key down and pressing the underlined letter in the field name. With the mouse, you simply point and click the left mouse button at the desired field.

Some dialogue boxes (such as the one shown in Fig. 2.6) contain List boxes which show a column of available choices. If there are more choices than can be seen in the area provided, use the scroll bars to reveal them. Such dialogue boxes may contain Check boxes which offer a list of features you can switch on or off. Selected options show a tick in the box against the option name. Another type of dialogue box option is the Option button (sometimes called Radio button) with a list of mutually exclusive items. The default choice is marked with a black dot against its name, while unavailable options are dimmed.

Another type of List box may display a column of document files. To select a single file from such a List box, either double-click the file, or use the arrow keys to highlight the file and press <Enter>. Again, if there are more files than can be seen in the area provided, use the scroll bars to reveal them.

Other dialogue boxes may contain groups of options within a field. In such cases, you can use the arrow keys to move from one option to another. Having selected an option or typed in information in a text box, you must press a command button, such as the **OK**, **Cancel** or **Apply** button (unavailable options or command buttons are dimmed), or choose from additional options. To select the **OK** button with the mouse, simply point and left-click, while with the keyboard, you must first press the <Tab> key until the focus moves to the required button, and then press the <Enter> key.

To cancel a dialogue box, either press the **Cancel** button, or the <Esc> key enough times to close the dialogue box and then the menu system.

Note: At this stage it might be a good time to change the default settings under the **View** tab of Fig. 2.6 by unchecking the **Hide file extensions for known file types** option, which could alert you to rogue and potentially lethal e-mail attachments (see the E-mail and Outlook Express chapter).

Desktop Icons

So far we have used the first and second of the four system icons (My Documents and My Computer) displayed at the top left corner of our computer's desktop, and shown below. Your desktop could be arranged differently from ours and could, indeed, have different icons on it as this depends on your settings prior to upgrading. For the sake of completeness we summarise below the function of the 'system' icons appearing on our desktop.

Double-click this for quick access to the list of documents, graphics, and other files you have saved in this folder and its sub-folders. Double-clicking a specific file in a list, opens the file and the program it was produced by, so you can carry on working with it.

Double-click this to graphically browse through all your discs, folders and files.

Double-click this to restore deleted folders and files to their original position on your hard disc.

Double-click this to set up your modem and your connection to MSN (Microsoft Network).

Double-click this to locate shared resources on the network to which you are connected, or create shortcuts to network, and Web servers.

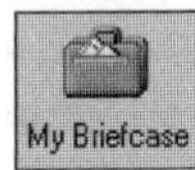

Double-click this when you want to work on your files on another computer.

Other icons, if any, that might appear on your desktop, will be 'shortcuts' to an object, such as an executable program file, an image file, or a document file. Double-clicking on such an icon opens the object itself or starts the application program. Later on we will discuss how to create such shortcuts.

Taskbar Buttons

At the bottom of the Desktop screen is the Taskbar. It contains the **Start** button which, as we shall soon see, can be used to quickly start a program, or to find a file, and it is also the fastest way to get Help.

When you open a program, or a window, a button for it is placed on the Taskbar, as shown below.

Fig. 2.7 The Windows Taskbar.

You can left-click your mouse on this button to make this the active program, or window. So, no matter how cluttered your screen is, you can always see what windows you have open and quickly switch between them. As more buttons are placed on the Taskbar their size shrinks.

If you need to see more details on a truncated button, hold the mouse pointer over it. You can also drag the top of the bar up and have multiple rows of buttons. Try it! However, this reduces the area of the Desktop.

Next to the **Start** button, there are four buttons (there could be more) placed there by the Windows Setup program. These, in order of appearance, have the following functions:

Show Desktop.

Launch the Internet Explorer Browser.

Launch Outlook Express.

Launch Windows Media Player

The Taskbar also shows the current time to the far right, the volume control, and the monitor setting icons. Moving the mouse pointer over the clock will display the date. Double-clicking the clock, opens the Date/Time Properties box, shown here, so that you can make changes, if necessary.

The Start Cascade Menu

Left-clicking the **Start** button at the bottom left corner of the Windows screen, displays the first column of a series of cascade menus. Moving the mouse pointer to the **Programs** menu option, displays the second column of the cascade menu where all Windows applications are to be found. In the screen dump below we show the menu options of the Windows Accessories menu option displayed on the third column.

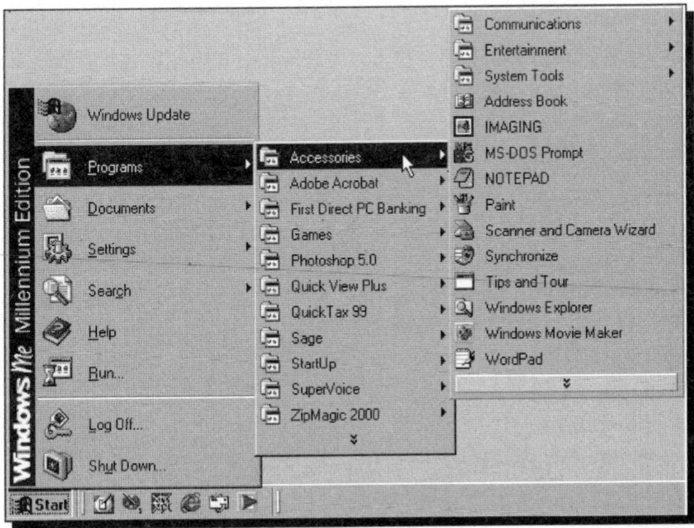

Fig. 2.8 The Start Cascade Menu.

New to Windows Me is the ability of its menus to adapt to the way you use your computer by keeping track of what features and programs you use the most. The result is that only the items used most regularly are displayed, while others are kept hidden from view. This saves time as you don't have to scroll through endless menu lists to find the one you want to use. However, if you rest the mouse pointer on the down-arrow bar at the bottom of a cascade menu, or part of the sub-menu, for a second or so, the hidden items of the menu are displayed automatically in a lighter shade of grey. Try it.

Exiting Windows Me

To exit Windows, you click the **Start** button and select the **Shut Down** option, as shown in Fig. 2.9.

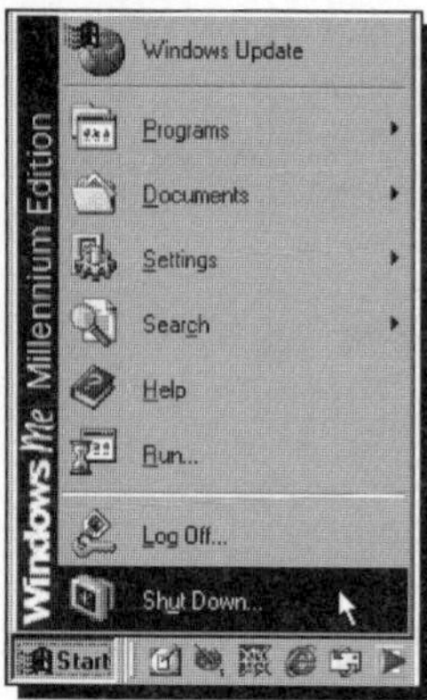

Fig. 2.9 The START Menu.

This opens the dialogue box below.

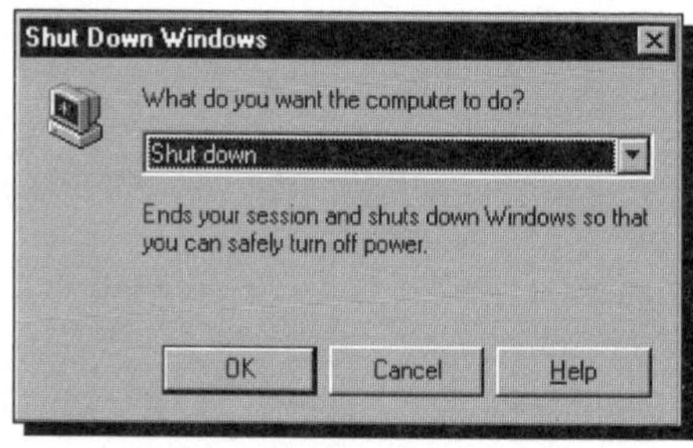

Fig. 2.10 The Shut Down Dialogue Box.

Selecting the default **Shut down** option in the dialogue box, exits all the open programs, carries out any file saves you require and then tells you when it is safe to switch off your computer. Clicking the down-arrow to the right of the text box reveals two other options, as shown here; one can exit Windows Me, but **Restart** it, while the other puts your PC in a **Stand by** mode. The **Restart** option is used if you want to clear the memory settings and restart Windows Me, while the **Stand by** mode (see Chapter 10, page 187), is used to save power by turning off your monitor and/or hard disc after a specified time interval.

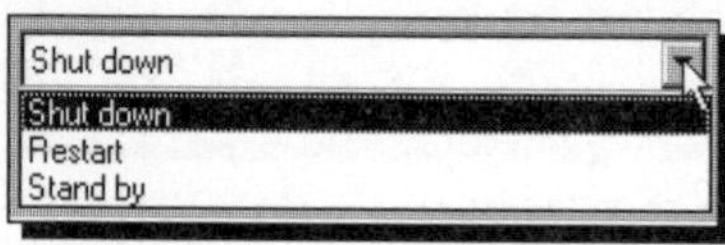

Note: This is the only way you should end a session - never just switch off your computer without going through this procedure. If you don't, next time you switch on your PC, Windows Me will scan your hard discs for errors, which takes an unnecessarily long time to complete.

3

The Windows Environment

Windows allows the display of multiple applications or multiple documents of a single application. Each of these Windows applications or documents displays on the screen in its own window, which can be full screen size or part screen size.

Manipulating Windows

To use any Windows program effectively, you will need to be able to manipulate a series of windows, to select which one is to be active, to move them, or change their size, so that you can see all the relevant parts of each one. What follows is a short discussion on how to manipulate windows.

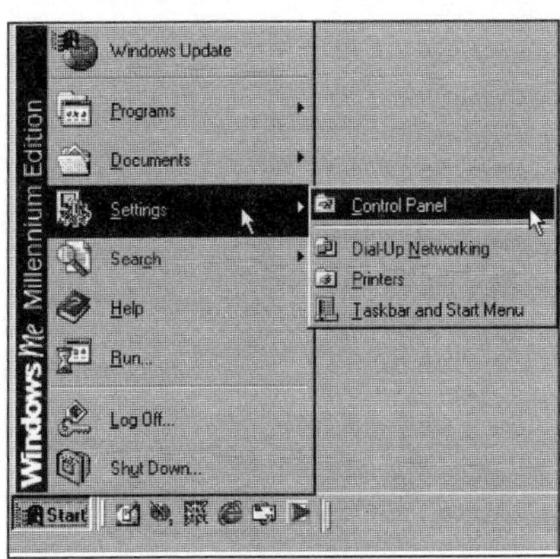

Fig. 3.1 The Start Menu.

To help with the illustration of the various points to be discussed, we will create three windows by first clicking the **Start** button to display the Start menu, then selecting the **Settings** option to reveal the cascade sub-menu, shown here, and clicking the **Control Panel** option. Repeat this process two more times, but click the **Printers** option on the sub-menu the second time and the **Taskbar & Start Menu** option on the third time. What you should see on your screen is shown on the next page. Don't worry about what these applications do; we will explain later.

All we are concerned with at the moment is to open three windows on the screen with each window containing a different application. If the contents of the Control Panel and Printers windows do not look exactly like ours, i.e., containing large icons, again don't worry as it is not important. We simply used the **View** command, as each window was being opened, then selected the **Large Icons** option.

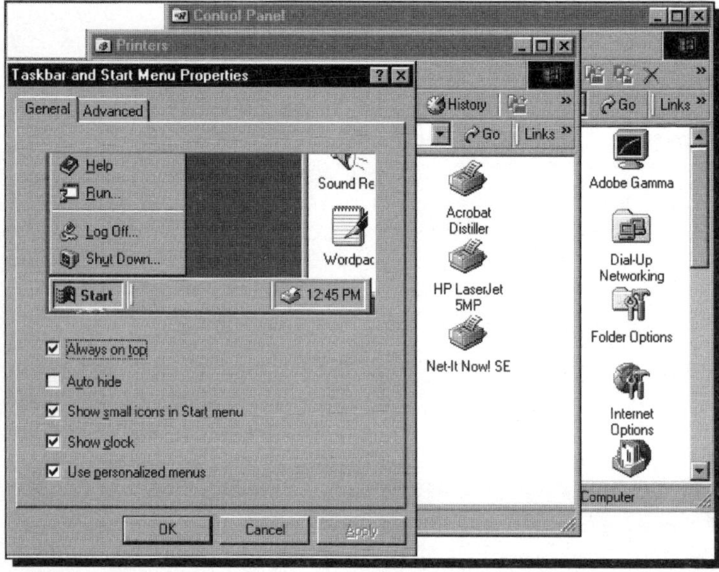

Fig. 3.2 Three Opened Application Windows on Screen.

If you followed the order we suggested for opening these application windows, then the active window (the last one to be opened) will display on top of the others, as shown in Fig. 3.2.

Changing the Active Window

To select the active window amongst those displayed on the screen, point to it and click the left mouse button, or, if the one you want to activate is not visible, click its icon on the Taskbar. Alternatively, hold down the <Alt> key and press the <Tab> key.

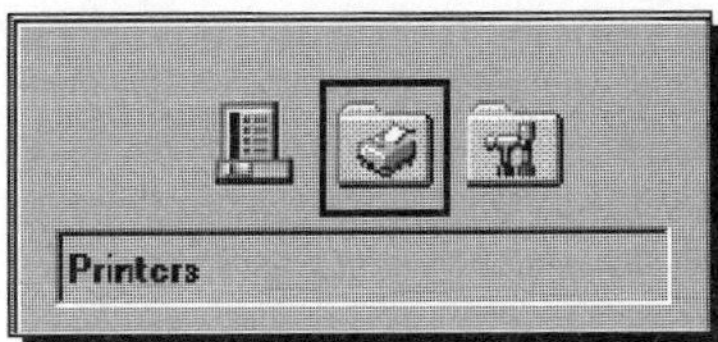

Fig. 3.3 List of Open Windows.

This opens the pop-up box shown here, which displays the icons of all open windows. As long as the <Alt> key is held down, the pop-up box remains visible. Pressing the <Tab> key moves the highlight through the listing and when the icon you want is selected, releasing the <Alt> key will make that the active window.

It is a good idea to practise what we are describing here. Do not be afraid if you make mistakes - the more mistakes you make the more you will learn!

Moving Windows and Dialogue Boxes

When you have multiple windows or dialogue boxes on the screen, you might want to move a particular one to a different part of the screen. This can be achieved with either the mouse or the keyboard, but not if the window occupies the full screen, for obvious reasons.

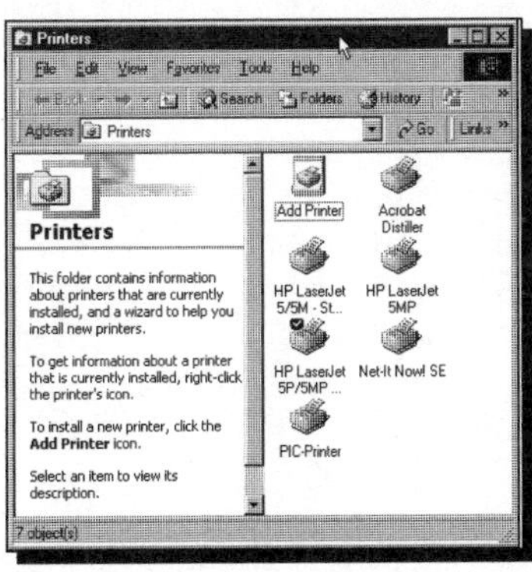

Fig. 3.4 Moving a Window.

To move a window, or a dialogue box, with the mouse, point to the title bar, as shown here, and drag it (press the left button and keep it pressed while moving the mouse) until the window is where you want it to be on the screen, then release the mouse button.

To move a window with the keyboard, press <Alt+Spacebar> to open the Application Control menu, or <Alt+-> to open the Document Control menu, then press **M** to select **Move,** which causes a four-headed arrow to appear in the title bar. Use the arrow keys to move the shadow border of the window to the required place and press <Enter>.

Sizing a Window

You can change the size of a window with either the mouse or the keyboard. With the mouse, move the window so that the side you want to change is visible, then move the mouse pointer to the edge of the window or corner so that it changes to a two-headed arrow, then drag the two-headed arrow in the direction you want that side or corner to move.

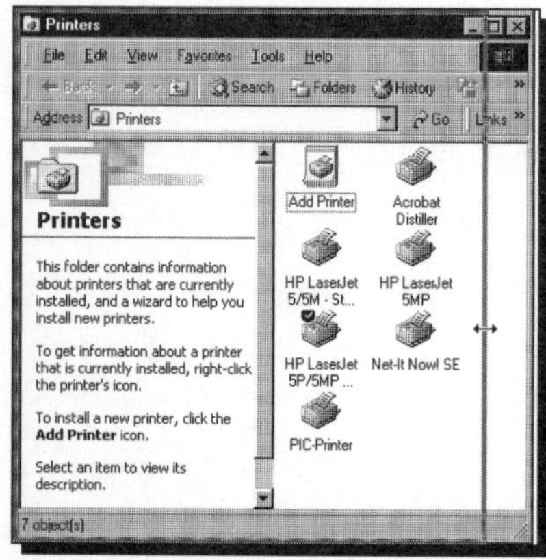

Fig. 3.5 Sizing a Window.

Here we are moving the right side of the window towards the left, thus making it smaller. Continue dragging until the shadow border is the size you require, then release the mouse button.

To size a window with the keyboard, press either <Alt+Spacebar> or <Alt+-> to reveal the Application Control menu or the Document Control menu, then press **S** to select **Size** which causes the four-headed arrow to appear. Next, press the arrow key that corresponds to the edge you want to move, or if a corner, press the two arrow keys (one after the other) corresponding to the particular corner, which causes the pointer to change to a two-headed arrow. Having pressed the appropriate arrow key in the direction you want that side or corner to move, continue to do so until the shadow border is the size you require, then press <Enter> to fix the new window size.

Minimising and Maximising Windows

Windows can be minimised into Taskbar icons to temporarily free desktop space. This can be done either by using the mouse to click the 'Minimise' button (the negative sign in the upper-right corner of the window), or by pressing <Alt+Spacebar> or <Alt+-> to reveal the Application Control menu or the Document Control menu, and selecting **n** for **Minimise**.

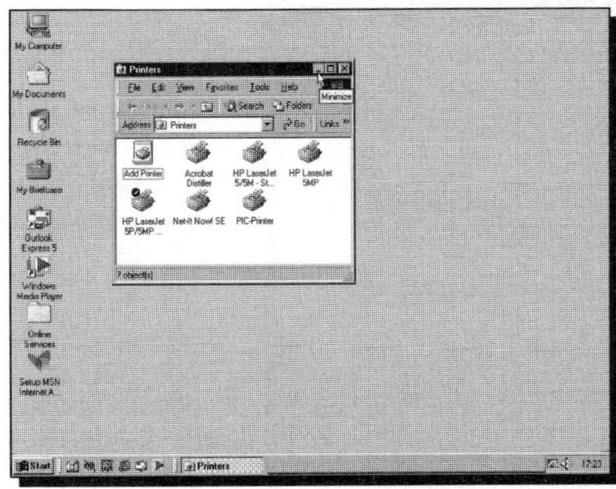

Fig. 3.6 Minimising a Window.

In the above screen dump we show the Printers window open with the mouse pointer pointing at the minimise button and also its icon on the Taskbar.

To maximise a window so that it fills the entire screen, either click on the 'maximise' button (the rectangle in the upper-right corner of the window), or press <Alt+Spacebar> or <Alt+-> to display the Application Control menu or the Document Control menu, and select **x** for **Maximise**.

An application which has been minimised or maximised can be returned to its original size and position on the screen by either clicking on its Taskbar icon to expand it to a window, or clicking on the 'Restore' button in the upper-right corner of the maximised window, to reduce it to its former size. With the keyboard, press <Alt+Spacebar>, then select **R** for **Restore** from the Control menu.

Closing a Window

A document window can be closed at any time to save screen space and memory. To do this, either click the X Close button (on the upper-right corner of the window), or double-click on the Control menu button (the icon in the upper-left corner of the window title bar). With the keyboard, press <Alt+–> and select **C** for **Close** from the window Control menu.

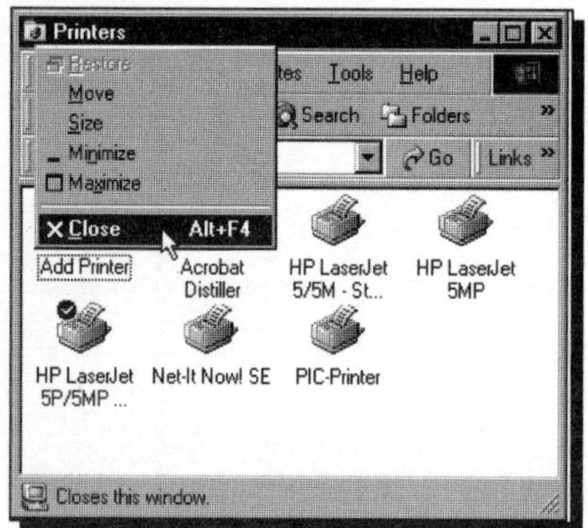

Fig. 3.7 Closing a Window.

If you try to close a window of an application document, such as that of a word processor, in which you have made changes since the last time you saved it, you will get a warning in the form of a dialogue box asking confirmation prior to closing it. This safeguards against loss of information.

Windows Display Arrangement

In Windows and most Windows application programs, you can display multiple windows in both tiled and cascaded (overlapping) forms - the choice being a matter of balance between personal preference and the type of work you are doing at the time. If you want to organise these automatically, right-click on an empty part of the Taskbar which opens the menu shown here.

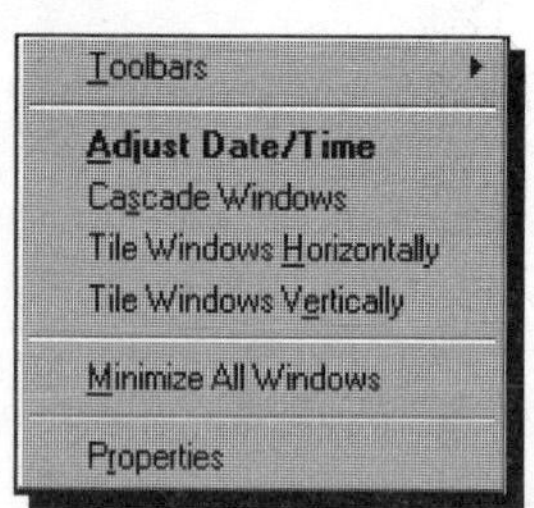

On the next page, we show two forms of windows display; the **Cascade Windows** option and the **Tile Windows Vertically** option.

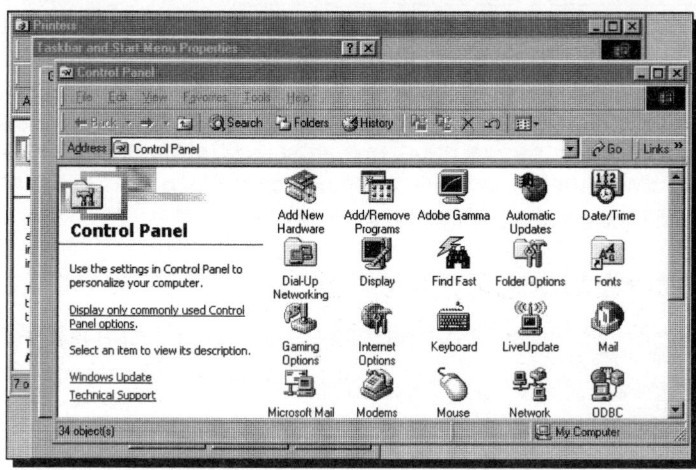

Fig. 3.8 Windows Displayed in Cascade Form.

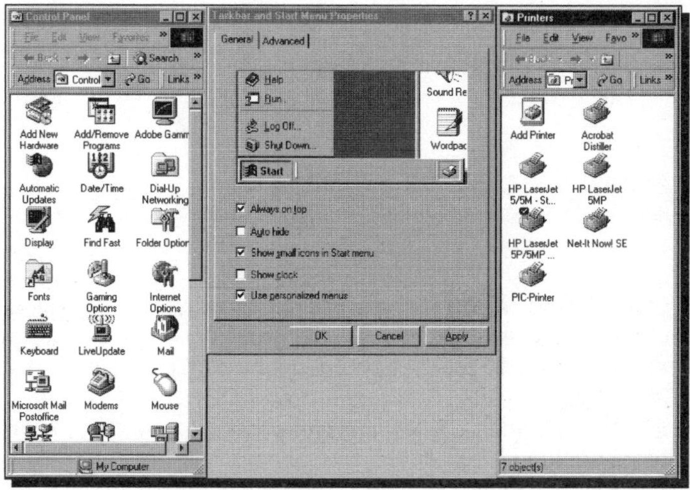

Fig. 3.9 Windows Displayed in Vertical Tile Form

As you will have discovered by now, the size of the **Taskbar & Start Menu Properties** window cannot be changed, hence you might have to alter the size of the other two to get exactly what is displayed in Fig. 3.9.

The Windows Control Panel

The Control Panel provides a quick and easy way to change the hardware and software settings of your system. To access it, either click the **Start** button, then select **Settings** followed by **Control Panel**, or double-click the Control Panel icon in the My Computer window. Either way opens the Control Panel window shown below from which the various Control Panel options can be accessed.

Fig. 3.10 The Control Panel Window.

Double-clicking at the Control Panel icons allows you to add new hardware, add or remove programs, change the display type and its resolution, change the printer fonts, and change the keyboard repeat rate. Further, you can change the settings of your mouse, install and configure your printer(s), specify regional settings, such as the formatting of numbers and dates, and access a variety of system administrative tools. If your system is connected to the outside world or supports multimedia, then you can also configure it appropriately.

All of these features control the environment in which the Windows application programs operate and you should become familiar with them.

Changing your Display

If your VDU (visual display unit or screen) is capable of higher resolution than the often used 640 by 480 pixels (picture elements), you might like to increase its resolution to, say, 800 by 600 pixels, or higher. This will allow you to see a larger number of icons on a screen when a given application is activated. To do this, follow the steps below.

- Click the **Start** button, then select **Settings** followed by **Control Panel**.
- In the Control Panel window, double-click the Display icon.
- In the Display Properties dialogue box, click the Settings tab.

The last dialogue box is shown below with the settings changed appropriately.

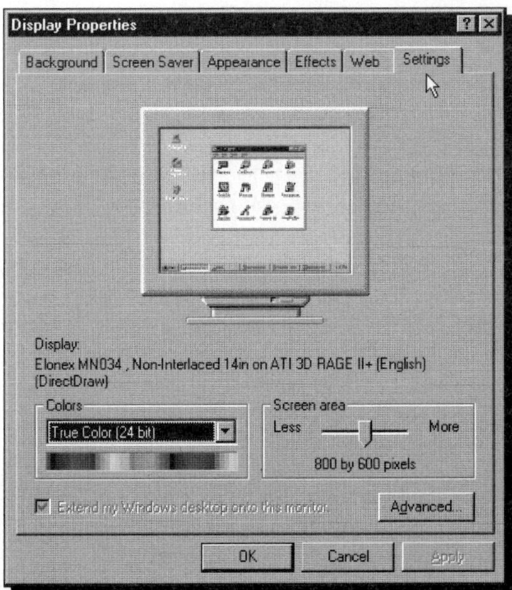

Fig. 3.11 The Display Properties Dialogue Box.

Changing the Default Printer

If you want to change the default printer, you can do so by carrying out the following steps:

- Click the **Start** button, then select **Settings, Printers** to display the Printers folder, shown below. Folders will be discussed in detail in the next chapter.

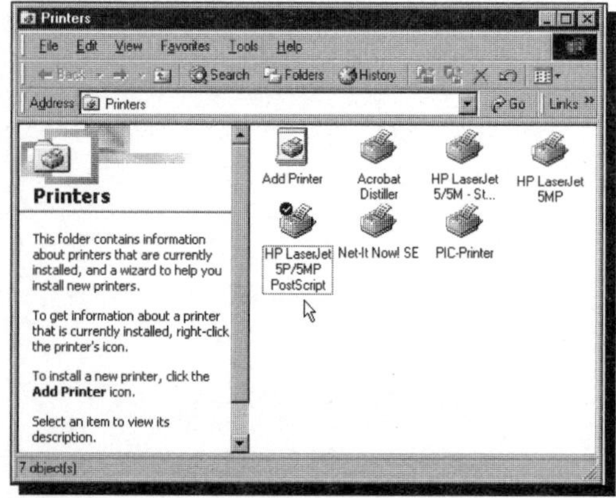

Fig. 3.12 The Printers Folder.

Here it shows that several printer drivers were installed; the fifth printer (currently the default, hence the small tick against it), is an HP LaserJet 5P/5M PostScript, configured for output via the parallel printer port LPT1. By the way, resting the mouse pointer on a printer icon whose label ends with three dots displays a banner with its full name in it.

- Next, right-click the icon of the printer you want to make the default printer in the Printers folder, and choose the **Set as Default** option, as shown here to the right. A small tick will appear against the printer indicating its status.

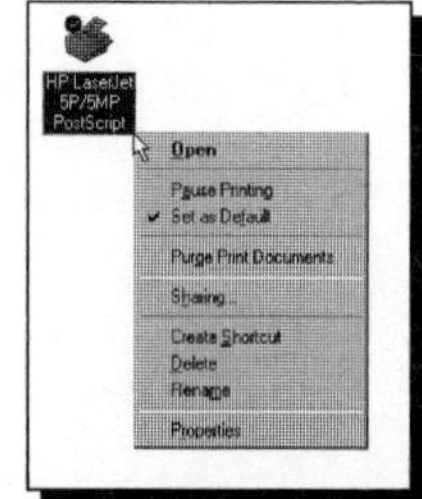

Additional Plug and Play printers are automatically detected at installation time or during the boot-up process. You will be prompted for the necessary driver files if they are not already in the Windows folder. Such printer drivers are normally supplied with all new Plug and Play printers. For other situations the Add Printer Wizard steps you through the printer installation process. You can invoke this Wizard by double-clicking the Add Printer icon in the Printers dialogue box.

The choice of installing an additional printer driver could be dependent on whether such a printer was connected to your system but was not of the Plug and Play variety, or the printer was available to you at, say, your office on a shared basis. This latter option would allow the preparation of documents incorporating fonts and styles not available on your local printer, to be saved with your file and printed later on a printer which supports such enhancements. This is discussed in Chapter 6.

The Common User Interface

The front end of Windows Me remains identical to that of Windows 98 with the user interface resembling that of the Internet Explorer which is bundled with it. You must have noticed by now that the My Computer, My Documents, Recycle Bin, Control Panel, and Printers folder windows, to mention but a few, have a toolbar with browser-style forwards and backwards arrows. The My Computer window is shown below fully extended so that all the toolbar icons are visible.

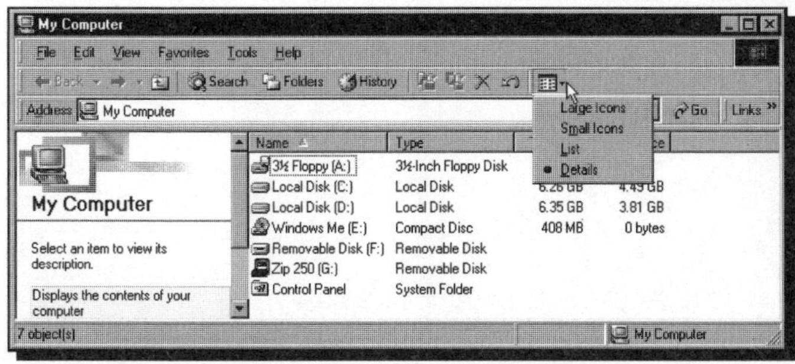

Fig. 3.13 The Toolbar of the Common Windows User Interface.

Note that to see the display exactly as it appears in Fig. 3.13, you need to click the down arrow against the Views button on the toolbar and select the **Details** option from the drop-down menu, as shown. Try the different display options available to you and see which one you prefer. For the display in Fig. 3.14, we chose the **List** option. Highlighting an item, in whichever display option you operate, gives you information about that item (the C: drive in this case).

Fig. 3.14 The List View Option.

If you have upgraded from a previous Windows version, to see a folder's contents you might have to use the **View, Customize This Folder** command and choose a standard template from the displayed Wizard.

Additional information can be obtained from the Properties dialogue box, shown in Fig. 3.15. First select a hardware item (such as a drive, a specific printer, or a document/program file), then use the **File, Properties** command.

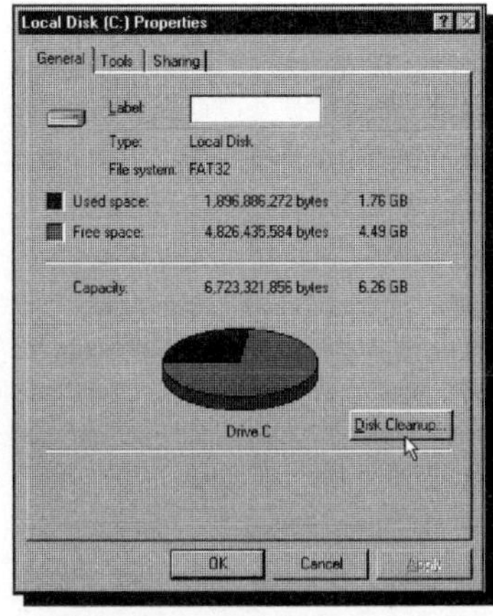

Fig. 3.15 The Properties Dialogue Box.

As you can see, the Properties dialogue box for the C: drive not only contains information about it, but also gives you the option to **Label** it (give it a name), and delete unwanted files to recover precious disc space. Pressing the **Disk Cleanup** button displays a dialogue box which can be used to recover disc space by helping you to delete programs you no longer use.

Pressing the Tools tab of the Properties dialogue box (Fig. 3.15), allows you to check your drive for errors, and defragment your disc (more about this later).

Returning to the common user interface toolbar, apart from the default buttons appearing on it, there are several others which can be added to invoke extra facilities. To do this, use the **View, Toolbars, Customize** command to display the following screen.

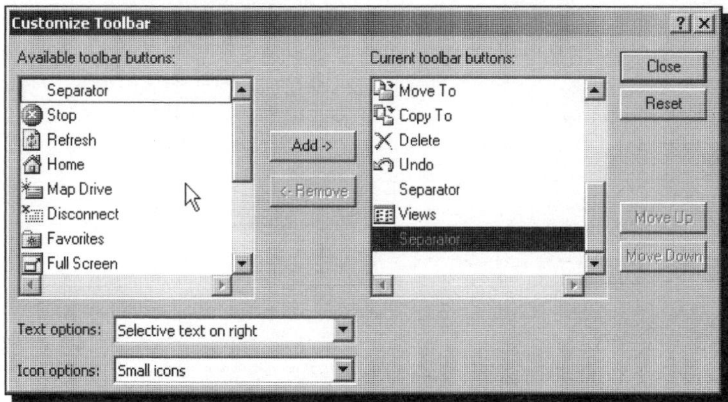

Fig. 3.16 The Customize Toolbar Dialogue Box.

To place an additional button on to the Toolbar, select it in the left pane, and press the **Add** button. Its place on the Toolbar depends on the position of the focus in the right pane. Try adding the 'Home' button to the Toolbar at a position to the left of the 'Search' button.

One interesting aspect of this common user interface is, that no matter which application you used to add the extra button to its Toolbar, the same button will appear on the Toolbar of all other program applications that use the same common user interface. Furthermore, if this was the 'Home' button, clicking it on any of these program applications, will cause the application to attempt to connect you to the Internet, provided your system is geared up to it, and will jump to a Web site without you having to load up a browser. The default Web site is that of Microsoft's MSN, as shown on the next page.

Fig. 3.17 The Default Home Web Site.

If you are connected to the Internet, it is worth examining this facility. If not, you can always use this facility off-line and give it an address pointing to your own Home page on your hard disc, as shown below. How to design this, is another story!

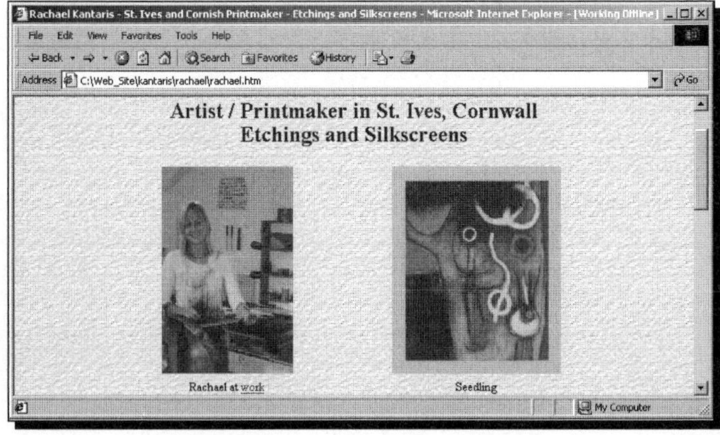

Fig. 3.18 Your Own Home Page.

Using the Help System

To obtain help in Windows Me, click the **Start** button, then select the **Help** menu command which opens the main Help window, shown below.

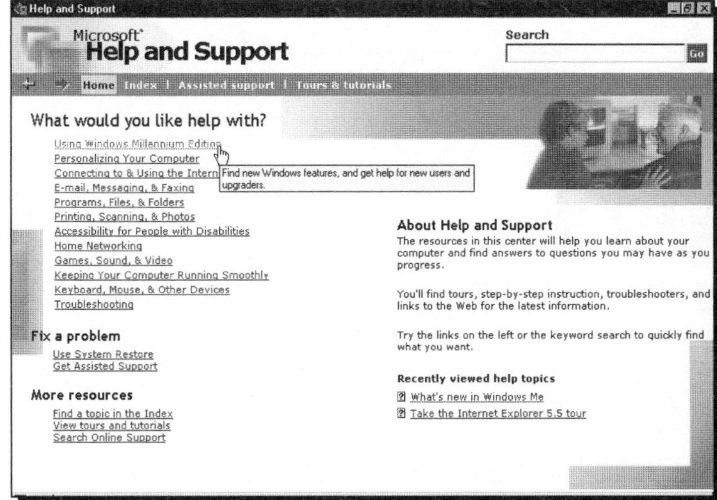

Fig. 3.19 The Windows Me Help System.

The **Home** and **Index** options give you off-line help, while the **Assisted support** and **Tours & tutorials** provide online help. With all options you get a 'Search' facility, and with all but the **Index** option you are presented with an extraordinary number of hypertext links to various topics. Clicking such a hypertext link, can open up a further list of hypertext links until you home onto a specific subject when a short page of text is displayed in the right pane of the Windows Help dialogue box.

The **Index** option opens up a Help index facility. If this option is selected and you type the first few letters of a word in the input box, it homes onto the available topics in the list. Selecting one and clicking the **Display** button opens its page, as shown on the next page.

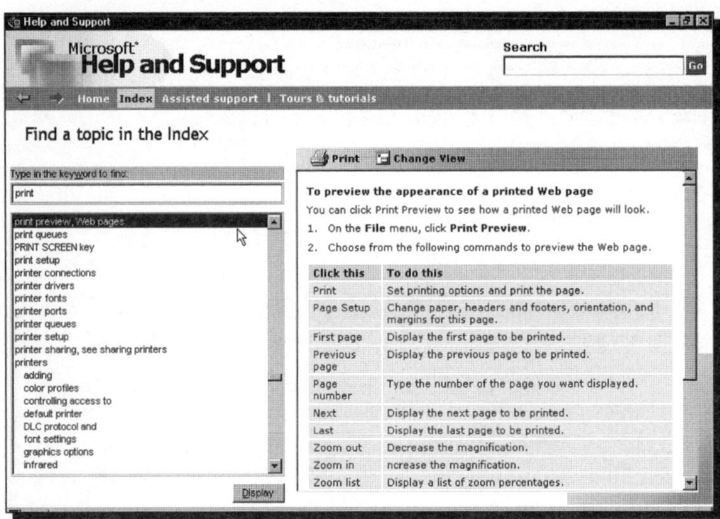

Fig. 3.20 Using the Help Index Facility.

The Search facility gives you access to a very powerful individual word search of the Help system, as shown below.

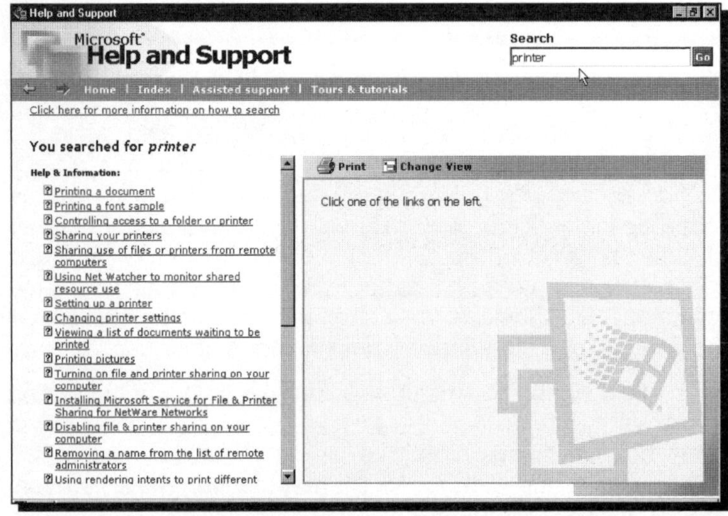

Fig. 3.21 Using the Help Search Facility.

4

Discs, Folders and Files

Windows Me, being an operating system, controls the use of your system's disc drives and allows for the manipulation of the data stored on them. With pre-Windows 95 versions of the program you would have used the semi-graphical File Manager to look after your discs, directories and files.

With Windows Me (and Windows 95/98 & NT/2000), the way discs, folders (the old directories) and files can be handled on your PC has been changed. In the 'My Computer' facility almost everything is done graphically, by clicking and dragging icons between windows, folders and the desktop itself. In Windows Me, as we have seen in the previous chapter, My Computer appears under the common user interface and is, therefore, capable of delivering more facilities than before.

Discs and Folders

To see all the folders held on your computer's drive, double-click the My Computer icon on your desktop, and click the appropriate disc icon that holds Windows Me (in our case this is Local Disc C:, yours could be different). Note that for this display, we have clicked the **Folders** icon on the Toolbar.

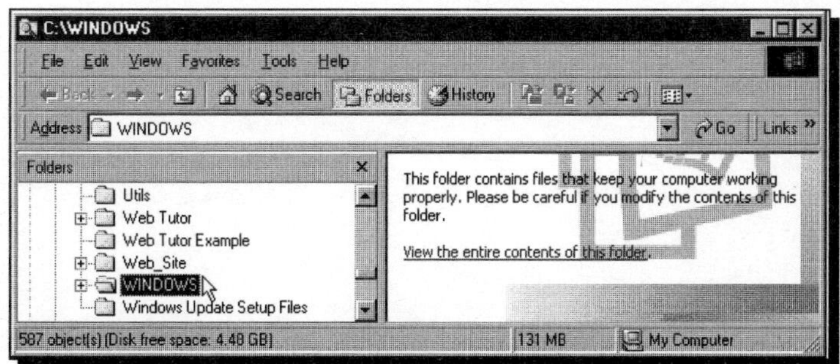

Fig. 4.1 Using My Computer to Look at the WINDOWS System Folder.

Note: Because we have selected to open the WINDOWS folder that holds Windows Me system files, the message 'This folder contains files that keep your system working properly ...' appears in the right pane of the displayed window. Left-clicking the View the entire contents of this folder link allows you to have a look (Fig. 4.2). But, as the warning tells you, do not move, delete, or in any way change the content of these folders or files - just look.

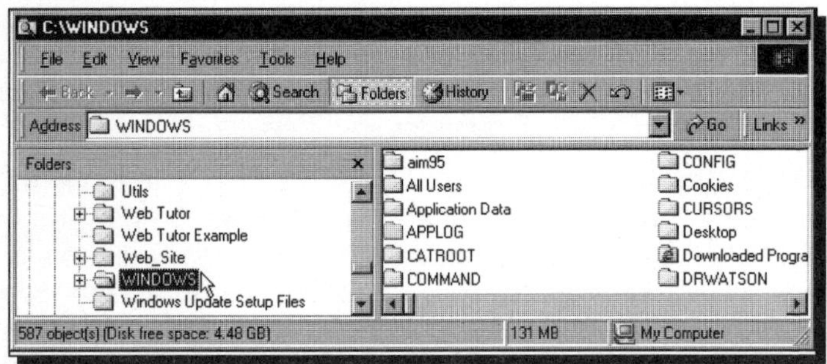

Fig. 4.2 The Contents of the WINDOWS Folder.

Note the Back icon on the toolbar has been activated. Pressing this icon returns you to the previous display and in doing so, activates the Forward icon on the toolbar. This simulates the way a Web browser works.

Folders are graphical devices, as shown here, similar to directories in that they can contain files, other folders and also icons. To examine this, locate the Program Files folder on your drive (ours is found several folders above the WINDOWS folder) and click it to display the following:

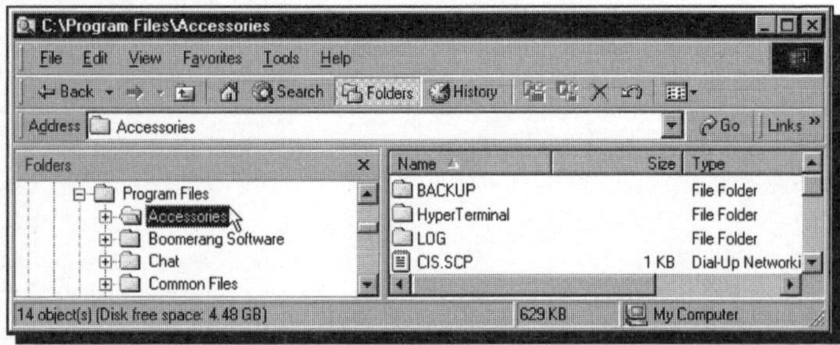

Fig. 4.3 The Contents of the Program Files Folder.

The My Computer Utility

In Windows Me you can work with files using the My Computer utility, which Microsoft have spent much time and effort making as intuitive as possible. In addition, all the advanced features only found in the Windows Explorer of previous versions of Windows, have now been incorporated in the My Computer utility.

As we have seen, double-clicking the My Computer icon on the desktop, gives you immediate visual access to all the disc drives in your computer, as well as the Control Panel folder. The My Computer window opens with default settings consisting of large icons, a Web browser type toolbar, and each time you double-click an icon its contents are shown in the same window.

Icon settings are easy to change, not only from the Views button on the toolbar, but also from the **View** menu. However, to control general settings, view options and edit the files you view, use the **Tools**, **Folder Options** menu command, which opens the Folder Options dialogue box shown in Fig. 4.4.

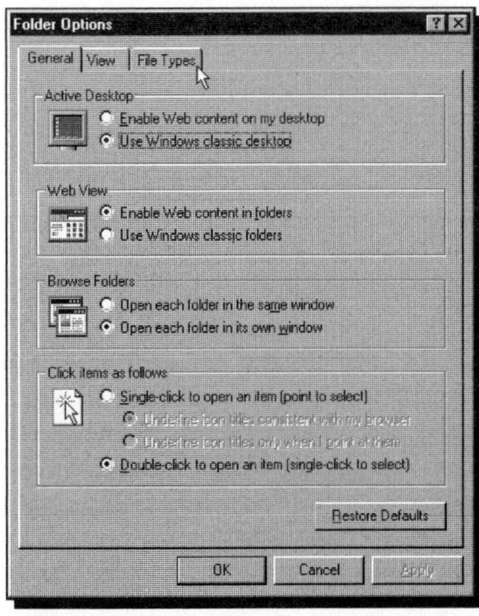

Fig. 4.4 The Folder Options Dialogue Box.

To see what program associations are valid on your system, click the File Types tab. This will open the dialogue box window shown in Fig. 4.5 on the next page. If you work your way down the list of **Registered file types** you can see the association details in the lower half of the box. Our example shows that a file with the .AU extension is a sound file.

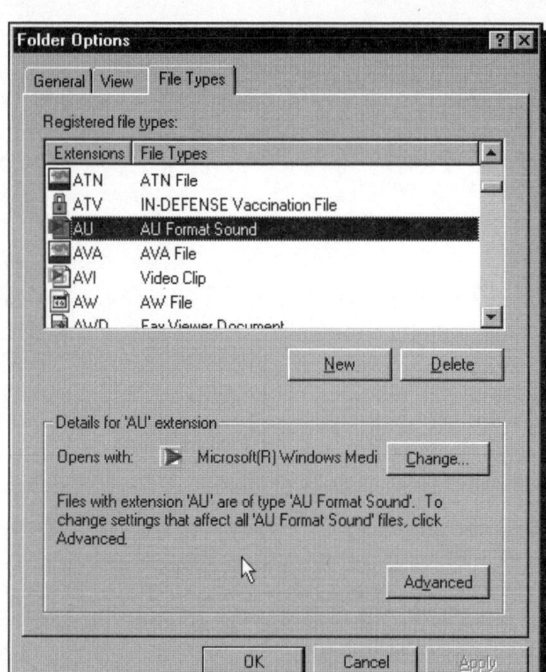

Fig. 4.5 Program File Associations.

From this box you can add new associations by clicking the **New** button, delete them with the **Delete** button and change them with the **Change** button. Without getting too involved at this stage, it is worth spending a few minutes just browsing through the list. It will help you to recognise the icons. These extensions are used by Windows Me to associate files with the application that they are used with.

Any file displayed within the My Computer window, whether with its extension showing or not, can be opened by double-clicking its icon. If it is a program file, the program will run. If it is a document, it will be opened in a running version of its application program.

Creating a New Folder

Before you start manipulating any files, create a new folder to hold copies of some existing files. It should then be safe to 'play around' with them.

To create a new folder:

- Open in succession by double-clicking, the Program Files folder, then the Common Files folder, and finally the Services folder. Next, right-click on an empty part of the right pane of the window. This opens the command menu shown to the left of the screen dump below.

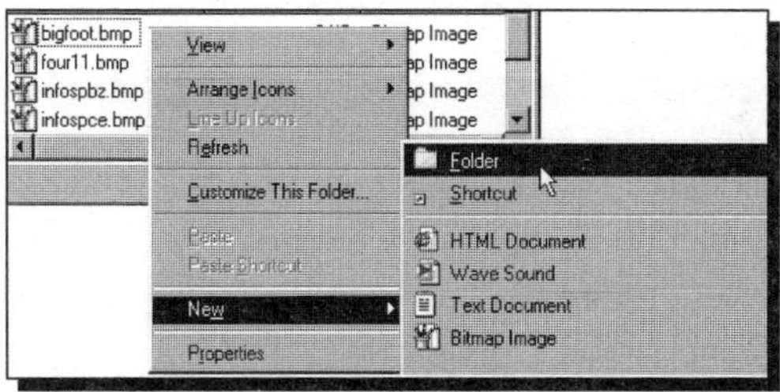

Fig. 4.6 Creating a New Folder.

- Holding the pointer over **New** opens the cascade menu. Clicking the **Folder** option places a 'New Folder' inside the currently active window, as shown below. Its temporary name is highlighted ready for you to type its proper name.

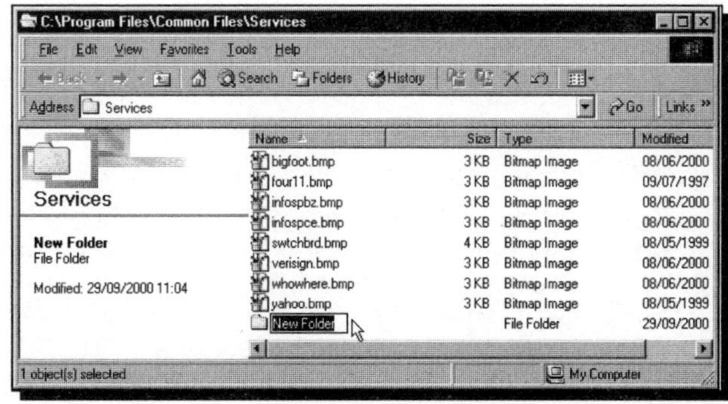

Fig. 4.7 A New Folder Added Inside the Active Window.

- Next, type **Test Folder** into the name slot and click at an empty area of the window. It's as easy as that to create and name a folder. At any time in the future you can rename it by clicking its existing name and typing in the new one. This works for files too.

Selecting Folders and Files

What we demonstrate below with files could also be done with folders, or a mixture of folders and files within any folder. Before selecting such items you would like to copy, arrange the new Test Folder next to the other icons in the Services folder (viewed as large icons) as shown below.

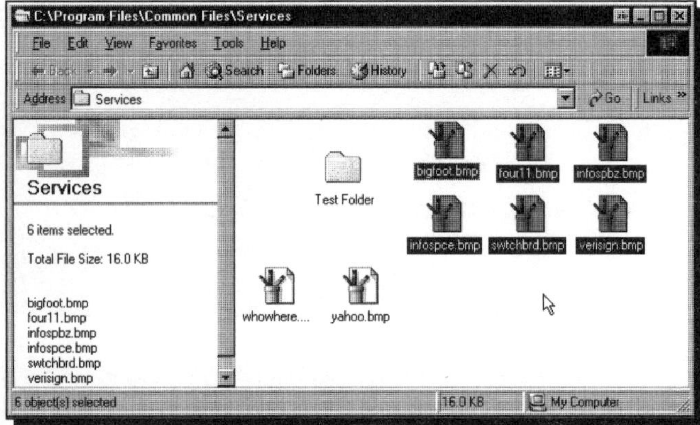

Fig. 4.8 Selecting Items in a Folder.

To select several objects, or icons, you have three options:

- If they form a rectangle, as above, left-click one corner, then with the <Shift> key depressed, click the opposite corner.
- To select random objects hold the <Ctrl> key down and left-click them, one by one.
- To select all the items in a window use the **Edit**, **Select All** menu command, or the keyboard shortcut <Ctrl+A>.

To cancel a selection, click in an empty area of the window.

Copying Folders and Files

There are several ways to copy selected items from one window into a target folder.

- ***Using the menu bar icon:*** If the destination folder is on a different drive or in a folder which is not displayed in the current window, then select the object you want to copy and left-click the Copy To menu bar icon pointed to below. This opens the Browse For Folder dialogue box for you to locate the required destination.
- ***Using the menu:*** Select the objects you want to copy, then use the **Edit**, **Copy** command from the menu bar. Double-click the folder into which you want to insert a copy of the selected objects, and use the **Edit**, **Paste** command.
- ***Using the keyboard:*** Select the objects to copy and press the <Ctrl+C> keyboard shortcut. Double-click the destination folder and press <Ctrl+V> to paste the objects there.
- ***Using the mouse:*** Press and hold down the <Ctrl> key, then drag the selected objects to the destination folder.

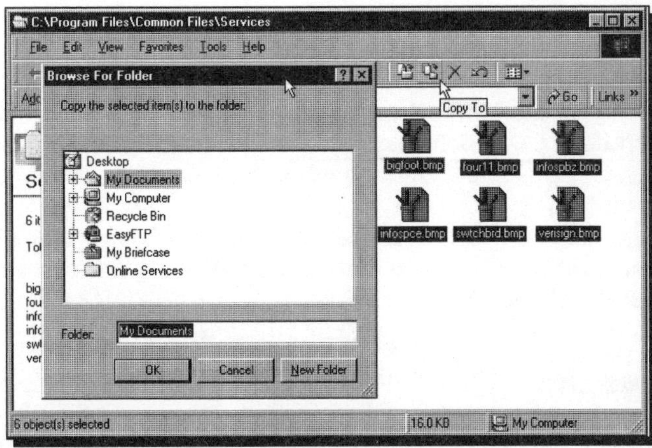

Fig 4.9 Using the My Computer Menu Bar Copy To Icon.

Moving Folders and Files

When you **copy** a folder or file to somewhere else, the original version of the folder or file is not altered or removed, but when you **move** a folder or file to a new location, the original is actually deleted. As with the copy operation there are several ways to move selected folders or files.

- ***Using the menu bar icon:*** If the destination folder is on a different drive or in a folder which is not displayed in the current window, then select the object you want to move and left-click the Move To menu bar icon (the one to the left of the Copy To icon pointed to in Fig. 4.9). This opens the Browse For Folder dialogue box for you to locate the required destination.
- ***Using the menu:*** Choose the **Edit**, **Cut** command from the source window, then use the **Edit**, **Paste** command from the destination window menu bar.
- ***Using the keyboard:*** Select the items to move and press the <Ctrl+X> keyboard shortcut. Then select the destination window and press <Ctrl+V> to paste them there.
- ***Using the mouse:*** Drag the selected items to the destination folder. This will move files between windows, or folders, **of the same drive** (see note below).

Note: It is possible to use the drag and drop technique to copy or move objects between different drives. However, dragging can be a little confusing until you get used to it. To drag-copy objects to a folder or window of *another disc drive*, you don't have to hold down the <Ctrl> key. This is the same action as drag-moving objects between folders of the *same* drive. Therefore, take special care or you will end up moving objects instead of copying them.

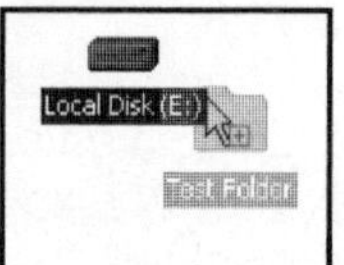

One easy way of telling what action a drag operation will result in, is to look for a + sign on the drag pointer. This indicates that a copy will take place, as shown here, where the Test Folder is about to be copied to the E: drive.

Perhaps a safer way of copying or moving objects with the mouse is to drag them with the *right* mouse button depressed to the desired destination. Releasing the mouse button produces a menu which gives you a choice between **Copy Here** and **Move Here**. Clicking one of these, completes the required task.

Renaming Folders and Files

Before you rename folders or files, copy a folder into your Test Folder. Anything done to it in the Test Folder should not have any effect on the rest of your system.

To rename a folder or file, first click on it to select it, then click the existing name below the icon. This will place a rectangle around the name and put you into edit mode. Type a new name and click somewhere else, or press <Enter>, to finish the task. Try renaming the Test Folder to Practice Folder.

File Properties

If you want to know more about a particular file, first select it, then either use the **File, Properties** menu command, or right-click the filename and select **Properties** from the drop-down menu to open the Properties dialogue box. Here, the full properties of the file are listed, including its name, type, location, size, the date when it was created, last modified, etc. You can also change the file's attributes, by making it, say, **Read-only**, to prevent accidental changes to its contents.

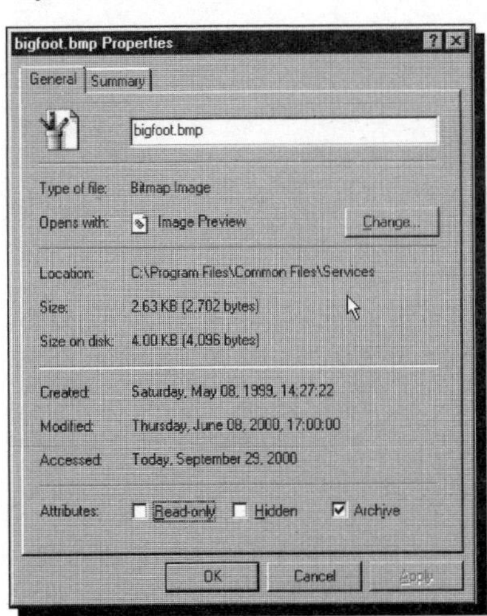

Fig. 4.10 Properties Display Box.

The Properties dialogue box of some types of files has an extra tab which allows you to preview, or even play, their contents.

Creating Shortcuts

With Windows Me, just as with Windows 95/98, you can put a shortcut to any program, document, or printer on your desktop or in any folder. Shortcuts are quick ways to get to the items you use often; they save you having to dig deep into your system files to access them.

One program we seem to use a lot to process our system text files is the Notepad (we will discuss its use later), so we will step through the process of placing a shortcut to it onto the desktop.

You must first find the actual program. An easy way is to use the **Start, Search, For Files or Folders** command and look in the C: drive (or whichever drive Windows is installed on). Soon enough the NOTEPAD.EXE file is found, and you can select it, right-click it and drag it onto the desktop. Releasing the right mouse button displays the drop-down menu shown below.

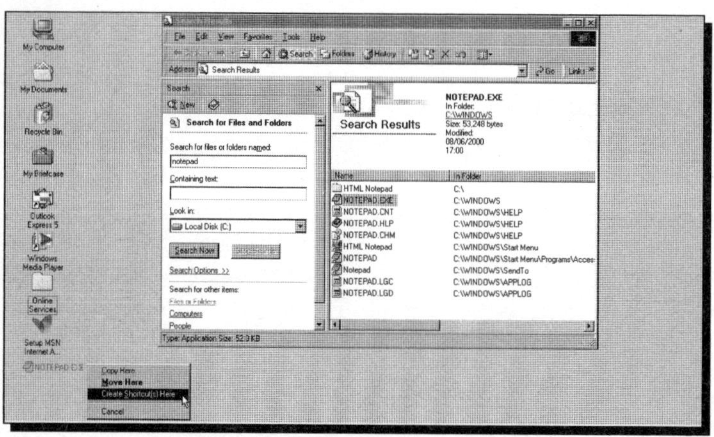

Fig. 4.11 Placing Notepad on the Desktop.

Click the **Create Shortcut(s) Here** option to place the new shortcut icon on the desktop. Note that the icon has a right pointer arrow on it. This is how you can tell that an icon is a shortcut, not the actual file. If you find the icon name a little lengthy, you can rename it, using the same procedure as described earlier for renaming files.

If your desktop does not let you place the icons where you want them, you need to change its settings. Right-click on the desktop, click the **Arrange Icons** option on the command menu and click **Auto Arrange** to remove the tick mark alongside it (Fig. 4.12).

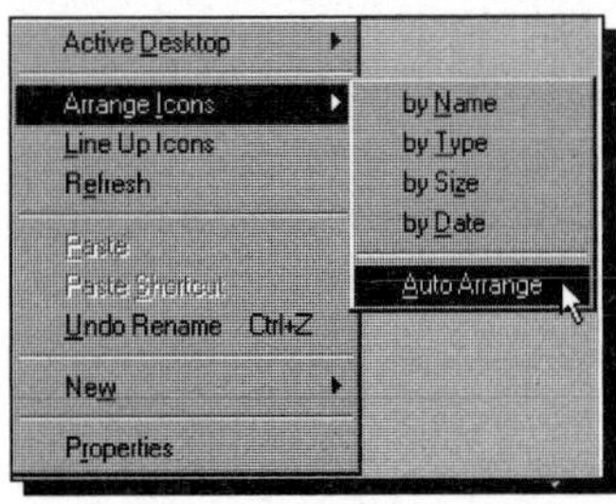

Fig. 4.12 Controlling Icon Position.

You should now be able to arrange your desktop icons in any way you wish, by simply dragging them around the desktop.

Sending Folders and Files

A very useful feature of Windows Me is the ability to quickly send files and folders to specific destinations.

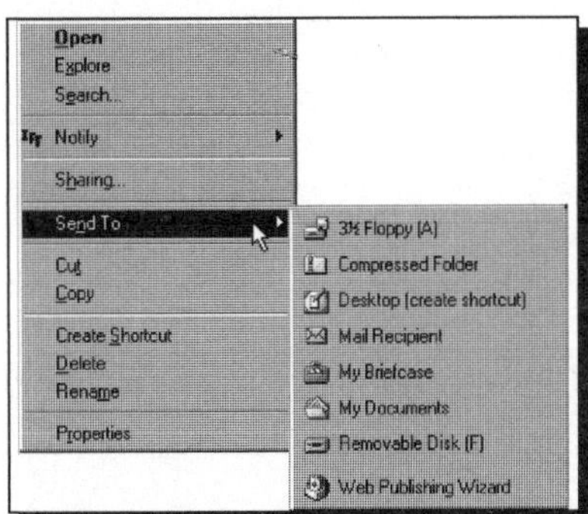

Fig. 4.13 Sending Folders and Files.

Right-clicking selected folders, or files, will open the menu shown in Fig. 4.13 on the left. Selecting the **Send To** option opens the list of available destinations. In your case these are bound to be different, for example, the last option might not be available to you.

Selecting the **3½ Floppy (A)** option will copy any selected folders and files to a removable disc in the (A:) drive, as shown by the very decorative animated window that appears while the process is being carried out.

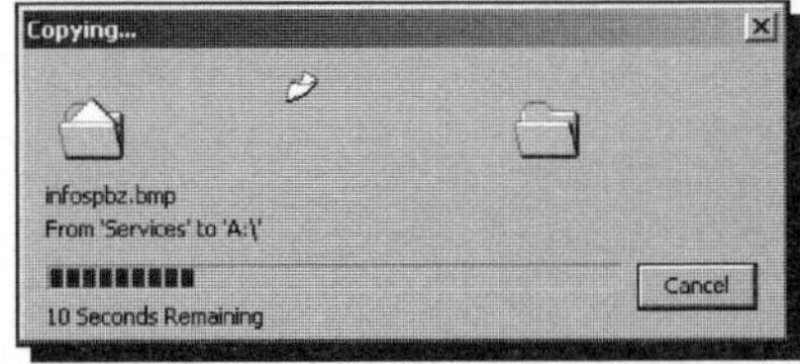

Fig. 4.14 Copying Folders and Files.

It is easy to add more locations to the Send To menu, as it is controlled by the contents of the SendTo folder, which is itself in the Windows folder. However, the SendTo folder is hidden by default, so if you use the **Start, Search** command, you may not find it. To make it visible, double-click on the My Computer icon on your desktop, then use the **Tools, Folder Options** command, click the View tab and finally click the **Show hidden files and folders** option.

To add a destination to the Send To menu do the following:

- Click the Documents and Settings folder on the drive where Windows Me is installed.
- Double-click the SendTo folder.
- Use the File, New, Shortcut command.
- Follow the instructions on your screen.

It is useful to be able to send text files straight to the Notepad so that you can see, and maybe edit, their contents. To add Notepad to the Send To menu, you don't have to go through the above procedure because you already have a shortcut to it on your desktop. Instead, copy this shortcut icon from your desktop to the SendTo window, as shown below.

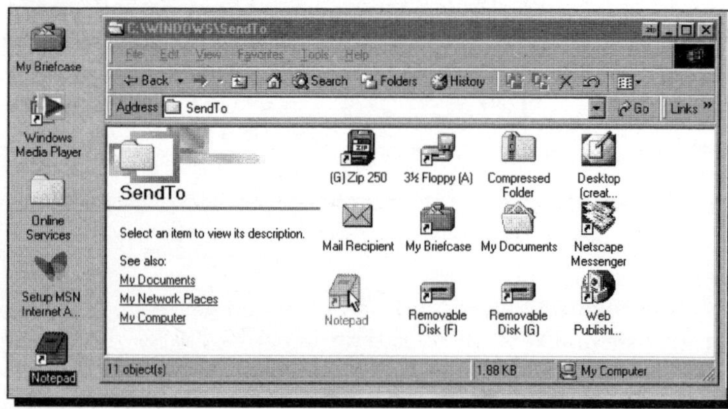

Fig. 4.15 Adding a Shortcut to the SendTo Folder.

When you next open the Send To menu it should have the extra item as shown here to the right. As you can see, we have renamed the shortcut to simply 'Notepad'.

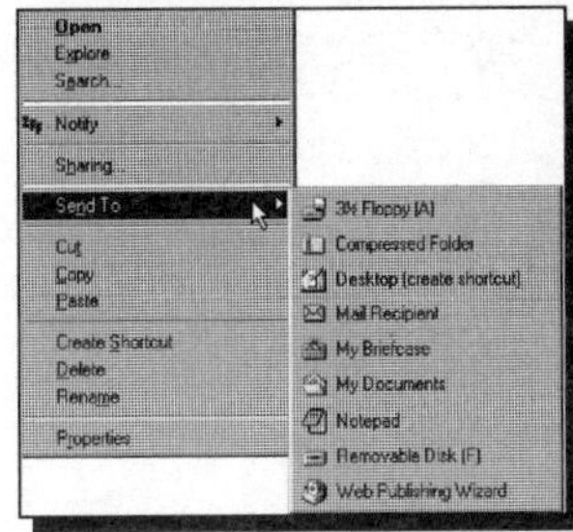

Deleting Folders and Files

The operations described here must only be carried out on the folders or files held in the Test Folder, unless you really want to delete specific items. To experiment, copy all the files in the Services folder into the Test Folder first (see page 49).

- To delete or remove files, first highlight them, and then either press the <Del> key on the keyboard, or press the Delete button on the toolbar, shown here, or use the **File**, **Delete** command from the window menu bar.

Either method opens the message box shown here which gives you the chance to abort the operation by selecting **No**.

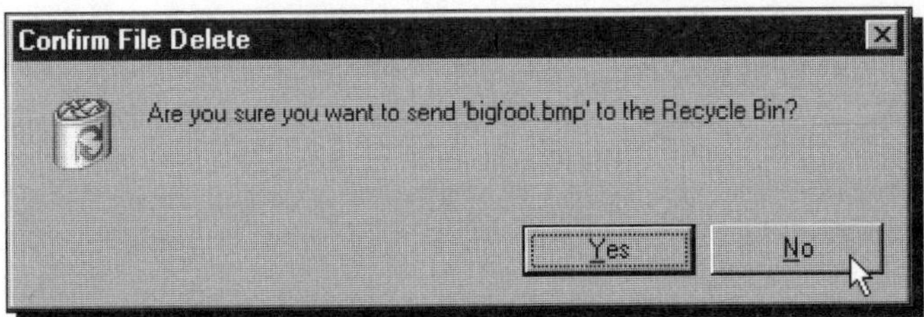

Fig. 4.16 The Delete File Warning Dialogue Box.

To delete folders, follow the same procedure as for files. A similar dialogue box to the one in Fig 4.16 will be displayed. The only difference is that the word 'File' is replaced by the word 'Folder'.

To carry on with the deletion in either case, select **Yes**.

The Recycle Bin

As you can see from the message boxes on the previous page, by default all files or folders deleted from a hard disc, are actually placed in a holding folder named the Recycle Bin.

If you open the Recycle Bin, by double-clicking its Desktop icon, shown here, you will see that it is just a special folder. It lists all the files, folders, icons and shortcuts that have been deleted from fixed drives since it was last emptied, as shown below.

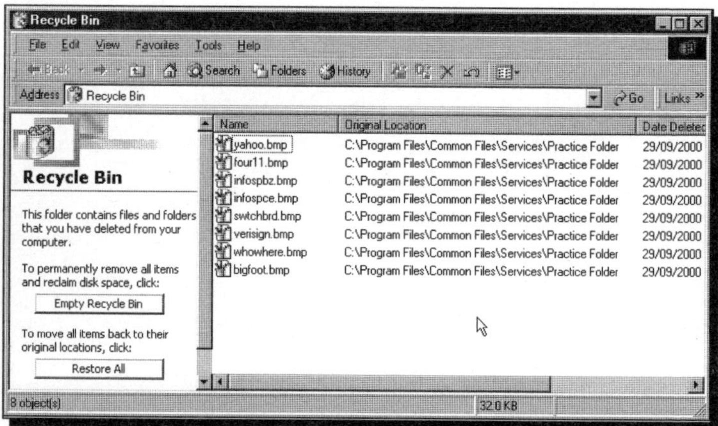

Fig. 4.17 The Recycle Bin Folder Showing Deleted Files.

Note that Windows keeps a record of the original locations of the deleted files, so that it can restore them if necessary.

To restore all files and folders in the Recycle Bin, click the **Restore All** button on the left pane of the displayed window. To restore certain files or folders, first select them which causes the **Restore All** button on the left pane to change to **Restore**, then either click this button or use the **File, Restore** menu command.

To save disc space, every now and then, open the Recycle Bin and click the **Empty Recycle Bin** button on the left pane.

Formatting Discs

We assume, here, that your hard disc has already been formatted according to your manufacturer's instructions when setting up the system. New floppy discs, if not already pre-formatted, must be formatted before they can be used by your computer's operating system. A floppy disc that has been formatted in one type of computer, can only be used in another computer if they are compatible and use the same operating system.

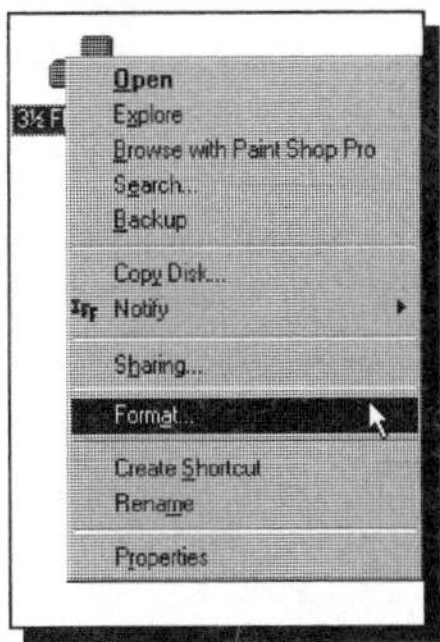

To format a floppy disc, put it into the correct disc drive, open My Computer by double-clicking its icon on the desktop and right-click on the icon for the drive. In our case, this would be the (A:) drive, as shown to the left. From the displayed drop-down menu, select the **Format** option, which opens the dialogue box below (Fig. 4.18). It only remains now to choose options in this box and press **Start** to carry out the formatting.

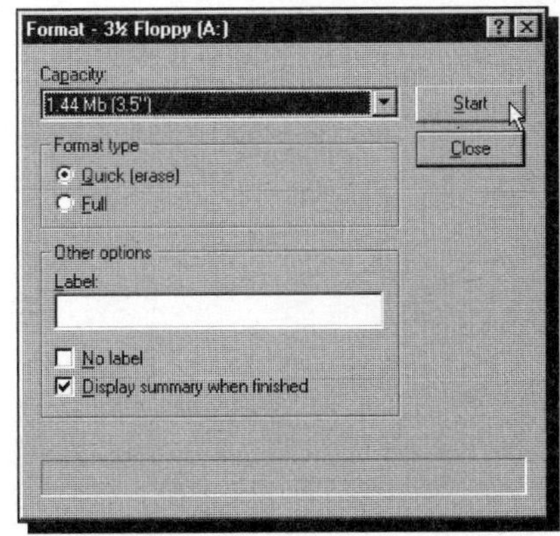

Fig. 4.18 The Format Dialogue Box.

The **Capacity** drop-down list lets you select the size of disc to format. If you want to name your disc, so that the system will recognise it by that name (in the My Computer windows, for example), enter the name in the **Label** text box. Choosing **Quick (erase)** in the **Format type** section, deletes the File Allocation Table of a previously formatted disc - you cannot use this option on a new disc.

Formatting will destroy any files on the disc, so take care.

Copying Discs

Copying whole floppy discs is quite straightforward with Windows Me. It is best carried out from the menu opened when you right-click the disc drive icon from within My Computer. Put the disc to copy into the drive and select **Copy Disk** from the menu.

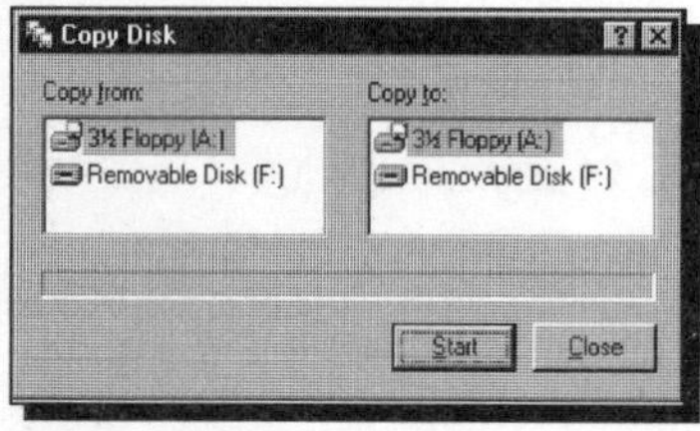

Fig. 4.19 The Copy Disk Window.

A box, similar to that shown here, will open with your floppy disc drives listed. In our case, only one drive type shows on each side. If you have more, select the drive to **Copy from** and that to **Copy to**, but the discs must be of the same type. You can't carry out this operation between different capacity discs. When ready, click the **Start** button. You will be told when to insert the destination disc, but be warned, any files already on this disc will be lost.

Additional Features of My Computer

Microsoft has upgraded the functionality of the My Computer facility and added features previously only found in the Windows Explorer. These are mainly available in the **View, Explorer Bar** menu options, as shown here, and include:

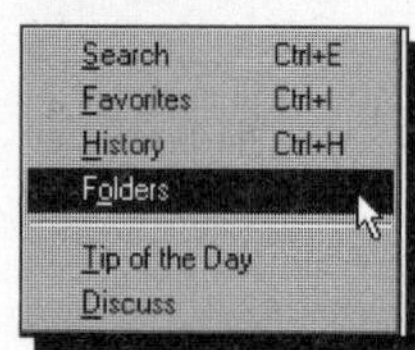

- ***Search*** - clicking this, displays the **Search** facility in the left pane of the My Computer window. This is identical in functionality to the **Start, Search** command.
- ***Favorites*** - clicking this, displays the **Favorites** facility in the left pane of the My Computer window, and allows you to add and organise useful URL addresses, or access various pre-set media addresses on the Internet.

* ***History*** - Clicking this, displays the **History** facility in the left pane of the My Computer window, and allows you to see which 'pages' (includes files and folders on your system, other computers connected to your system or sites on the Internet) were visited recently.

* ***Folders*** - Clicking this, displays a hierarchical 'system tree' on the left panel of the My Computer window showing all the resources of your computer, as well as those of a network you might be connected to. In your case, the display to the right will obviously have different contents from ours, as your system is bound to be structured differently.

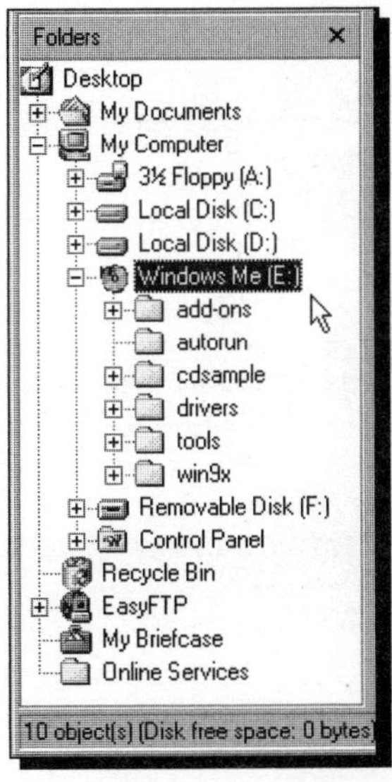

Fig. 4.20 The System Tree.

The system tree lists Objects which are marked with a plus sign (+), and contain sub-folders. Clicking a (+) sign, opens it up to reveal the sub-folders beneath. When sub-folders are displayed, the (+) sign changes to a minus sign (–), indicating that the parent folder can be collapsed. This is shown in the example above, where the drive (E:) (containing the Windows Me CD-ROM) is expanded.

The right-hand, or contents, pane is automatically displayed when you select a folder from the tree. As with most Windows Me system windows, you can change the format of the information shown in the contents pane by using the **View** commands from the menu bar, or clicking the Views button on the toolbar. All the powerful right-click and properties features described previously are supported in My Computer.

Windows Explorer

Windows Explorer is the other way of manipulating your system data. However, there doesn't seem to be any advantage to using Windows Explorer over My Computer, because Microsoft has made their features identical.

Nevertheless, to open Windows Explorer from the desktop, click the **Start** button, point to **Programs**, then **Accessories** and click **Windows Explorer**, which is probably very near the bottom of the cascade menu list, with the identifying icon shown here. When it starts, Windows Explorer shows a split window with the hierarchical 'system tree' appearing on the left panel of its window by default.

To get used to the Windows Explorer, we suggest you open it, maximise its window, set the contents format to **Details** from the **View** menu, and then slowly work your way down the system tree viewing in detail all your folders and files.

5

Controlling Information

When you are using Windows Me or one of its applications, you will invariably come across a **Readme.txt** file which contains last minute information not available in printed form in the User Guides. Vendors create such text files which can be read by either the WordPad or the Notepad accessories. What follows will show you how to read such files, print them, or copy them onto the Clipboard, so that you can transfer the information into another package.

Microsoft's WordPad

WordPad supports mainly text document formats, plus Word 6 documents, but has no pagination features. It is a useful accessory for writing and reading simple documents or memos.

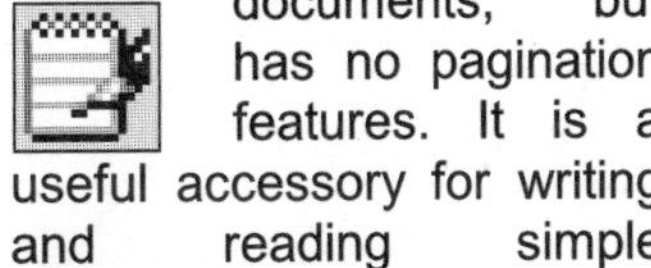

To access WordPad, click the **Start** button, and select **Programs, Accessories, WordPad**, as shown to the right in Fig. 5.1.

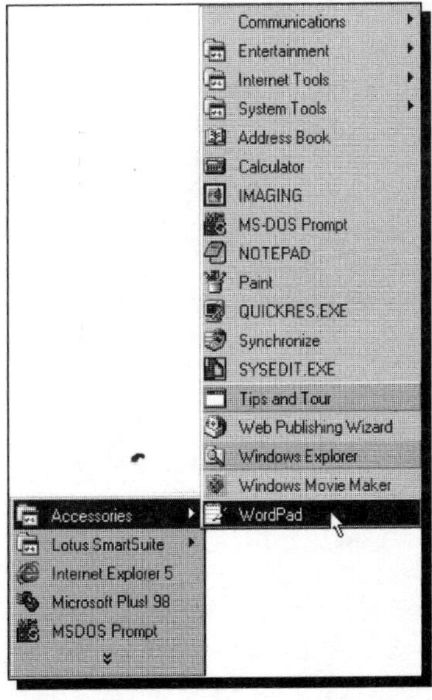

Fig. 5.1 Accessing the Text Editor WordPad.

The WordPad Window

Opening the WordPad accessory, displays an application window similar to the one below.

The top line of the WordPad window is the 'Title' bar which contains the name of the document, and if this bar is dragged with the mouse the window can be moved around the screen. Also, just like any other window, its size can be changed by dragging any of its four sides in the required direction.

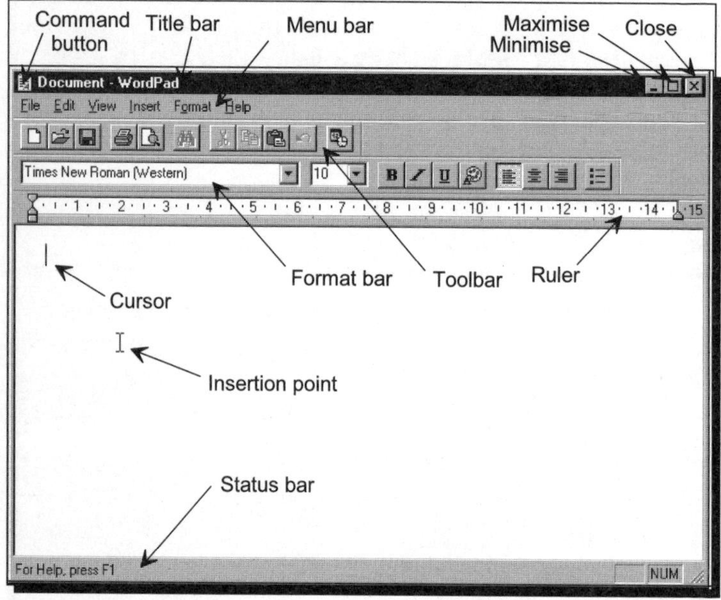

Fig. 5.2 The WordPad Window.

The second line of the window displays the 'Menu' bar which allows access to the following sub menus:

File Edit View Insert Format Help

As described in Chapter 2 - 'Starting Windows Me' - the sub-menus are accessed either with your mouse, or by pressing the <Alt> key (which underlines one letter per menu option) followed by the underlined letter.

The Toolbar

As with most Windows applications, the Toolbar contains a set of icon buttons that you click to carry out some of the more common menu functions. The actions of each icon are outlined below.

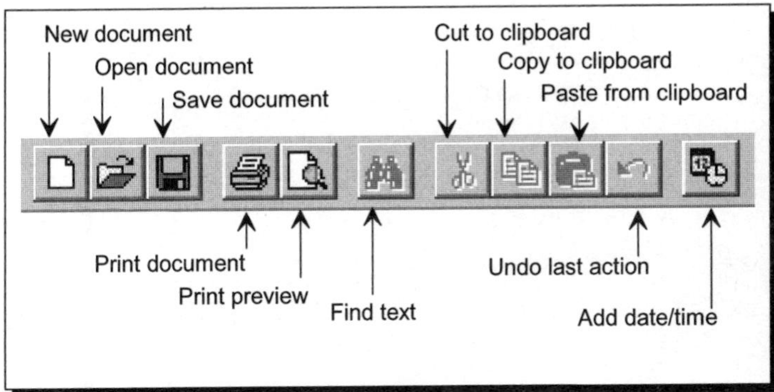

Fig. 5.3 The WordPad Toolbar.

The Format Bar

WordPad has an extra bar of icons that are used to more easily control the format of text in a document.

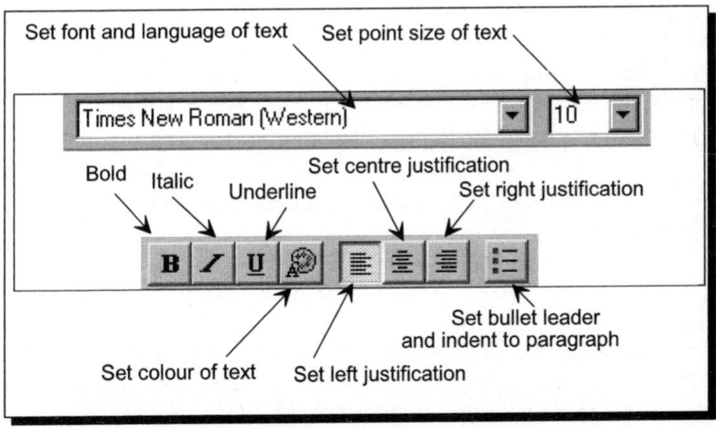

Fig. 5.4 The WordPad Format Bar.

Opening a WordPad Document

In order to illustrate this section, either type in a short letter, or if

you have the Windows Me CD, place it in the CD Drive and left-click the Open button on WordPad's Toolbar, shown here, which displays the following dialogue box.

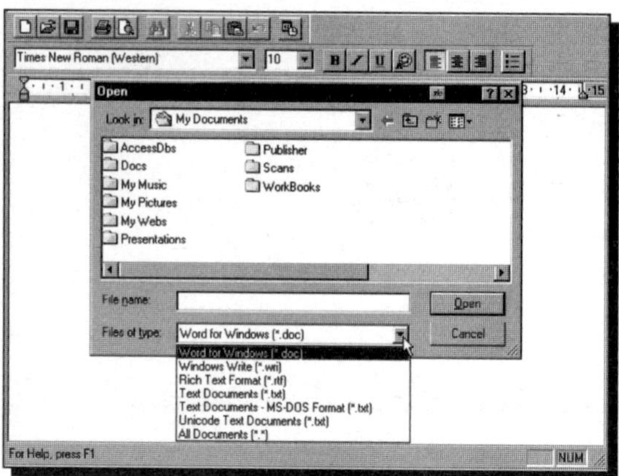

Fig. 5.5 The WordPad Open Dialogue Box.

You can use this Open box to open documents that might have been created by different applications, as shown on the drop-down list against **Files of type**, or documents that are kept in different locations. For example, you can open a document which might be on your computer's hard disc, or on a network drive that you have a connection to. To locate other drives, simply click the Up One Level button pointed to below.

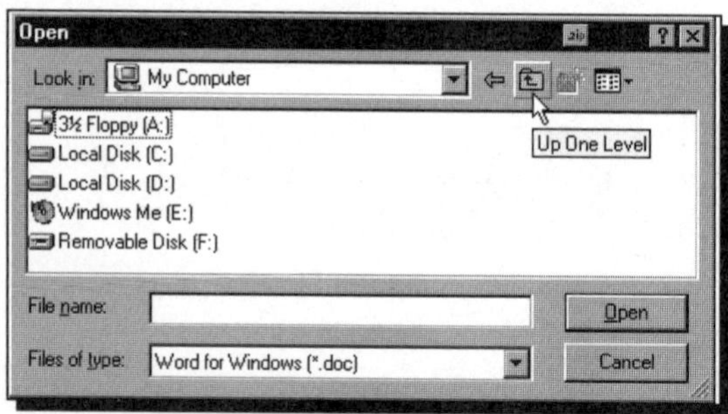

Fig. 5.6 Moving Up One Level in the Open List.

Having selected a drive, you can then select the folder within which your document was saved, select its filename and click the **Open** button on the dialogue box. For our example, first choose the CD-ROM drive (if not already selected), then choose 'All Documents' (*.*) in the **Files of type** box to reveal the **setuptip.txt** file, as shown below.

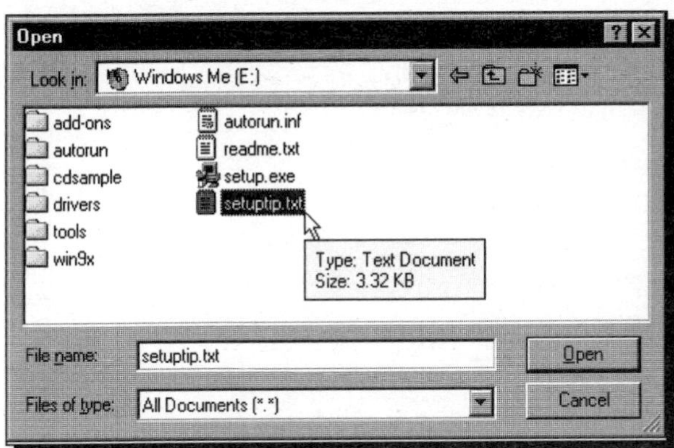

Fig. 5.7 Selecting the Setuptip.txt File.

Select this file and click the **Open** button to display:

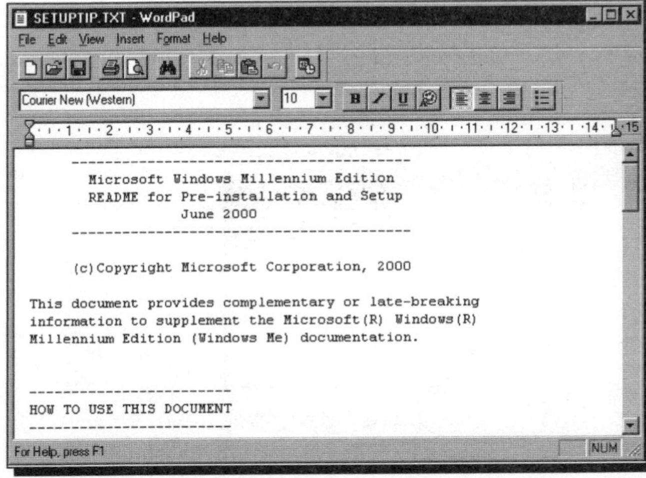

Fig. 5.8 The Setuptip Text File Opened in WordPad.

WordPad can read six types of file formats; Word for Windows (.doc) files, Windows Write (.wri) files, Rich Text Format (.rtf) files, Text Document (.txt - both ANSI and ASCII formats), Text Document - MS-DOS Format (.txt) files, and Unicode Text Document (.txt) files.

Moving Around a WordPad Document

You can move the cursor around a document with the mouse, the normal direction keys, and with key combinations, the most useful of which are listed below.

To move	*Press*
Left one character	←
Right one character	→
Up one line	↑
Down one line	↓
To beginning of line	Home
To end of line	End
Up one window	Page Up
Down one window	Page Down
To beginning of file	Ctrl+Home
To end of file	Ctrl+End

Saving to a File

To save a document, click the Save Toolbar icon, shown here, or use the **File, Save** command. A dialogue box appears on the screen with the cursor in the **File name** field box waiting for you to type a name. You can select a drive or a folder, other than the one displayed, by clicking the 'Up One Level' icon on the Toolbar - the one we are pointing to.

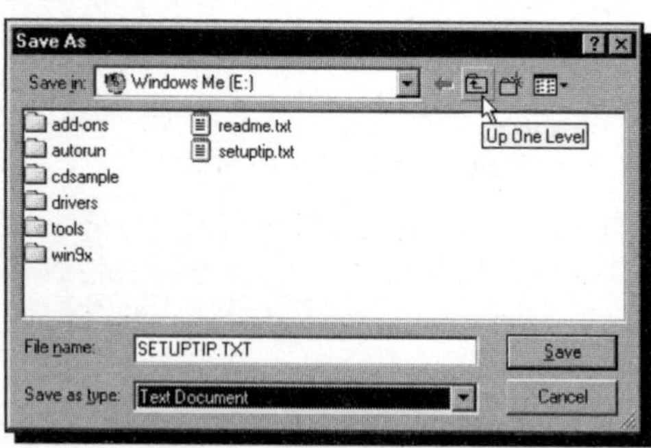

Fig. 5.9 The Save As Dialogue Box.

There are five formatting choices in the **Save as type** box when you first save a WordPad document. These are:

(i) Word for Windows 6 which can then be read by Microsoft Word, (ii) Rich Text Format (.rtf) which retains most of its text enhancements and can be imported into many other applications, (iii) Text Document which is a Windows ANSI file to be used if your document is a program or you intend to telecommunicate it, (iv) Text - MS-DOS format which is an unformatted ASCII file, and (v) Unicode Text Format which is another type of text file.

To save your document in the future with a different name use the **File**, **Save As** menu command.

Document Editing

For small deletions, such as letters or words, the easiest way is to use the <Delete> or <BkSp> keys. With the <Delete> key, position the cursor on the first letter you want to remove and press <Delete>; the letter is deleted and the following text moves one space to the left. With the <BkSp> key, position the cursor immediately to the right of the character to be deleted and press <BkSp>; the cursor moves one space to the left pulling the rest of the line with it and overwriting the character to be deleted. Note that the difference between the two is that with <Delete> the cursor does not move at all.

Text editing is usually carried out in the insert mode. Any characters typed will be inserted at the cursor location and the following text will be pushed to the right, and down. Pressing the <Insert> key will change to Overstrike mode, which causes entered text to overwrite any existing text at the cursor.

When larger scale editing is needed, use the **Cut, Copy** and **Paste** operations; the text to be altered must be 'selected' before these operations can be carried out. These functions are then available when the **Edit** sub-menu is activated, or Toolbar icons are used.

Selecting Text

The procedure in WordPad, as in all Windows applications, is that before any operation such as formatting or editing can be carried out on text, you first select the text to be altered. Selected text is highlighted on the screen. This can be carried out in several ways:

a. **Using the keyboard**; position the cursor on the first character to be selected, hold down the <Shift> key while using the direction keys to highlight the required text, then release the <Shift> key. Navigational key combinations can also be used with the <Shift> key to highlight blocks of text.

b. **With the mouse**; click the left mouse button at the beginning of the block and drag the cursor across the block so that the desired text is highlighted, then release the mouse button. To select a word, double-click in the word, to select a larger block, place the cursor at the beginning of the block, and with the <Shift> key depressed, move the mouse pointer to the end of the desired block, and click the left mouse button.

   Using the 'selection area' and a mouse; place the mouse pointer in the left margin area of the WordPad window where it changes to a right slanting arrow, and click the left mouse button once to select the current line, twice to select the current paragraph, or three times to select the whole document.

Try out all these methods and find out the one you are most comfortable with.

Copying Blocks of Text

Once text has been selected it can be copied to another location in your present document, to another WordPad document, or to another Windows application. As with most of the editing and formatting operations there are many ways of doing this.

The first is by using the **Edit, Copy** command sequence from the menu, or clicking the Copy Toolbar icon, moving the cursor to the start of where you want the copied text, and using the **Edit, Paste** command, or clicking the Paste icon. Another method uses the quick key combinations, <Ctrl+C> to copy and <Ctrl+V> to paste.

To copy the same text again to another location in the document, move the cursor to the new location and paste it there with either of the above methods.

Drag and Drop - Maybe the easiest way to copy selected text, or an object such as a graphic, is to drag it with the left mouse button and the <Ctrl> key both depressed and to release the mouse button when the vertical line that follows the pointer is at the required destination.

As you get used to Windows application packages you will be able to decide which of these methods is best for you.

Moving Blocks of Text

Selected text can also be moved, in which case it is deleted in its original location. Use the **Edit, Cut,** command, or the <Ctrl+X> keyboard shortcut, or click the Cut icon, move the cursor to the required new location and then use the **Edit, Paste** command, <Ctrl+V>, or click the Paste icon. The moved text will be placed at the cursor location and will force any existing text to make room for it. This operation can be cancelled by simply pressing <Esc>.

Drag and Drop - Selected text, or an object such as a graphic, can be moved by dragging it with the left mouse button depressed and releasing the button when the vertical line that follows the mouse pointer is at the required destination.

Deleting Blocks of Text

When text is deleted it is removed from the document. With WordPad any selected text can be deleted with the **Edit, Cut** command, or by simply pressing the <Delete> key. However, using **Edit, Cut** (or <Ctrl+X>) places the text on the Windows clipboard and allows you to use the **Edit, Paste** (or <Ctrl+V>) command, while using the <Delete> key, does not.

The Undo Command

As text is lost with the delete command you should use it with caution, but if you do make a mistake all is not lost as long as you act immediately. The **Edit, Undo** command (or <Ctrl+Z>), or clicking the Undo Toolbar button, reverses your most recent action, so you need to use it before carrying out any further operations.

Finding and Changing Text

WordPad allows you to search for specified text, or character combinations. In the 'Find' mode it will highlight each occurrence in turn so that you can carry out some action on it. In the 'Replace' mode you specify what replacement is to be carried out.

For example, in a long memo you may decide to replace every occurrence of the word 'program' with the word 'programme'. To do this, first go to the beginning of the document, as searches operate in a forward direction, then choose the **Edit, Replace** menu command to open a dialogue box, like the one shown in Fig. 5.10.

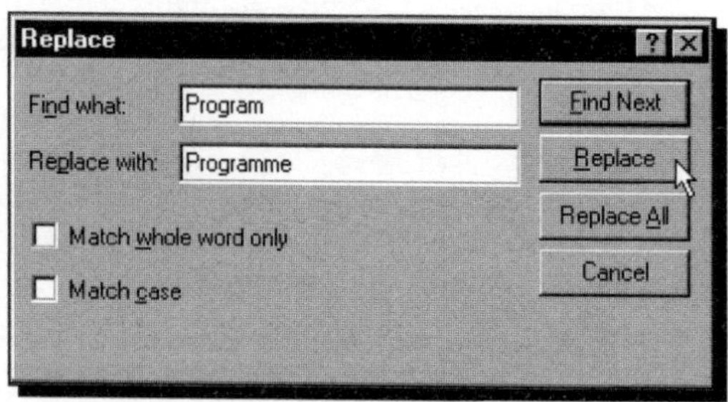

Fig. 5.10 The Replace Dialogue Box.

You type what you want to search for in the **Find what** box. You can then specify whether you want to **Match whole word only**, and whether to **Match case**, (upper or lower case) by check-marking the appropriate boxes. Type the replacement word in the **Replace with** box, and then make a selection from one of the four buttons provided. Selecting **Replace** requires you to manually confirm each replacement, whilst selecting **Replace All** will replace all occurrences of the word automatically.

Formatting your Work

When working with text files you cannot format your documents, but in Microsoft Word, or RTF modes, you can. Such formatting can involve the appearance of individual characters or words, and the indentation, addition of bullet leaders and the alignment of paragraphs. These functions are carried out in WordPad from the **Format** menu options or from the Format bar. To activate the latter, use the **View** command and click the **Format Bar** option, as shown in Fig. 5.11.

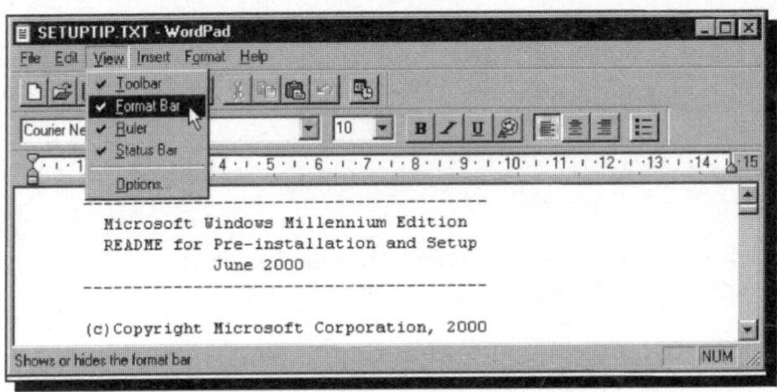

Fig. 5.11 Activating the Formatting Bar.

As an example of some of the formatting options, we have carried out a few changes to the **Setuptip** document opened earlier. First, we used the **Save As** command to save the document as an RTF type file on our hard drive, say within the Windows folder, so that we could carry out certain formatting commands (such as justification) which are not available to a TXT type file.

We then removed the dotted line above and below the title and all spaces before each of the three title lines. Then we highlighted the three title lines, and changed their point size to 16, then emboldened them and centre justified them by clicking appropriate format bar options.

The date was then added below the title by clicking the Date/Time icon on the Toolbar and choosing the date format required.

The two main paragraphs were then selected and the Bullet icon clicked on the Format bar. This indented the paragraphs and gave them bullet leaders.

Finally, the whole document was selected and its font changed from Courier New to Arial by choosing the font type from the drop-down list shown to the left. To get the formatted document shown in Fig. 5.12, we found it necessary to remove hard returns at the end of each line so word wrap could display correctly.

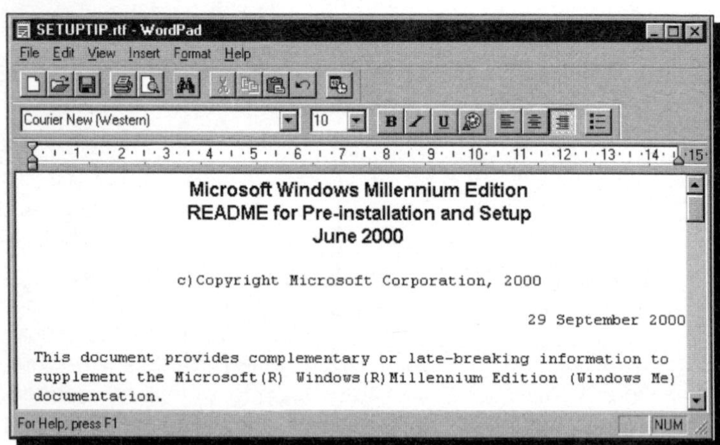

Fig. 5.12 The Display of a Formatted Document.

Try these features out for yourself. They are quite powerful.

The Ruler

To activate the ruler, use the **View** command, then click the **Ruler** option on the drop-down sub-menu. The Ruler displays at the top of the text area of the WordPad window (see Fig. 5.12), and lets you set and see Tab points for your text, or visually change the left and right margins, (the empty space to the left and right of the text area) of your document.

Setting your own tabs is easy by clicking within the ruler where you want to set the tab. Tabs can be moved within the ruler by dragging them with the mouse to a new position, or removed by simply dragging them off the ruler. Default tab settings do not show on the ruler, but custom tabs do.

Printing Documents

As long as your printer has been properly installed and configured (see Chapter 6), you should have no problems printing your document from the WordPad application.

Setting up your Page

Before attempting to print, make sure that WordPad is set to the same page size as the paper you plan to use. To do this, use the **File**, **Page Setup** menu command to open the dialogue box to the left. From here you can control the paper **Size** and **Source**, the size of all the **Margins** around the edge of the sheet, and the **Orientation** of the paper. The **Printer** button lets you select between different printers, including network printers (if you are connected to any), and set their properties.

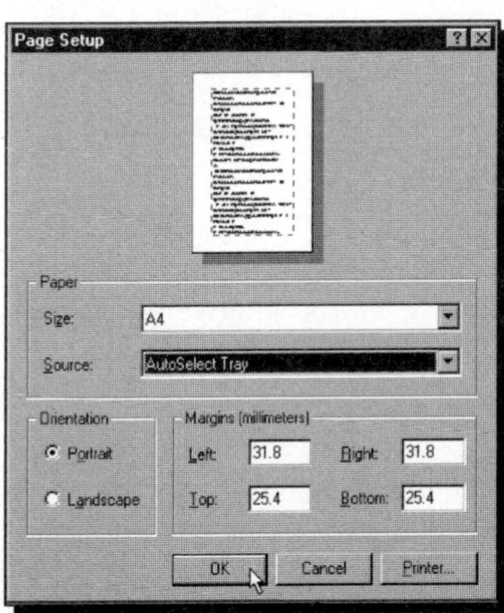

Fig. 5.13 The Page Setup Screen.

Print Preview

Before actually committing yourself and printing your document to paper, it is always best to look at a Preview on the screen. This can save both your paper and printer toner or cartridge bills.

To preview the current document and settings, either click the Print Preview icon on the Toolbar, or use the **File, Print Preview** menu command to display the following screen.

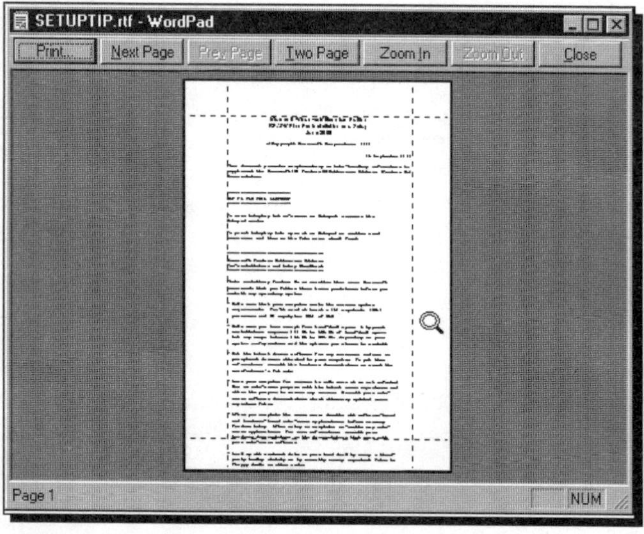

Fig. 5.14 The Print Preview Screen.

The preview screen, shown above, is the only place in WordPad that you can actually see your document's pagination, and then you have no control over it! A dreadful omission, but perhaps intentional, to make sure everyone buys Microsoft Word instead!

To zoom in on the document, just click the pointer on it, or use the **Zoom In** button. If your document has several pages you can select a **Two Page** view of it. When you are happy your document is perfect, press the **Print** button.

Using the Clipboard

In Windows Me, you have access to the Clipboard utility which is a temporary storage location for information you want to cut or copy. This information can be viewed using the Clipboard viewer, the icon of which is shown here.

We have already used the Clipboard when using the **Cut** and **Paste** features found in WordPad, and in most other Windows programs. Apart from cutting, copying and pasting operations in Windows applications, you can also use the Clipboard to copy the contents of an application's window, or to copy Windows graphics images, so that you can transfer such information to other applications. There are two ways of copying information:

- Press the <Print Screen> key to copy onto the Clipboard the contents of a whole Windows screen, even if that screen is a DOS application.
- Press the <Alt+Print Screen> key combination to copy onto the Clipboard the contents of the current open window, or dialogue box.

To illustrate these techniques follow the step-by-step instructions given below.

To Copy a Full Windows Screen:

- Close all running applications and double-click the My Computer icon on the desktop.
- Move the My Computer displayed dialogue box to the top left corner of the screen so that it does not obscure any icons on the desktop.
- Press the <Print Screen> key, then click the **Start** button and select **Programs, Accessories, System Tools** and click the **Clipboard Viewer** option. The following, or something like it, will be displayed:

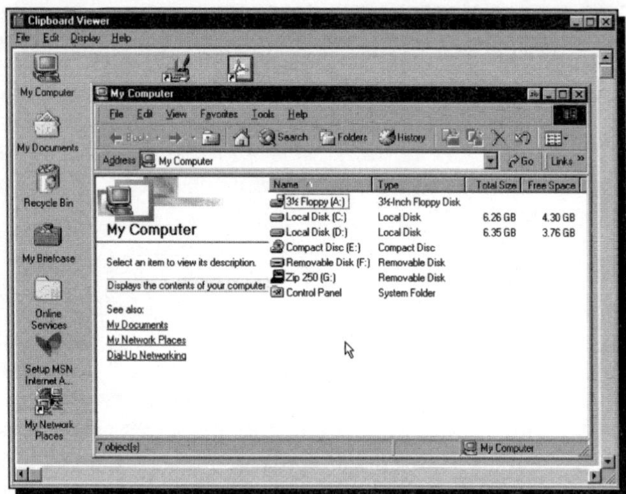

Fig. 5.15 The Contents of the Clipboard.

To Copy the Contents of a Current Open Window:

- Close all running applications and double-click the My Computer icon on the desktop.
- Press the <Alt+Print Screen> key, then click the **Start** button and select **Programs, Accessories, System Tools** and click the **Clipboard Viewer** option to display the current window only.

To copy a DOS screen:

- Close all running applications, click the **Start** button and select **Programs, Accessories, System Tools** and click the DOS Prompt option, the icon of which is shown here.

- DOS applications can run in a window or in full screen. You can switch from one to the other by pressing <Alt+Enter>. Then continue as above.

The contents of the Clipboard can be saved in a file (with the .CLP extension). The Clipboard's Menu bar supports the usual options, which are self-explanatory.

The Windows Paint Program

Paint is a 32-bit Windows application, first introduced with Windows 95 and improved in Windows 98. You can use Paint to create, view and edit, simple or complicated graphics.

Paint is an OLE (Object Linking and Embedding) program, and allows the creation of OLE object information that can be embedded or linked into other documents, as we shall see at the end of the chapter. It can read and write a number of file formats, namely, bitmap (.bmp) files (monochrome, and 16, 256 & 24-bit colour), File Interchange Format (.jpg & .jpeg) files, and Graphics Interchange Format (.gif) files.

Starting Paint

To start Paint, use the **Start**, **Programs** command, select **Accessories** from the cascade menu and click the **Paint** entry. In Fig. 5.16, we show the **Iceberg.jpg** file to be found in My Pictures folder which itself is in My Documents folder.

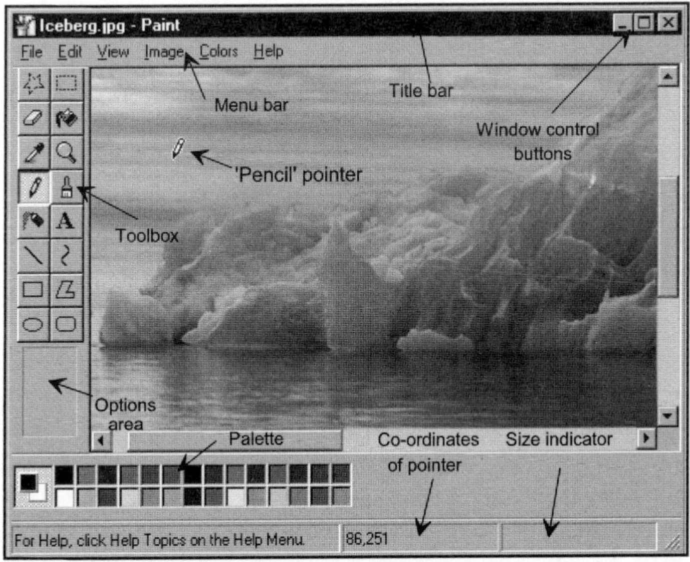

Fig. 5.16 The Paint Opening Window.

The window is divided into a 'drawing' area (the default size of which depends on your video display), surrounded by the Menu bar at the top, the Palette at the bottom, the Options box at the bottom-left corner, with the Toolbox above it.

The Paint Toolbox

The drawing area is where you create your drawings with the help of various tools from the Toolbox. Note that the pencil tool is always selected when you start Paint, and that the function of a Toolbox icon is flagged when you move the mouse pointer over it.

To select a tool, simply point to it and click. Several of them have extra functions you can also select in the Options area. Some tools can work with either of the current foreground or background colours - dragging the tool with the left mouse button uses the foreground colour and with the right one the background colour.

More detail of the Toolbox functions is listed below.

Tool	*Function*
Free Form select	Used to cut out an irregular-shaped area of a picture, with either an opaque or transparent background, which can then be dragged to another part of the drawing, or manipulated using the **Edit** menu commands.
Rectangle select	Used to cut out a rectangular-shaped area of a picture, with either an opaque or transparent background, which can then be dragged to another part of the drawing, or manipulated using the **Edit** menu commands.

Eraser

Used to change the selected foreground colours under the eraser icon to a background colour, or automatically change every occurrence of one colour in the drawing area to another.

Colour fill

Used to fill in any closed shape or area with the current foreground or background colour.

Pick colour

Used to set the foreground or background colour to that at the pointer.

Magnifier

Used to zoom the image to different magnifications. Choose from 1x, 2x, 6x or 8x magnification in the options area.

Pencil

Used to draw free-hand lines in either the foreground or background colour.

Brush

Used to draw free-hand lines with a selection of tools and line thickness shown in the options area.

Airbrush

Used to produce one of three available circular sprays in the foreground or background colours.

Text

Used to add text of different fonts, sizes and attributes in the current foreground colour, with either an opaque or transparent background.

Line

Used to draw straight lines between two points in the current foreground or background colours and drawing width.

Curve

Used to draw curved lines in the current colours and drawing width.

Rectangle

Used to draw hollow and filled rectangles or squares (<Shift> key depressed), in the current colours and drawing width.

Polygon

Used to draw hollow and filled triangles and other polygon shapes, in the current colours and drawing width.

Ellipse

Used to draw hollow and filled ellipses or circles (<Shift> key depressed), in the current colours and drawing width.

Rounded Rectangle

Used to draw hollow and filled rectangles or squares (<Shift> key depressed), with rounded corners, in the current colours and drawing width.

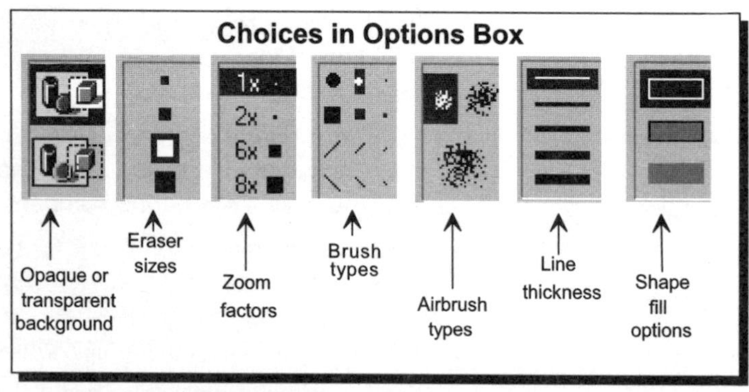

Fig. 5.17 Choices Available in the Options Area of the Toolbox.

Preparing for a Drawing

Before you start drawing, you may need to set the size of the image you want. To do this, use the **Image**, **Attributes** menu command to open the dialogue box shown here.

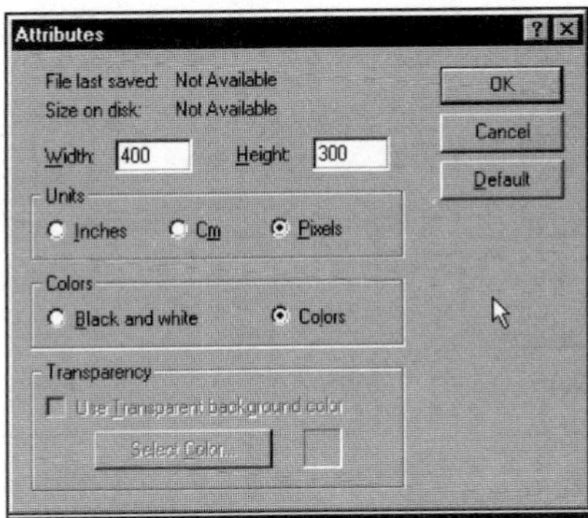

Fig. 5.18 The Attributes Dialogue Box.

The default **Width** and **Height** settings for a new image are given in **Pixels**. If you need a specific image size when it is printed to paper, you can work in **Inches** or **Cm**. Lastly in this box, you can set whether to work in colour or in black and white. Clicking the **Default** button will make your new settings the default for any new working sessions.

Selecting Working Colours

The current background and foreground colour settings are always shown in the two squares to the left of the palette, as shown here.

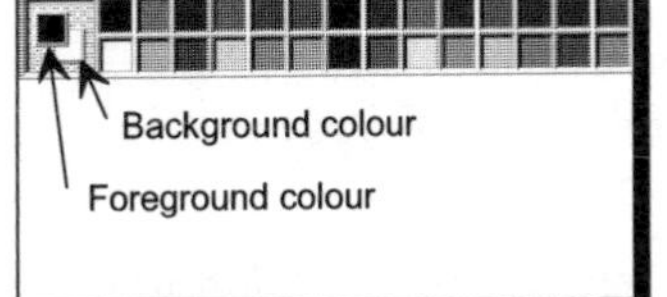

To select a new background colour, point to the colour in the Palette and click the right mouse button. If you now select the **File**, **New** command, Paint will open a new document with the selected background colour. Alternatively you could 'flood' the existing background by selecting the Colour fill icon and right-clicking it on the background of the drawing area.

To select a different foreground colour to be used with any of the drawing tools in the Toolbox, left-click the colour in the Palette.

Entering Text in a Drawing

If you intend to enter text within a drawing, carry out the following steps:

- Select the foreground colour for the text.
- Select the **Text** tool from the Toolbox.
- Select opaque or transparent from the options box.
- Click the pointer on the working area to open the text box, drag it to the correct size and type the text.
- Open the text toolbar, if not already opened, with the **View**, **Text Toolbar** menu command.
- Select the font, point size or other style you want to use from the text toolbar, as shown below.

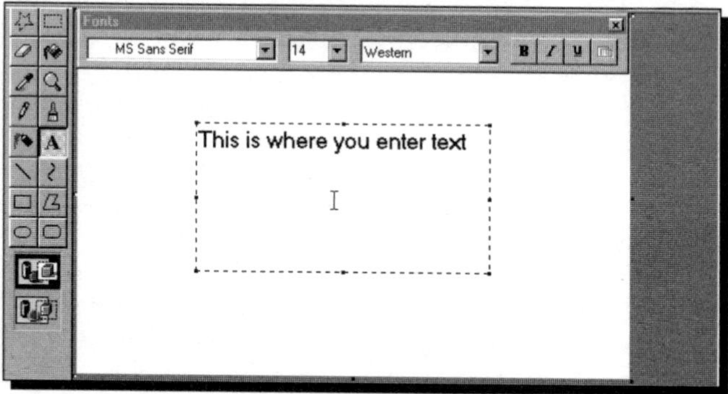

Fig. 5.19 Inserting Text in a Drawing Area.

- When you are happy with the text, click outside the text box to 'fix' it in the drawing and close the toolbar.

While the text toolbar is open you can change any of its options, or use the palette, and see the entered text change straight away.

In the future, as long as the **Text Toolbar** option is ticked in the **View** menu, the toolbar will open whenever you start to enter text.

Using the Paint Tools

Most of the other tools in Paint's Toolbox are quite easy and straightforward to use. To select a tool, point to it and click the left mouse button which depresses its icon in the Toolbox. To use them, you move the pointer to a suitable position within the drawing area and drag the tool around to accomplish the required task.

With most of the Toolbox options, dragging with the left mouse button uses the active foreground colour, and with the right button the active background colour. Releasing the mouse button stops the action being performed. If you make a mistake, you can select the **Edit, Undo** command from the menu bar up to three times, to cancel the last three actions you carried out.

To complete this discussion, we need to describe how to use the 'Curve' and 'Polygon' tools, which differ slightly from the rest. For example:

To draw a curve, first click the Curve toolbar icon, choose a line thickness in the options box, left-click the pointer in the required starting position within the drawing area, then press the left mouse button to anchor the beginning of the curve and move the mouse to the required end of the eventual curve and release it. A 'flexible' line in the current foreground colour will be produced between the two points. Next, click the mouse buttons away from the line and drag it around the window, which causes the line to curve as you move the pointer. When you are happy with the produced curvature, release the mouse button.

To draw a polygon, place the Polygon pointer in the required starting point in the drawing area, left-click and drag the mouse to the required end of the first side of the polygon and release it. A line in the foreground colour is produced between the two points. Next, continue adding sides to the polygon in this way until you complete it, at which point you should double-click the mouse button.

Embedding a Graphic into WordPad

Embedding a graphic into WordPad is similar to copying, but with the important advantage that you can actually edit an embedded object from within WordPad.

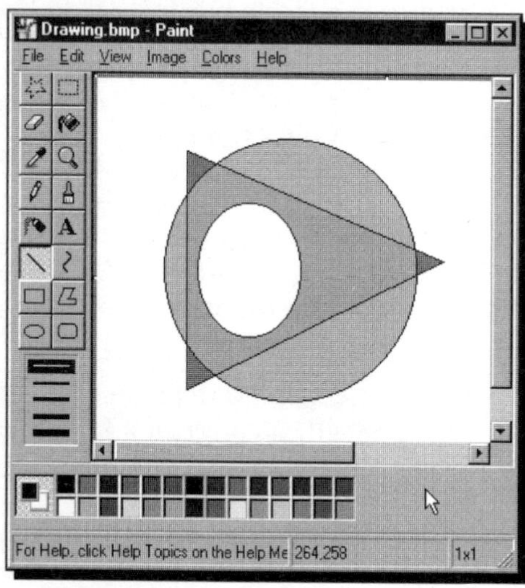

Fig. 5.20 Creating a Graphic in Paint.

To embed a Paint image, first create it in Paint (we created the object shown to the left in order to illustrate the process), then save it as a bitmap file. Next, start WordPad, open the letter or memo you want to embed a graphic into (or just use an empty document), place the cursor where you want to embed it, and press the <Enter> key twice to make some room for it.

Now from the WordPad menu bar, use the **Insert, Object** command which displays the Insert Object dialogue box shown in Fig. 5.21. Click the **Create from File** radio button, **Browse** to locate your bitmap drawing, and press **OK** to place the selected graphic into the WordPad document, as shown on the next page.

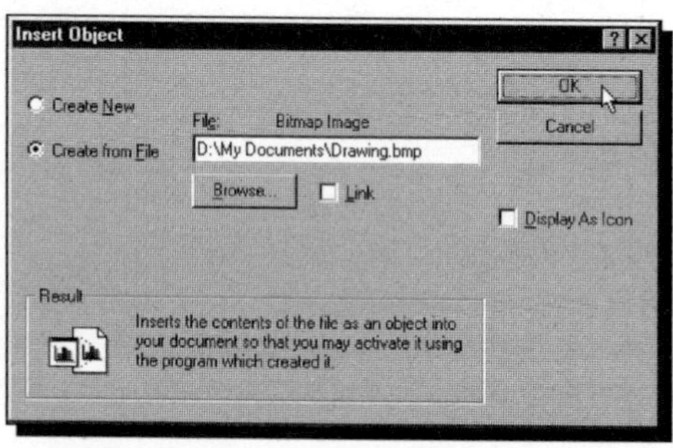

Fig. 5.21 The Insert Object Dialogue Box.

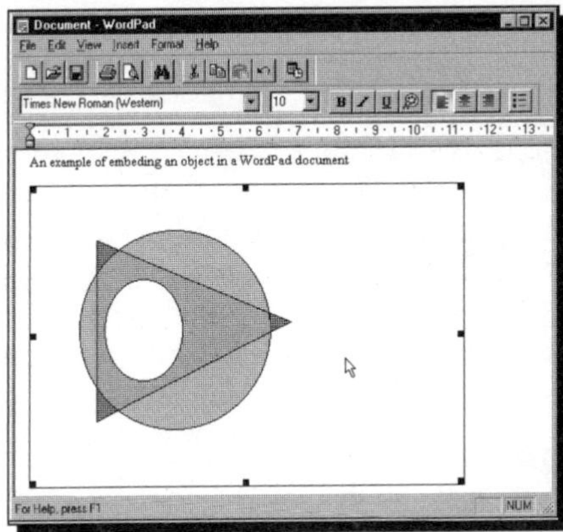

Fig. 5.22 An Embedded Graphic in WordPad.

What has happened here is that the graphic has been embedded in the WordPad document. If you double-click it, the WordPad window will change to a Paint window. You can then edit the image without leaving WordPad, and clicking outside the image will bring WordPad's features back.

The **Display As Icon** option in the Insert Object dialogue box, embeds an icon in the destination document. Not much help in our example, but useful for embedding speech or movie clips in a document. Double-clicking the icon would then play the sound, or movie.

Linking a Graphic into WordPad

Linking, the other main OLE feature, links files dynamically so that information held in one file is automatically updated when the information in the other file changes.

To link our graphic to WordPad, select the **Link** option in the Insert Object dialogue box before clicking the **OK** button. When you double-click a linked image, its file is opened into a separate Paint window. Any changes made are saved in this file as well as being reflected in the document.

These are very clever features that can save a lot of time with full Windows applications. What we have covered here should be a good grounding for the future. You must try these features for yourself, the time will be well spent.

The Notepad

Notepad is a text editor which can be used to write short notes, or create and edit script files. The program, which supports different fonts and their modifications (bold, underline, italic) is usually used to read text files (with the extension **.txt** of less than 64 KB) supplied by different vendors, or to make short text notes. You read such files by double-clicking their filename - trying to read larger files than 64 KB causes WordPad to be activated instead.

To see Notepad in operation, click its entry in the **Accessories** group of **Programs** in the **Start** menu. When Notepad is activated, use the **File, Open** command and look in the WINDOWS folder of the drive it was installed on, probably (C:). There should be several text files there. Double-clicking the filename **Support.txt**, displays:

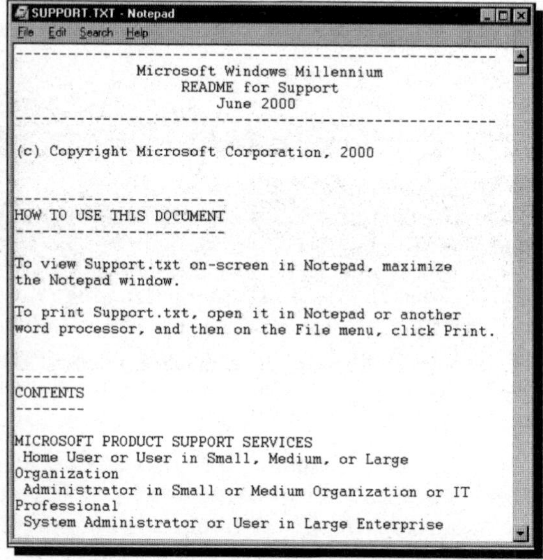

Fig. 5.23 The Task Scheduler Text File.

It is worth reading this file, particularly if you would like to know how to get support from Microsoft on any aspect of running Windows Me.

Notepad's Edit Features

Although Notepad is not as powerful as WordPad, it has some interesting features, such as the ability to turn on word wrap which causes words that will not fit within its page margins to be placed on the next line automatically. You can turn word wrap on by selecting the **Edit, Word Wrap** menu command. Another Notepad feature is the **Select All** option from the **Edit** menu which allows you to highlight a whole document at a stroke in order to, say, copy it onto the Clipboard.

To change the font of a selected text, use the **Edit, Set Font** command to display the Font dialogue box shown in Fig. 5.24:

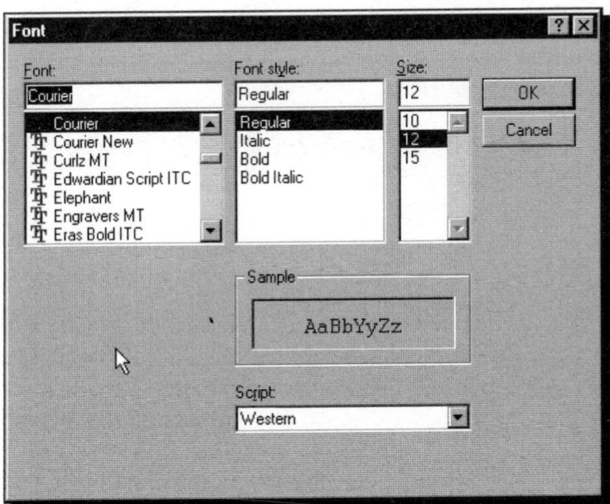

Fig. 5.24 Notepad's Font Dialogue Box.

From here you can also change the **Font style** and font **Size**. However, any changes you make here are reflected in the whole document, as well as all other documents you open using Notepad. In other words, you are configuring Notepad to the font, font style and font size you would like to use when reading or writing text files, rather than applying these changes to individual documents or parts within these documents.

Notepad supports the usual edit features which are useful when working with files, such as cut, copy, paste, and delete, all of which are options of the **Edit** menu. You can even use Notepad to search and find text, by selecting the **Search, Find** command. Once the text is found, pressing the **F3** function key finds the next occurrence. You can also control the **Direction** of the search and use the **Match case** facility.

As you can see, Notepad is a simple text editor and nothing more. If you want more formatting capabilities, use WordPad, or your own word processor.

6

Controlling your System

Controlling Printers

When you upgraded to Windows Me your printers should have been installed automatically. If not, you would have been stepped through the Add Printer Wizard, described later.

Nearly 1,000 different printers are supported by Windows Me so, hopefully, you shouldn't have too much trouble getting yours to work. The printer and printing functions are included in a single Printers folder, which you can open by clicking the icon, shown to the left, in the **Start, Settings** cascade menu. Our Printers folder, shown in Fig. 6.1, has several printers available for use, and an Add Printer icon. This folder provides an easy way of adding new printers, configuring existing ones, and managing all your print jobs.

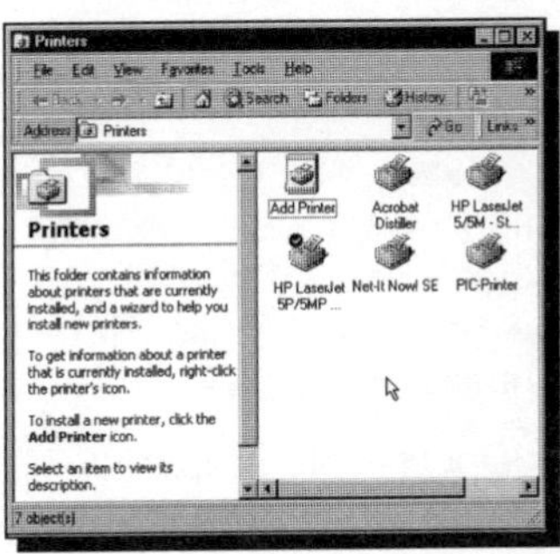

Fig. 6.1 The Printers Folder.

Windows Me, just like Windows 95/98 and Windows NT/2000, supports the following printer set-up methods:

- Plug and Play printers are automatically detected at installation time, or during the boot-up process. You will be prompted for the necessary driver files if they are not already in the Windows directory, these should be supplied with a new Plug-and Play printer.
- Point and Print printing enables you to quickly connect to, and use, printers shared on some other networked PCs.

* For other situations, the Add Printer Wizard steps you through the printer installation process, whether the new printer is connected to your PC, or on a network.

Installing an additional printer (not connected to your system, but available to you, say, at work) allows you to use the additional fonts available to this printer (we will discuss fonts shortly). Below we will step through the procedure of installing such a printer to your system.

To start installation, double-click the **Add Printer** icon in the Printers window, shown in Fig. 6.1. This opens the Add Printers Wizard, which really makes the installation procedure very easy indeed. As with all Wizards, you progress from screen to screen by clicking the **Next** button. The first time you activate the Add Printer Wizard, and after pressing the **Next** button on the first screen, the Wizard scans your computer for installed printers and updates its built-in database.

On the next Wizard screen select the desired printer from the displayed extensive list. If your printer is not on the list, then either use the disc provided by the manufacturer of your printer, or go to the Internet for an update on the list of printers. On the next screen choose FILE: as the port you want to use with the printer.

Documents prepared with this printer selection, can then be printed to file on a 3½" floppy disc, and later printed out on the selected printer (even if it is not connected to your computer and does not itself have access to the particular application you are using). Later you can copy that file to the selected printer from its attached PC by issuing the simple command

```
COPY A:\Filename LPT1: /B
```

The /B switch in this command tells the printer to expect a binary file (with embedded printer codes).

Note that the PC which is connected to the additional printer does not even have to operate under Windows for you to print your work, as the command is given at the Command prompt. If the PC does operate under Windows Me, you will need to use the **Start, Programs, Accessories, MS-DOS Prompt** command, then issue the COPY command.

Configuring your Printer

All configuration for a printer is consolidated onto a tabbed property sheet that is accessed from its icon in the Printers folder. Right-clicking a printer icon opens the object menu, shown on the left, which gives control of the printer's operation. If you click the **Properties** option, the window shown below (Fig. 6.2) opens and lets you control all the printer's parameters, such as the printer port (or network path), paper and graphics options, built-in fonts, and other device options specific to the printer model. All these settings are fairly self explanatory and as they depend on your printer type, we will let you work them out for yourselves.

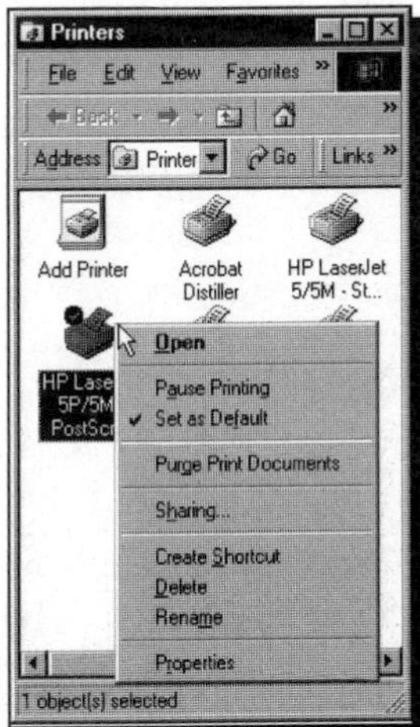

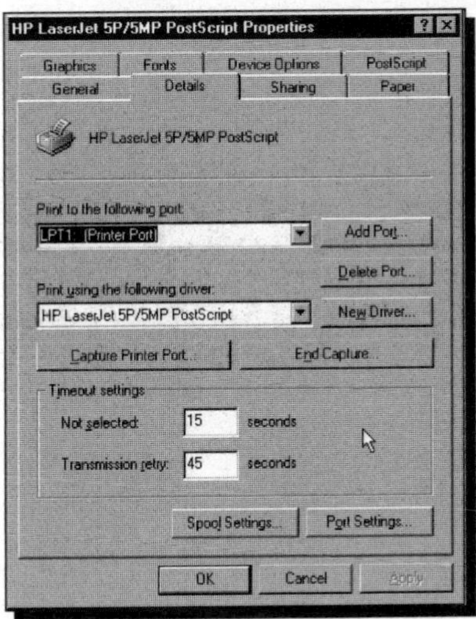

Fig. 6.2 The Printer Properties Window.

If you use one printer all, or most of the time, you should make it the default printer, by selecting **Set as Default** from its right-click menu. This saves continually having to select that printer from within your applications.

Once you have installed and configured your printers in Windows they are then available for all your application programs to use. If Windows is happy with your printer set-up, all its applications should be as well. Just make sure that the correct printer is selected by the program, which is usually one of the program's **File** menu options.

Managing Print Jobs

If you want to find out what exactly is happening while a document or documents are being sent to your printer, double-click the printer icon, to open its window.

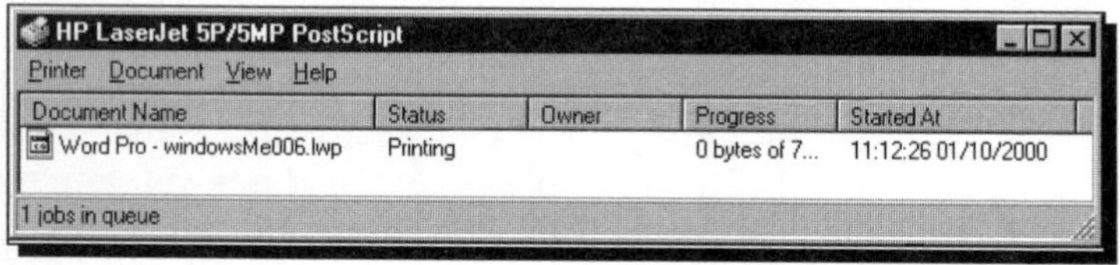

Fig. 6.3 The Print Queue Window.

As shown above, this displays detailed information about the contents of any work actually being printed, or of print jobs that are waiting in the queue. This includes the name of the document, its status and 'owner', when it was added to the print queue, the printing progress and when printing was started.

You can control the printing operation from the **Printer** and **Document** menu options of this window, or from the right-click object menu of a particular printer's icon. Selecting **Printer, Pause Printing** will stop the operation until you make the same selection again; it is a toggle menu option. The **Purge Print Documents** option will remove all, or selected, print jobs from the print queue.

Controlling Fonts

Windows Me uses a Font Manager program to control the installed fonts on your system. You can use the Font Manager to install new fonts, view examples of existing fonts, and delete fonts.

To open the Font Manager, click the **Start** button then select **Settings**, and click the **Control Panel** menu option to reveal the Control Panel window, as follows:

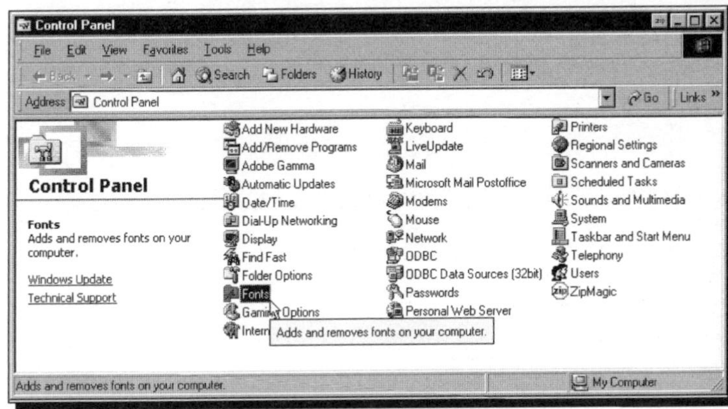

Fig. 6.4 The Control Panel Window.

Next, double-click the Fonts icon to display the Fonts window, shown in Fig. 6.5. To control what you see on the Fonts window, click **View** to display the drop-down menu, shown in Fig. 6.6. We have chosen **Status Bar**, **List** and **Hide Variations.**

Fig. 6.5 The Fonts Window.

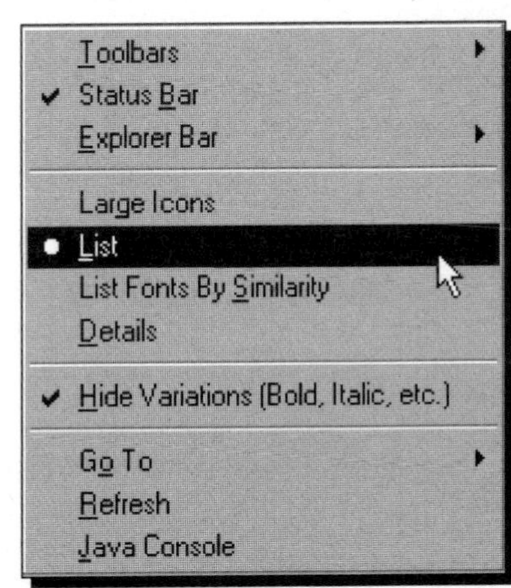

Fig. 6.6 The View Sub-menu.

To see an example of one of the listed fonts, double-click its icon in the Fonts window (Fig. 6.5). Below we show the Arial (TrueType) font in four different sizes.

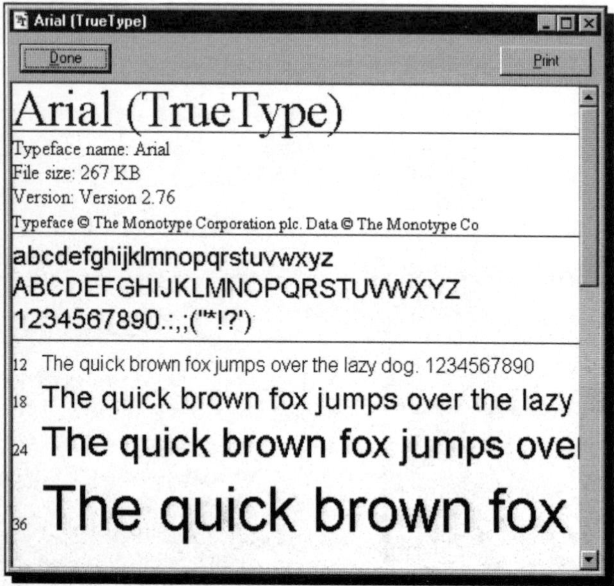

Fig. 6.7 Font Size Sample Window for a Selected Font.

You might find it interesting to know, that the Symbol font contains an abundance of Greek letters, while the Webdings and Wingdings Fonts contain special graphic objects, as shown below.

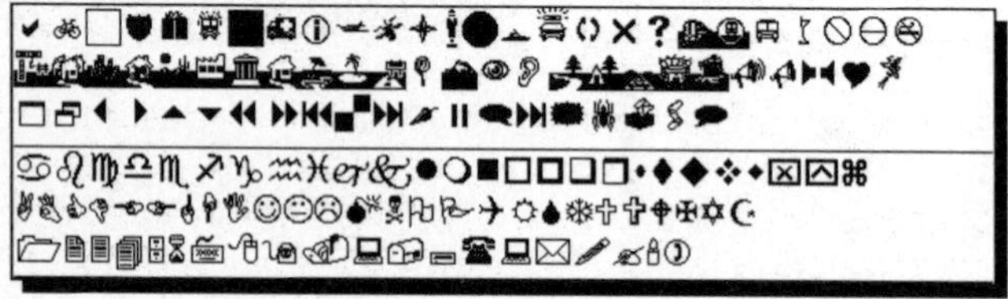

Fig. 6.8 Webdings (top) and Wingdings (bottom) Fonts.

We will explain shortly how such characters can be inserted into a document.

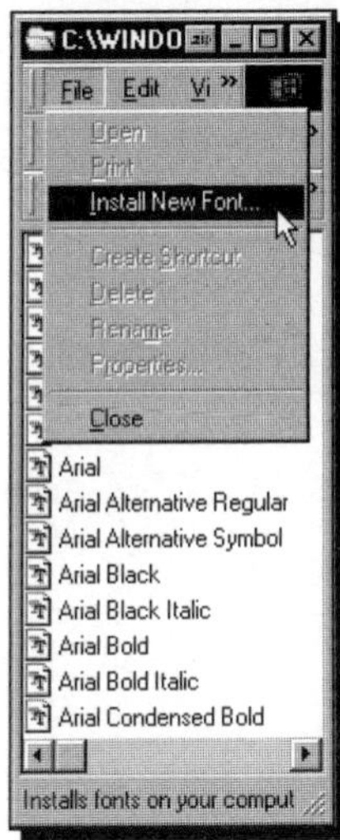

New fonts can be installed by selecting the **File, Install New Font** menu command in the Fonts window, shown to the left. This opens the Add Fonts dialogue box in which you have to specify the disc, folder and file in which the font you want to install resides.

Unwanted fonts can be removed by first highlighting them in the Fonts window, then using the **File, Delete** command. A warning box, as shown to the right, is displayed.

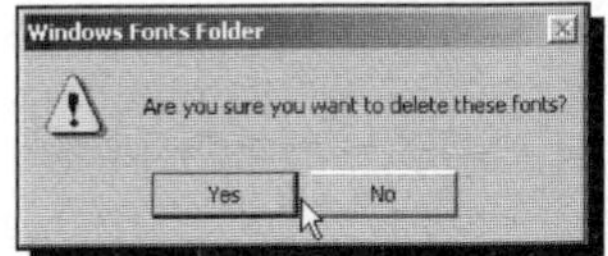

Some Font Basics: Font sizes are measured in 'points' (a point being, approximately 1/72 of an inch), which determine the height of a character. There is another unit of character measurement called the 'pitch' which is the number of characters that can fit horizontally in one inch.

The spacing of a font is either 'fixed' (mono spaced) or 'proportional'. With fixed spacing, each character takes up exactly the same space, while proportionally spaced characters take up different spacing (an 'i' or a 't' take up less space than a 'u' or a 'w'). Thus the length of proportionally spaced text can vary depending on which letters it contains. However, numerals take up the same amount of space whether they have been specified as fixed or proportional.

Windows Me makes available several 'TrueType' fonts which can be used by Windows applications, such as word processors. TrueType are outline fonts that are rendered from line and curve commands. These types of fonts are scalable to any point size, can be rotated, and look exactly the same on the screen as they do when printed.

Controlling Characters

A useful feature in Windows is the Character Map, shown open below. This should be found in the **Programs, Accessories, System Tools** menu.

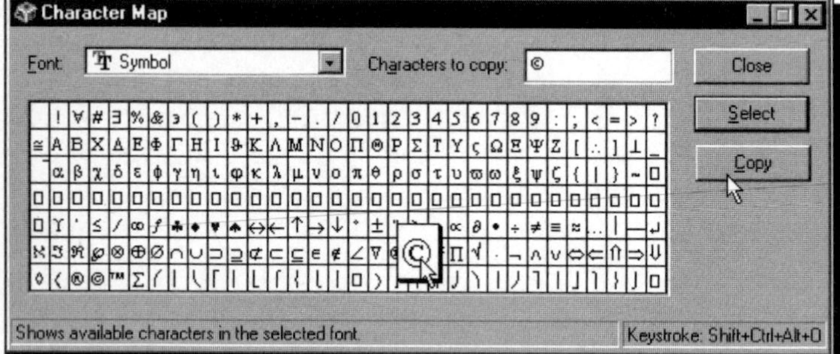

Fig. 6.9 Selecting a Character from the Character Map Utility.

You use this facility from an application, such as a word processor, when you need a special character, such as the 'copyright' sign © above, to be included in your document.

To copy a special character, not found on your keyboard, into your document, open the Character Map, select the **Font**, and look for that character. With high resolution monitors the characters are a little on the small side, so the one immediately under the pointer is automatically enlarged when the left mouse button is depressed, as shown above.

When you find the character you want, click the **Select** button, which places it in the **Characters to copy** box. When you have all you want in this box, clicking the **Copy** button will copy them to the clipboard. Now, return to your application, make sure the insertion point is in the correct position and paste the characters there.

If you are observant, you may have noticed the message **Keystroke: Shift+Ctrl+Alt+O** in the bottom right-hand corner of the above window. This is the keyboard code of the highlighted character.

Adding Hardware to your System

Prior to Windows 95, it was difficult to add new hardware to your PC, particularly if you did not understand how a PC works. Both Windows 95/98/Me and NT/2000 automate this process by including a set of software standards for controlling suitably designed hardware devices.

Plug-and-Play: Windows 95 was the first PC operating system to support what is known as Plug-and-Play compatible devices. Adding such hardware devices to your system is extremely easy, as Windows takes charge and automatically controls all its settings so that it fits in with the rest of the system. So, when you buy new hardware, make sure that it is Plug-and-Play compatible.

Add New Hardware Wizard: If you are not lucky and your new hardware is not Plug-and-Play compatible all is not lost, as there is a very powerful Wizard to step you through the process of installing new hardware. Fit the new hardware before you run the Wizard, as it is just possible that Windows will recognise the change and be able to carry out the configuration itself.

If the new hardware is not recognised, start the Wizard by double-clicking the Add New Hardware icon in the Control Panel, and follow the instructions. Make sure you have no applications running, and allow the Wizard to search your system for anything new. This can take a minute or two to complete. Eventually you should be given a list of any new hardware additions that are recognised, as shown in Fig. 6.10. Here the Advanced Power Management Support was detected as disabled.

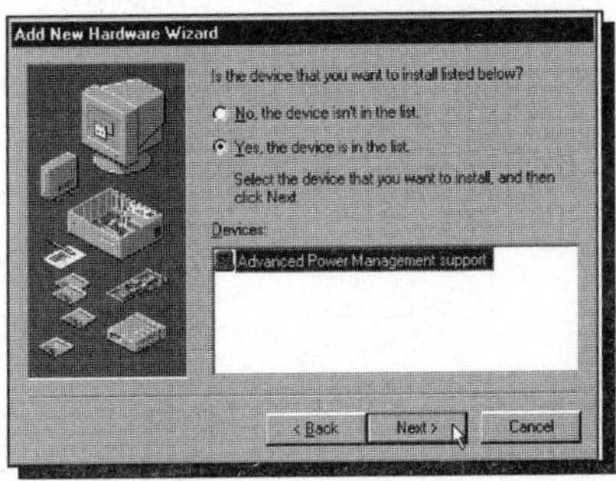

Fig. 6.10 The Add New Hardware.

Adding Software to your PC

Installing Windows applications is very easy with Windows Me.

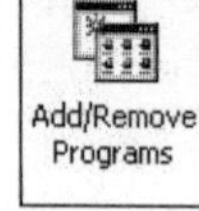

Place the first disc, or the CD-ROM, with the software on it in its drive, double-click the Add/Remove Programs icon in the Control Panel and select **Install** from the Install/Uninstall tabbed sheet, shown here. The disc drives will be searched and you will be asked to confirm what you want installed.

The Uninstall option only works for programs on your system that were specially written for Windows 95/98 or Windows Me and are listed at the bottom of the dialogue box (Fig. 6.11). This uninstall procedure removes all trace of the selected program from your hard disc. However, with earlier Windows programs, you will be left with the usual application set-up files on your system.

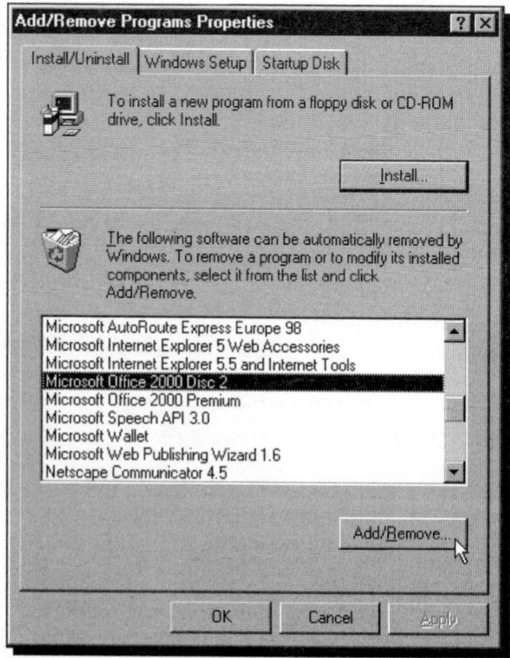

Fig. 6.11 The Add/Remove Programs Dialogue Box.

Adding/Removing Windows' Features

The Windows Setup tab of the Add/Remove Programs Properties dialogue box allows you to install, or remove, Windows components at any time. If you do not have a described feature on your system it may not have been installed. To install such features, open the tab sheet, shown to the left of Fig. 6.12, highlight the group that you think will contain them and click the **Details** button. This will list the components of the chosen group, shown to the right below. Clicking the box to the left of an item name will install the selected component, while any items with their ticks removed, will be uninstalled.

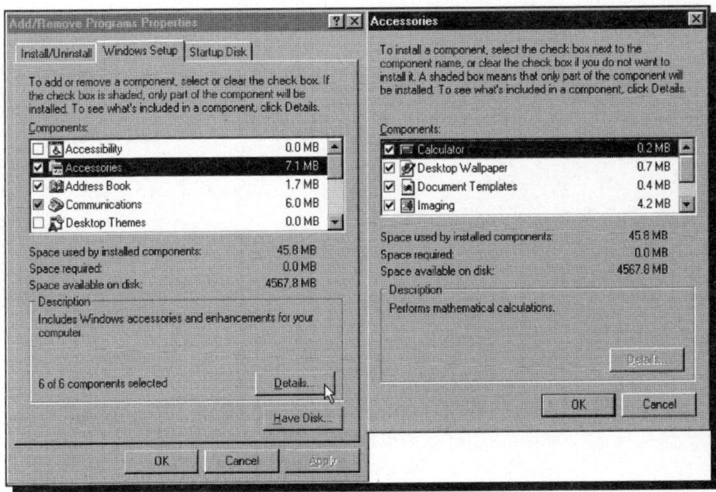

Fig. 6.12 The Windows Components Wizard.

You will need to have the original Windows Me CD-ROM system disc available, and when you have made the selections you want, keep clicking **OK** to carry out the required changes.

It is easy to use up too much hard disc space with Windows Me features, so keep your eye on the **Space required** entry.

Checking your Regional Settings

Most Windows application programs use Windows settings to determine how they display and handle, time, date, language, numbers, and currency. It is important that you ensure your system was correctly set up during the installation process.

Use the **Start**, **Settings**, **Control Panel** command, then double-click the Regional Settings icon, shown here, to open the Properties sheet shown below.

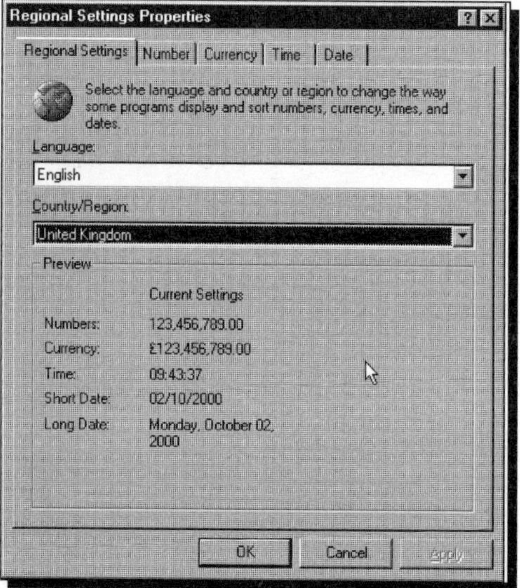

Fig. 6.13 The Regional Settings Properties Box.

Make sure the **Language** and **Country/Region** settings are correct. If not, change them by clicking the down-arrow to the right of each entry, in turn, to display a drop-down list and select the most appropriate language and country.

Before leaving the Properties box, work your way through the tabbed pages and make sure the selections are as you want them. If, in the future, you start getting '$' signs, instead of '£' signs, or commas in numbers where you would expect periods, check your regional settings. You will have to restart Windows before any changes become effective.

From this dialogue box you can also change the time and date of your computer's clock. The clock settings can also be reached by double-clicking the clock displayed at the bottom right corner of the Windows screen.

Changing the Taskbar Menus

The Taskbar menu system, as we saw in an earlier chapter, is set up originally when Windows Me is installed, the **Start** menu being standard, but the **Programs** cascade menus being based on any previous Windows set-up you had on your computer. Once you are a little familiar with Windows, we are sure you will want to tailor these menus to your own preferences.

Adding to the Start Menu

It is very easy to add extra programs to the top of the **Start** menu. This can be useful, as this menu opens with one click of the **Start** button which gives very rapid access to its contents.

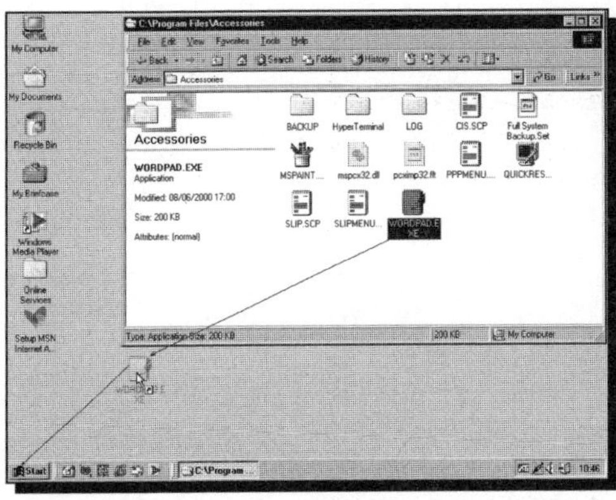

Fig. 6.14 Dragging the WordPad Icon on to Start.

To do this, you can simply drag the program icon, or a shortcut to it, onto the **Start** button itself. For example, to add the Windows text editor WordPad to the **Start** menu, use the My Computer facility to open the Program Files Folder, then the Accessories folder, as shown in Fig. 6.14. Next, find the WordPad icon and drag it with the left mouse button depressed. When you drag a single icon like this, the drag pointer changes as you move round the screen, to indicate what will happen if you release the mouse button at that location. As shown above, the pointer is over the desktop and the small black arrow '↗' in its bottom right corner shows that a shortcut would be produced.

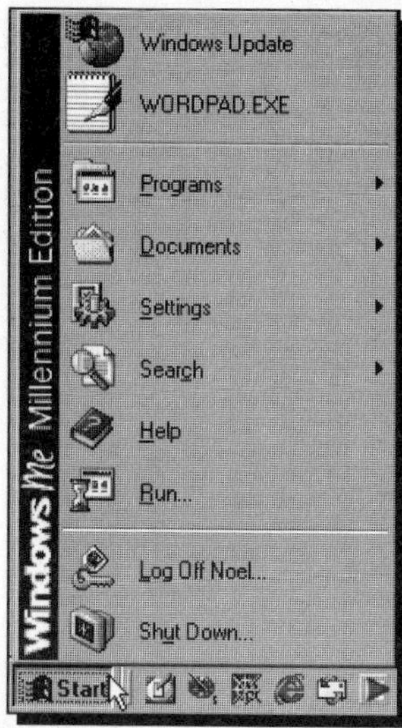

Fig. 6.15 The Start Menu.

Over some desktop features the arrow changes to a plus sign '+' showing that the file would be copied there. Drag the icon slowly over the **Start** button. It will first seem to go under the button, then it will change to a 'No entry' sign ⦸ when over the Taskbar border, but will finally show the shortcut arrow. At that point, release the mouse button. Your **Start** menu should now have an extra option near the top, as shown in Fig. 6.15. You can rename the added entry with a more appropriate name, such as WordPad, by right-clicking the entry and selecting **Rename** from the displayed menu.

Within reason, you can add as many extra items to the **Start** menu as you like and they will sort themselves in alphabetical order.

The Taskbar Properties sheet lets you both add and remove items to and from the **Start** and the **Programs** menu. To open this sheet, you select **Properties** from the Taskbar right-click menu shown in Fig. 6.16, which displays the Taskbar and Start Menu Properties dialogue box shown in Fig. 6.17 on the next page.

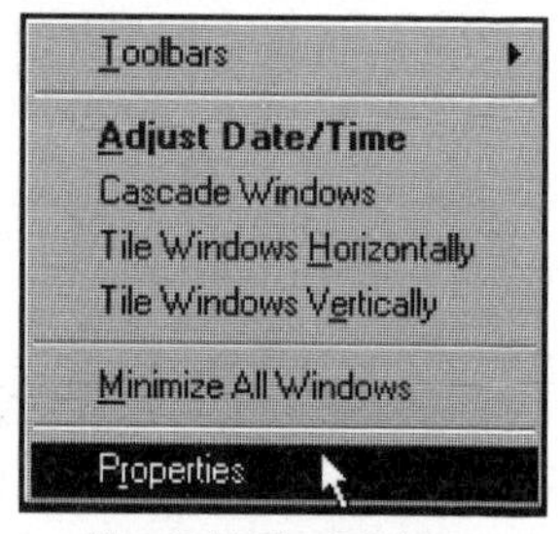

Fig. 6.16 The Taskbar Right-click Menu.

Clicking the **Add** button on the Advanced tab sheet, steps you in a 'Wizard like' way, through the process of creating a shortcut to the program you want, and adding it to the required menu position. The **Remove** button lets you choose a menu item and then deletes it from the menu system.

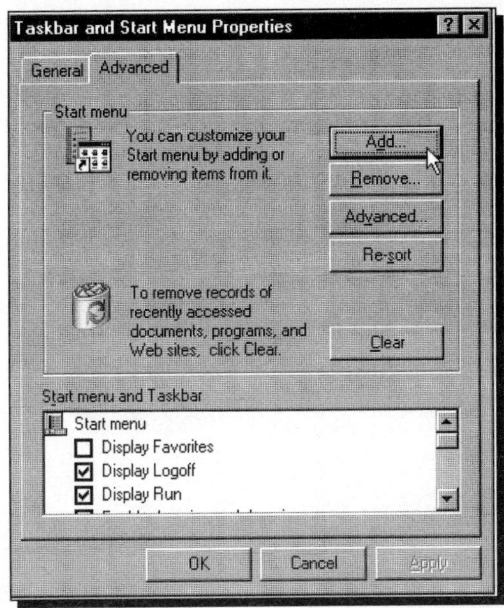

Fig. 6.17 The Taskbar and Start Menu Properties Dialogue Box.

Finally, the **Advanced** button can be used to manipulate the menus in a My Computer window, as shown below. If you are happy using the My Computer utility, this is by far the quickest way to customise your menus. This method is possible because these menus depend on the contents of the Start Menu sub-folder of the individual user's Documents and Settings folder. Menu items are stored here as shortcuts and you can add or delete them as you want.

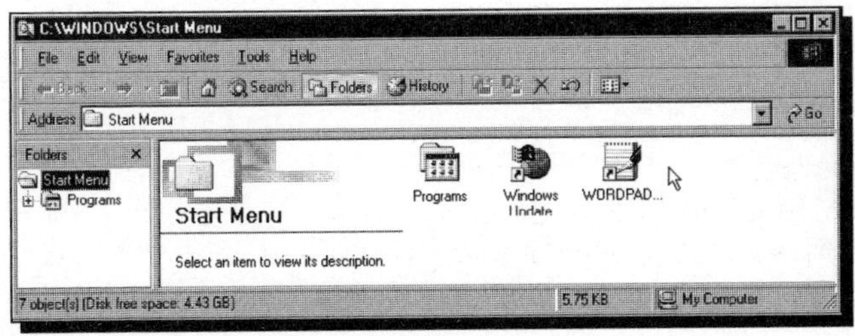

Fig. 6.18 The Start Menu Folder.

Controlling Images

Another Windows accessory can be used to control images. This program was originally designed for Microsoft by a subsidiary of Kodak. To run 'Imaging for Windows' use the **Start, Programs, Accessories** command, then left-click the **Imaging** option, the icon of which is shown here. After briefly showing an opening screen, the program displays its 'Untitled' screen. In Fig. 6.19, we show the **Clouds.jpg** file open which is to be found in My Pictures folder which itself is in My Documents folder.

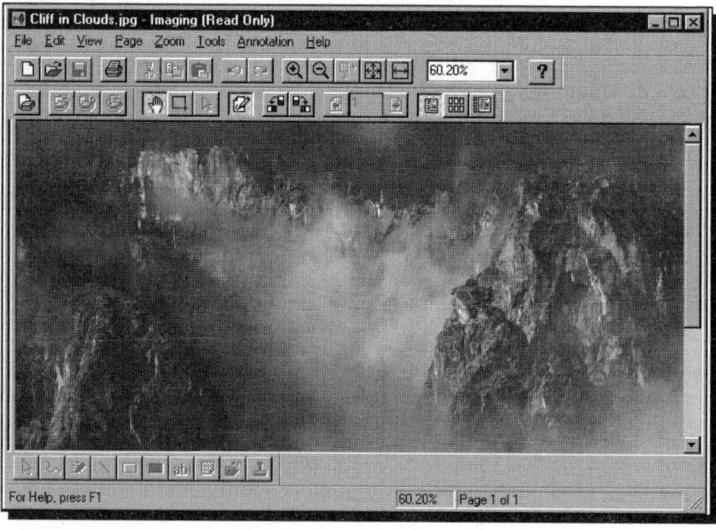

Fig. 6.19 The Imaging Screen.

The above screen contains the usual Menu bar command options with typical functions, such as **File** management, ability to **Edit** your image documents, select ways to **View** them, set your **Page** preview and print options, and select the **Zoom**, **Tools**, and **Annotation** preferences. To illustrate some of these commands, first open the drawing we created on page 84, then spend some time investigating the various sub-menu options available to you under each menu command.

We now draw your attention to the top two toolbars of the Imaging screen (if you do not have an image opened, then most of these toolbar buttons are greyed out, indicating unavailability of the command or option they represent). Below, we explain briefly the function of the first toolbar buttons.

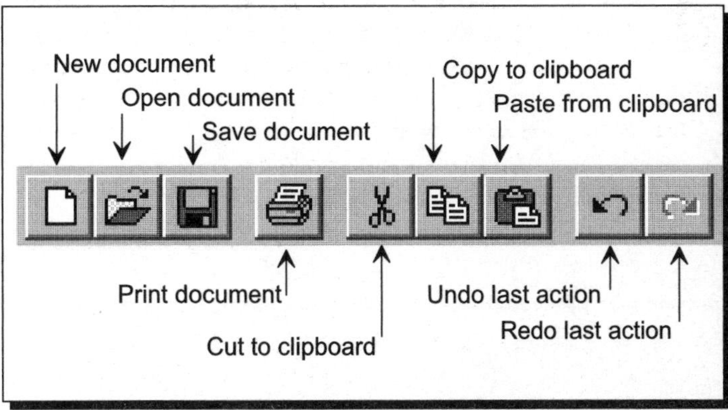

Fig. 6.20 The Editing Buttons of the Toolbar.

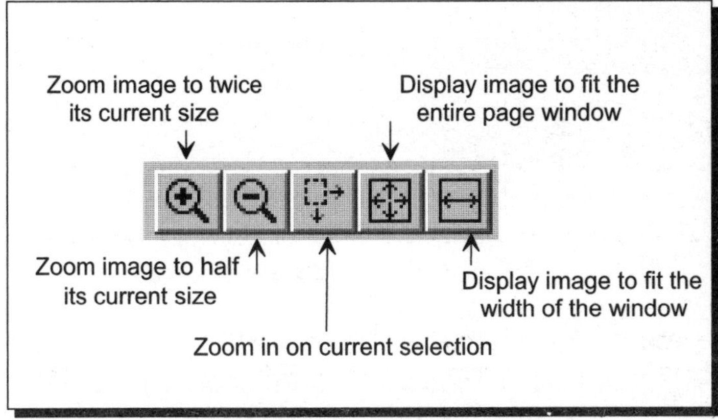

Fig. 6.21 The Zooming Buttons of the Toolbar.

The first four buttons on the second toolbar have functions which only become active if you have a scanner attached to your system.

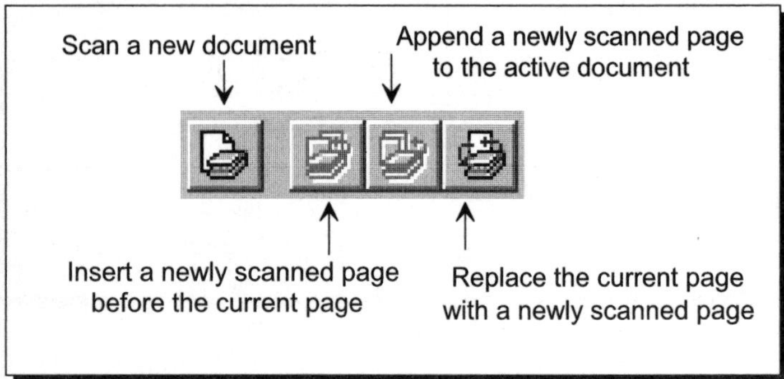

Fig. 6.22 The Scanning Buttons of the Toolbar.

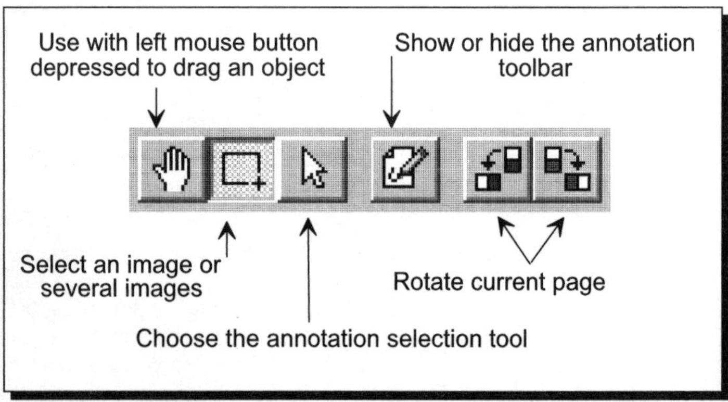

Fig. 6.23 The Image Manipulation Buttons of the Toolbar.

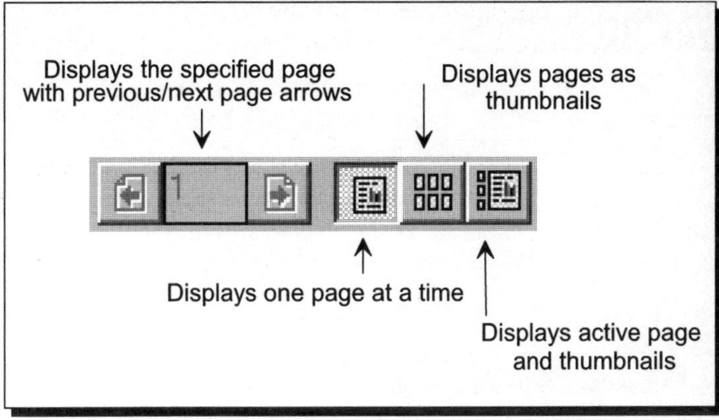

Fig. 6.24 The Display Buttons of the Toolbar.

Finally, if the 'show/hide annotation' button is selected (Fig. 6.23), then the annotation toolbar appears at the bottom of the screen, as shown on page 104. The buttons on this toolbar have the following functions.

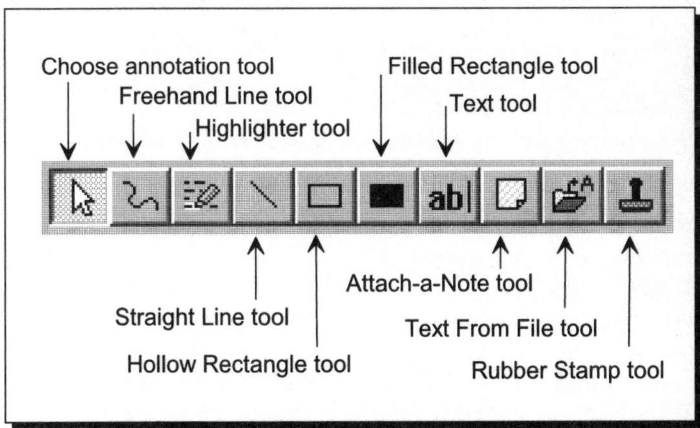

Fig. 6.25 The Buttons on the Annotation Toolbar.

The best way of becoming familiar with the various facilities provided by Imaging, is to use a drawing you have created or one of the images in My Pictures folder, and play with it. If you have a scanner, then so much the better.

Playing Games

We will not spend long on this topic, but many people only seem to have a PC to use it for playing games, but maybe not the ones provided with Windows!

Our version of Windows Me placed the eleven games shown below in the Games folder of the **Programs** menu.

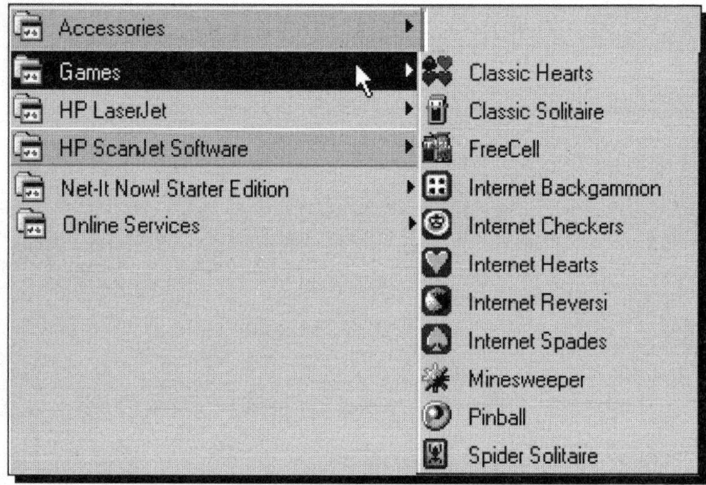

Fig. 6.26 The Games Folder.

Of these, five games require you to connect to the Internet to find opponents of different skill levels, while the other six can be played without additional expense. Classic Hearts can be played over a network against real opponents or against opponents supplied by the computer. FreeCell is a patience based game, while Classic Solitaire, Minesweeper, Spider Solitaire are designed to help with mouse skills. Pinball is a 3D arcade type game with impressive sounds that tests your reactions.

All of these games come with quite good Help sections and we will leave it to you to explore them if you want.

7

E-mail with Outlook Express

To be able to communicate electronically with the rest of the world many users will need to connect their PC through a modem to an active phone line. This is a device that converts data so that it can be transmitted over the telephone system. Installing such a modem is quite easy with Windows Me.

Modem Properties

Before using your modem you must check to ensure it is correctly configured. To do this, double-click the Modems icon in the Control Panel. If Windows finds that no modem has been installed, it will step you through the process, using the relevant parts of the Add New Hardware Wizard. Otherwise it will open the Modems Properties sheet shown below left. Clicking the **More Info** button will let you query your modem.

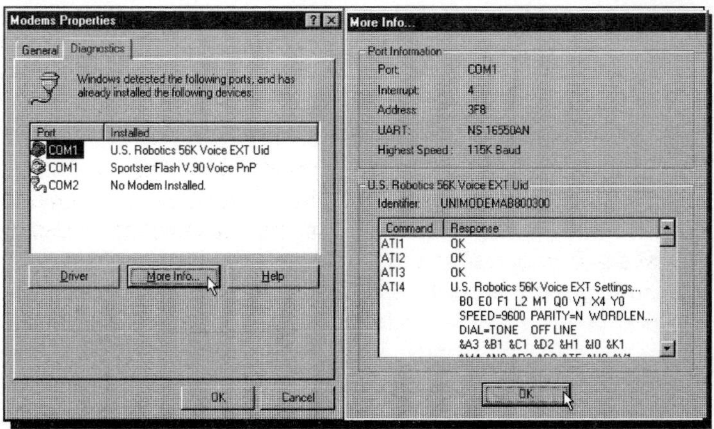

Fig. 7.1 Performing a Diagnostic Test on your Modem.

Microsoft Outlook Express

Windows Me comes with the very powerful mail and news facility, Outlook Express 5, built into it, which makes it very easy for you to send and receive e-mail messages. The program should already have been added to your PC by **Setup** (a shortcut icon being placed on the Taskbar - see Fig. 2.7, page 24). To start the program, left-click the launch icon on the Taskbar, shown here. The program starts and the opening screen is displayed as shown in Fig. 7.2 below.

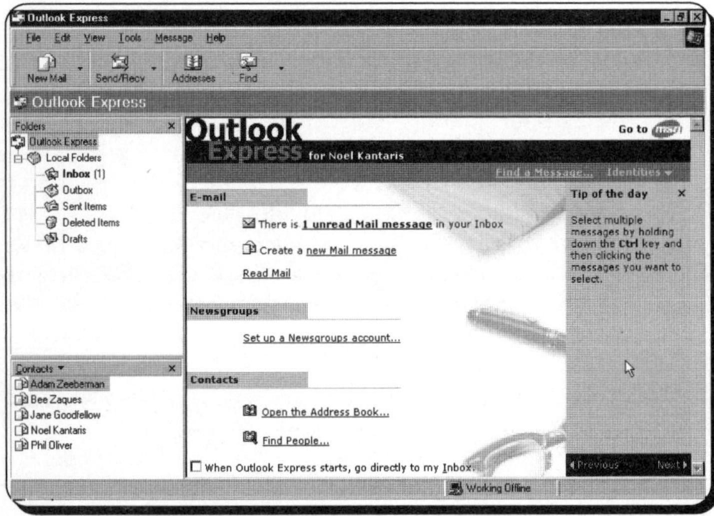

Fig. 7.2 The Outlook Express Opening Screen.

To send and receive electronic mail over a modem, you must make an arrangement with a commercial server. There are quite a few around now, and most have Internet options. Try and find one that can provide you with a reduced rate for local telephone calls, to reduce your phone bills. Once you have taken a subscription to such a service, you will be provided with all the necessary information to enter in the Internet Connection Wizard, so that you can fully exploit all the available facilities.

Connecting to your Server

To tell Outlook Express how to connect to your server's facilities, you must complete your personal e-mail connection details in the Internet Connection Wizard shown in Fig. 7.3, which opens when you first attempt to use the Read Mail facility.

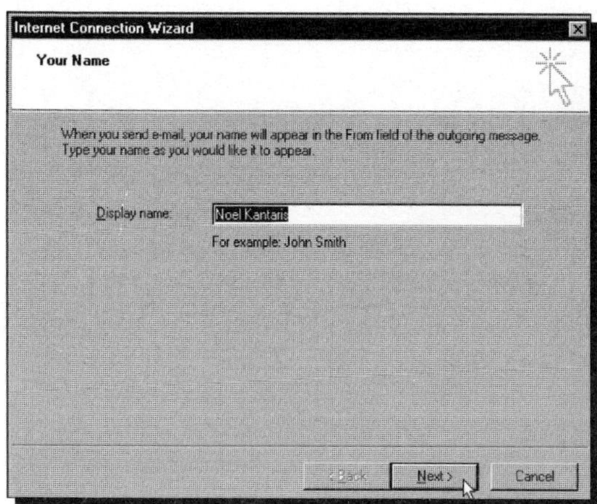

Fig. 7.3 The First Internet Connection Wizard Screen.

If the Wizard does not open, or if you want to change your connection details, use the **Tools**, **Accounts** menu command, select the mail tab and click **Add**, followed by **Mail**.

In the first screen of the Wizard, type your name in the text box, as shown above, and click the **Next** button to display the second screen, shown in Fig. 7.4 on the next page. Enter your e-mail address in the text box, if you have not organised one yet you could always click the **I'd like to sign up for a new account from Hotmail** option. Hotmail is a free browser-based e-mail service owned by Microsoft. Hence its inclusion!

In the third Wizard screen enter your e-mail server details, as shown for us in Fig. 7.5. To complete some of the details here you may need to ask your Internet Service Provider (ISP), or system administrator, for help.

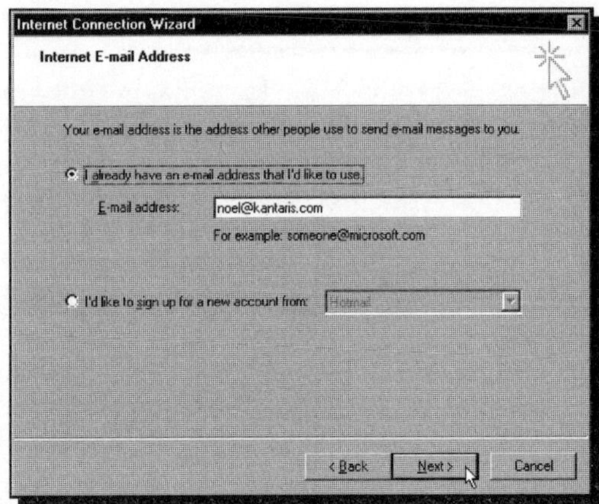

Fig. 7.4 The Second Internet Connection Wizard Screen.

The details shown below will obviously only work for the writer, so please don't try them!

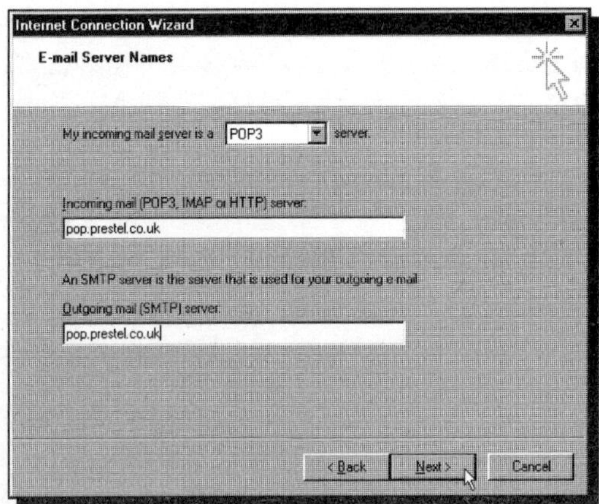

Fig. 7.5 The Third Internet Connection Wizard Screen.

The next Wizard screen asks for your user name and password. Both these would have been given to you by your ISP. Type these in, as shown for us in Fig. 7.6, and click the **Next** button.

If you select the **Remember password** option in this box, you will not have to enter these details every time you log on. **BUT** it may not be wise to do this if your PC is in a busy office - for security reasons.

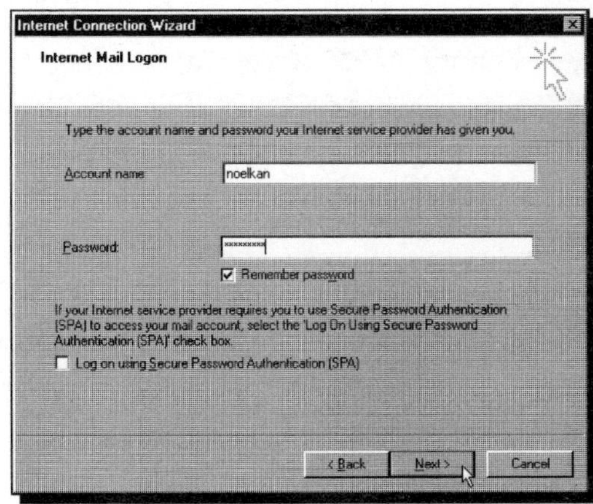

Fig. 7.6 The Fourth Internet Connection Wizard Screen.

This leads to the final Wizard screen informing you of your success, which completes the procedure, so press **Finish** to return you to the Internet Accounts dialogue box, with your new account set up as shown below for us.

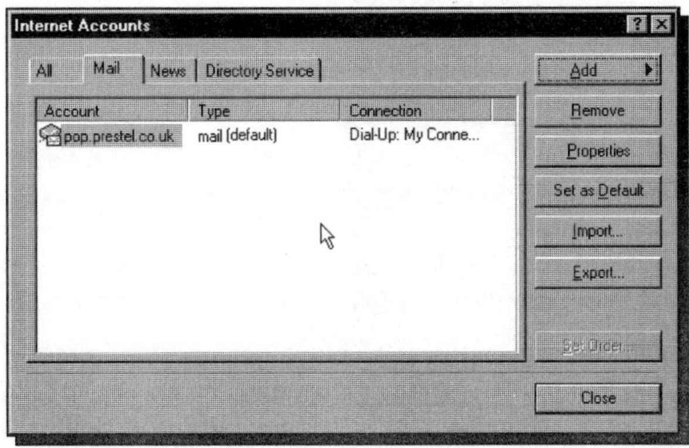

Fig. 7.7 The Internet Accounts Dialogue Box.

In the future, selecting the account in this box and clicking the **Properties** button will give you access to the settings sheets (to check, or change, your details).

Once your connection is established, you can click the Read Mail coloured link, or the **Inbox** entry in the Folder List on the left side of the Outlook Express 5 opening window. Both of these actions open the Inbox, which when opened for the first time, will probably contain a message from Microsoft, like that shown below.

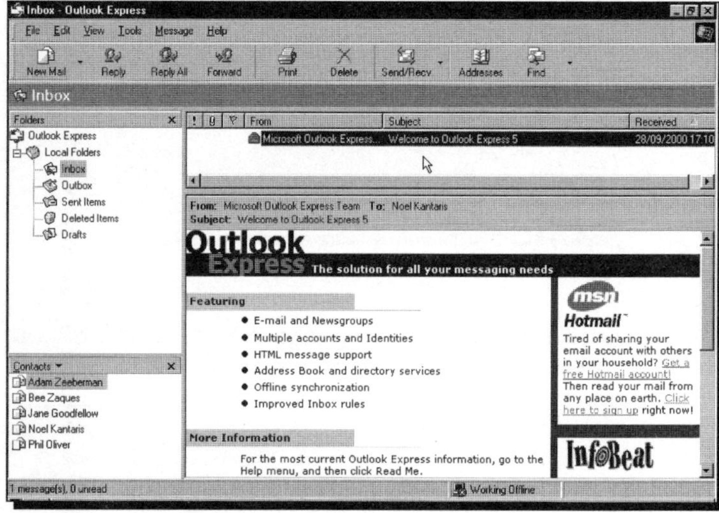

Fig. 7.8 The Inbox Outlook Express Screen.

This shows the default Outlook Express Main window layout, which consists of a Folders List to the left with a Contacts list (from the Address Book) below it, a Message List to the right and a Preview Pane below that. The list under Folders contains all the active mail folders, news servers and newsgroups.

Clicking on one of these displays its contents in the Message List, and clicking on a message opens a Preview of it below for you to see. Double-clicking on a message opens the message in its own window.

A Trial Run

To check your mail, click the Send/Recv Toolbar icon which will connect you to the Internet and download any new messages from your mailbox to your hard disc. You can then read and process your mail at your leisure without necessarily still being connected to the Internet.

Before explaining in more detail the main features of Outlook Express we will step through the procedure of sending a very simple e-mail message. The best way to test out any unfamiliar e-mail features is to send a test message to your own e-mail address. This saves wasting somebody else's time, and the message can be very quickly checked to see the results. To start, click the New Mail icon to open the New Message window, shown below.

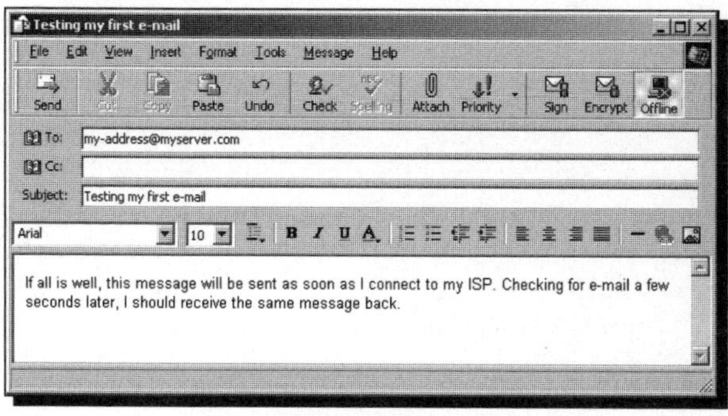

Fig. 7.9 Creating a New E-mail.

Type your own e-mail address in the **To:** field, and a title for the message in the **Subject:** field. The text in this subject field will form a header for the message when it is received, so it helps to show in a few words what the message is about. Type your message and when you are happy with it, click the Send Toolbar icon shown here.

By default, your message is stored in an Outbox folder, and pressing the Send/Recv Toolbar icon will connect to the Internet and then send it, hopefully straight into your mailbox. When Outlook Express next checks for mail, it will find the message and download it into the Inbox folder, for you to read and enjoy!

The Main Outlook Express Window

After the initial opening window, Outlook Express uses three other main windows, which we will refer to as: the Main window which opens next; the Read Message window for reading your mail; and the New Message window, to compose your outgoing mail messages.

The Main window consists of a Toolbar, a menu, and five panes with the default display shown in our example in Fig. 7.8. You can choose different pane layouts, and customise the Toolbar, with the **View**, **Layout** menu command, but we will let you try these for yourself.

The Folders List

The folders pane contains a list of your mail folders, your news servers and any newsgroups you have subscribed to. There are always at least five mail folders, as shown in Fig. 7.10. You can add your own with the **File**, **Folder**, **New** menu command from the Main window. You can delete added folders with the **File**, **Folder**, **Delete** command. These operations can also be carried out after right-clicking a folder in the list. You can drag messages from the Message list and drop them into any of the folders, to 'store' them there.

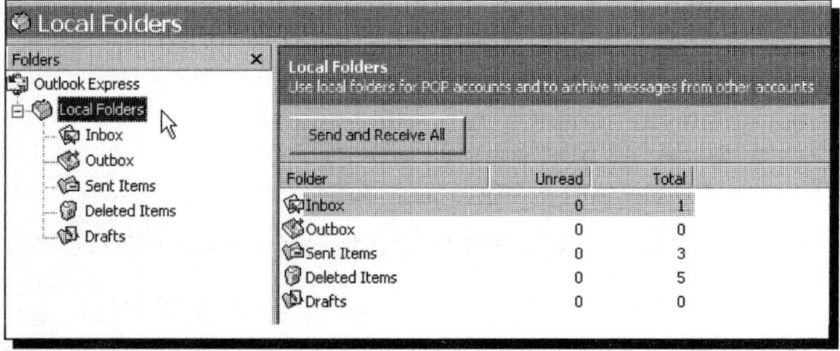

Fig. 7.10 The Local Folders Pane.

Note the icons shown above, any new folders you add will have the same icon as that of the first added folder.

The Contacts Pane

This pane simply lists the contacts held in your Address Book. Double-clicking on an entry in this list opens a New Message window with the message already addressed to that person.

The Message List

When you select a folder, by clicking it in the Folders list, the Message list shows the contents of that folder. Brief details of each message are displayed on one line, as shown below.

Fig. 7.11 Received Messages in Ascending Date Order.

The first column shows the message priority, if any, the second shows whether the message has an attachment, and the third shows whether the message has been 'flagged'. All of these are indicated by icons on the message line. The 'From' column shows the message status icon (listed on the next page) and the name of the sender, 'Subject' shows the title of each mail message, and 'Received' shows the date it reached you. You can control what columns display in this pane with the **View, Columns** menu command.

To sort a list of messages, you can click the mouse pointer in the title of the column you want the list sorted on, clicking it again will sort it in reverse order. The sorted column is shown with a triangle mark, as shown below.

Fig. 7.12 Received Messages in Descending Date Order.

As seen on the screen dump above, the received messages have been sorted by date, with the most recently received message appearing at the top. This is our preferred method of display.

Message Status Icons

This icon	Indicates this
	The message has one or more files attached.
	The message has been marked high priority by the sender.
	The message has been marked low priority by the sender.
	The message has been read. The message heading appears in light type.
	The message has not been read. The message heading appears in bold type.
	The message has been replied to.
	The message has been forwarded.
	The message is in progress in the Drafts folder.
	The message is digitally signed and unopened.
	The message is encrypted and unopened.
	The message is digitally signed, encrypted and unopened.
	The message is digitally signed and has been opened.
	The message is encrypted and has been opened.
	The message is digitally signed and encrypted, and has been opened.
	The message has responses that are collapsed. Click the icon to show all the responses (expand the conversation).
	The message and all of its responses are expanded. Click the icon to hide all the responses (collapse the conversation).
	The unread message header is on an IMAP server.
	The opened message is marked for deletion on an IMAP server.
	The message is flagged.
	The IMAP message is marked to be downloaded.
	The IMAP message and all conversations are marked to be downloaded.
	The individual IMAP message (without conversations) is marked to be downloaded.

Fig. 7.13. Table of Message Status Icons.

The Preview Pane

When you select a message in the Message list, by clicking it once, it is displayed in the Preview pane, which takes up the rest of the window. This lets you read the first few lines to see if the message is worth bothering with. If so, double clicking the header, in the Message list, will open the message in the Read Message window, as shown later in the chapter.

You could use the Preview pane to read all your mail, especially if your messages are all on the short side, but it is easier to process them from the Read Message window.

The Main Window Toolbar

Selecting any one of the local folders displays the following buttons on Outlook's Toolbar.

Opens the New Message window for creating a new mail message, with the To: field blank.

Opens the New Message window for replying to the current mail message, with the To: field pre-addressed to the original sender. The original Subject field is prefixed with Re:.

Opens the New Message window for replying to the current mail message, with the To: field pre-addressed to all that received copies of the original message. The original Subject field is prefixed with Re:.

Opens the New Message window for forwarding the current mail message. The To: field is blank. The original Subject field is prefixed with Fw:.

Prints the selected message.

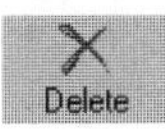

Deletes the currently selected message and places it in the Deleted Items folder.

Connects to the mailbox server and downloads waiting messages, which it places in the Inbox folder. Sends any messages waiting in the Outbox folder.

Opens the Address Book.

Finds a message or an e-mail address using Find People facilities of the Address Book.

The Read Message Window

If you double-click a message in the Message list of the Main window the Read Message window is opened, as shown below.

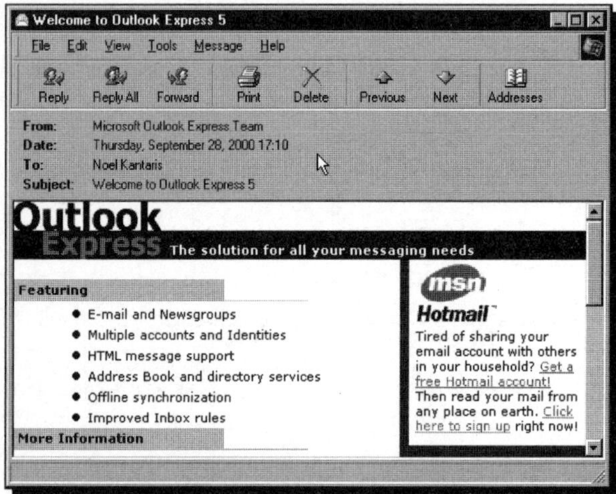

Fig. 7.14 The Read Message Window.

This is the best window to read your mail in. It has its own menu system and Toolbar, which lets you rapidly process and move between the messages in a folder.

The Read Message Toolbar

This window has its own Toolbar, but only two icons are different from those in the Main window.

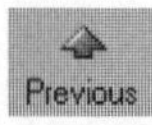

Previous - Displays the previous mail message in the Read Message window. The button appears depressed if there are no previous messages.

Next - Displays the next mail message in the Read Message window. The button appears depressed if there are no more messages.

Creating New Messages

We briefly looked into the creation of a new message and the New Message window earlier in the chapter (Fig. 7.9). However, before we activate this window again and discuss it in detail, let us first create a signature to be appended to all outgoing messages.

Your Own Signature

You create a signature from the Main window using the **Tools, Options** command which opens the Options dialogue box shown below when its Signature tab is selected and the **New** button is clicked.

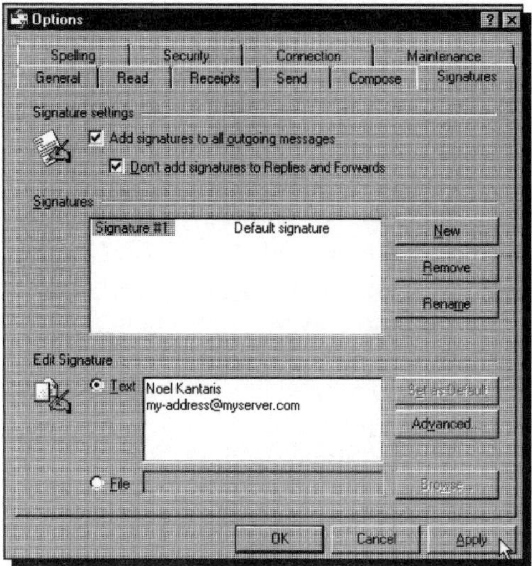

Fig. 7.15 The Options Dialogue Box.

You could also create a more fancy signature file in a text editor like Notepad, or WordPad, including the text and characters you want added to all your messages, and point to it in the **File** section of this box. We have chosen to **Add signatures to all outgoing messages**, but you could leave this option blank and use the **Insert, Signature** command from the New Message window menu system if you prefer.

The New Message Window

This is the window, shown below, that you will use to create any messages you want to send electronically from Outlook Express. It is important to understand its features, so that you can get the most out of it.

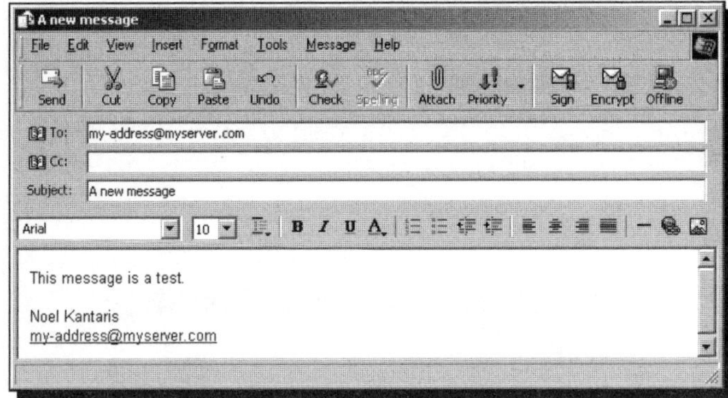

Fig. 7.16 The New Message Window.

As we saw, this window can be opened by using the New Mail Toolbar icon from the Main window, as well as the **Message**, **New Message** menu command. From other windows you can also use the **Message**, **New** command, or the <Ctrl+N> keyboard shortcut. The newly opened window has its own menu system and Toolbar, which let you rapidly prepare and send your new e-mail messages.

Message Stationery

Another Outlook Express feature is that it lets you send your messages on pre-formatted stationery for added effect.

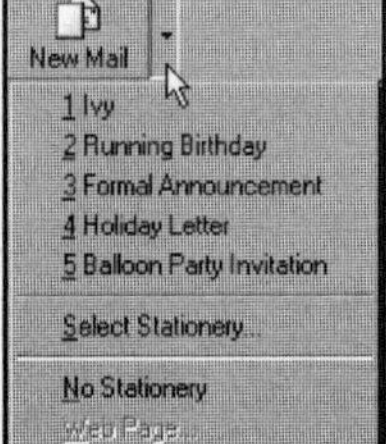

To access these, click the down arrow next to the New Mail button in the Main window and either select from the **1** to **5** list, as shown here, or use the **Select Stationery** command to open a box with many more stationery types on offer.

The New Message Toolbar

The icons on the New Message Toolbar window have the following functions.

Send Message - Sends message, either to the recipient, or to the Outbox folder.

Cut - Cuts selected text to the Windows clipboard.

Copy - Copies selected text to the Windows clipboard.

Paste - Pastes the contents of the Windows clipboard into the current message.

Undo - Undoes the last editing action.

Check Names - Checks that names match your entries in the address book, or are in correct e-mail address format.

Spelling - Checks the spelling of the current message before it is sent.

Attach File - Opens the Insert Attachment window for you to select a file to be attached to the current message.

Set Priority - Sets the message priority as high or low, to indicate its importance to the recipient.

Digitally sign message - Adds a digital signature to the message to confirm to the recipient that it is from you.

Encrypt message - Encodes the message so that only the recipient can read it.

Work Offline - Closes connection to the Internet so that you can process your mail offline. The button then changes to **Work Online.**

Message Formatting

Outlook Express provides quite sophisticated formatting options for an e-mail editor from both the **Format** menu and Toolbar. These only work if you prepare the message in HTML format, as used in Web documents. You can set this to be your default mail sending format using the Send tab in the **Tools**, **Options** box.

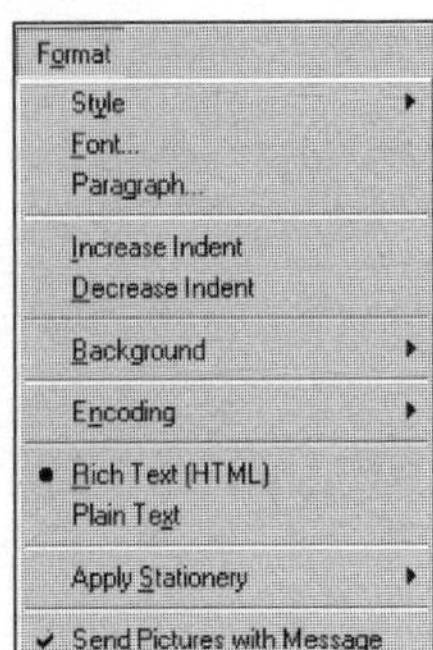

To use the format for the current message only, select **Rich Text (HTML)** from the **Format** menu, as we have done here. If **Plain Text** is selected, the black dot will be placed against this option on the menu, and the formatting features will not then be available.

The Format Toolbar shown below is added to the New Message window when you are in HTML mode and all the **Format** menu options are then made active.

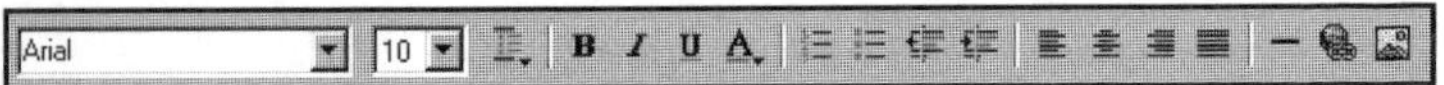

All of the formatting features are well covered elsewhere in the book so we will not repeat them now. Most of them are quite well demonstrated in Microsoft's opening message to you. You should be able to prepare some very easily readable e-mail messages with these features, but remember that not everyone will be able to read the work in the way that you spent hours creating. Only e-mail programs that support MIME (Multi-purpose Internet Mail Extensions) can read HTML formatting. When your recipient's e-mail program does not read HTML, and many people choose not to, the message appears as plain text with an HTML file attached.

Note: At the risk of being called boring we think it is usually better to stick to plain text without the selection of any message stationery; not only can everyone read it, but it is much quicker to transmit and deal with.

Using E-mail Attachments

If you want to include an attachment to your main e-mail message, you simply click the **Attach** Toolbar button in the New Message window, as shown below.

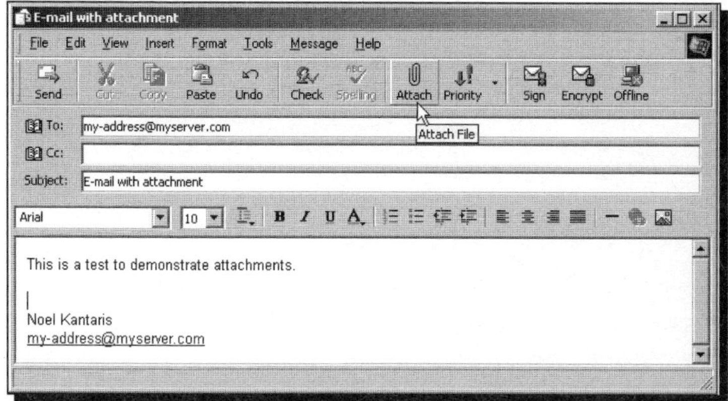

Fig. 7.17 Adding an Attachment to an E-mail.

This opens the Insert Attachment dialogue box, for you to select the file, or files, you want to go with your message.

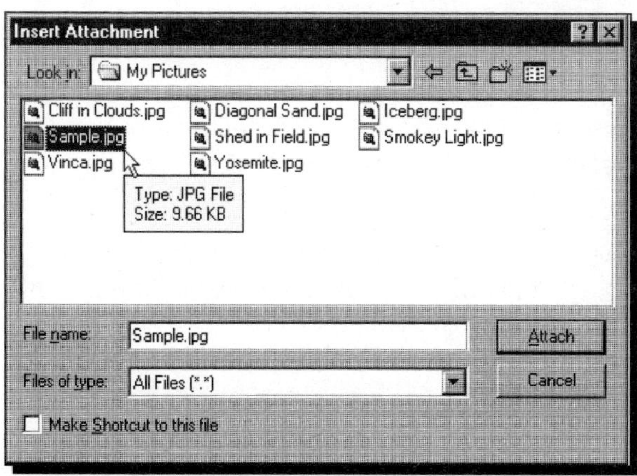

Fig. 7.18 The Insert Attachment Dialogue Box.

In Outlook Express the attached files are 'placed' below the **Subject** text box. Below we have shown two attachments, each with a distinctive icon that tells the recipient what each file is; the first a graphics .jpg file, the second a Word .doc document. It is only polite to include in your e-mail a short description of what the attachments are, and which applications were used to create them; it will help the recipient to decipher them.

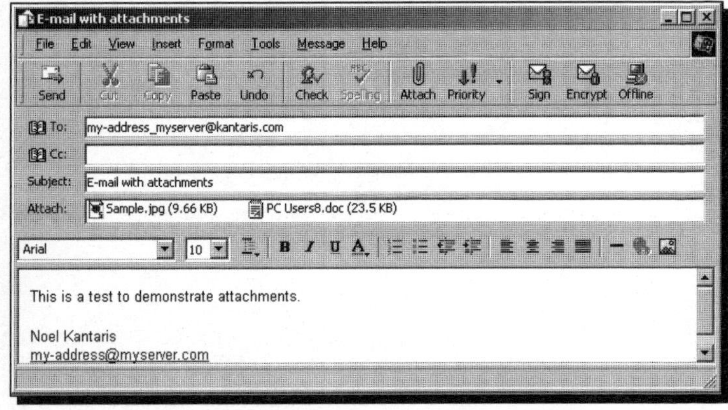

Fig. 7.19 Adding an Attachment to an E-mail.

Clicking the **Send** icon on the Toolbar, puts each e-mail (with its attachments, if any) in Outlook's **Outbox** folder. Next time you click the **Send/Recv** Toolbar icon, Outlook Express connects to your ISP and sends all the e-mails stored in it.

Receiving Attachments with an E-mail

To demonstrate what happens when you receive an e-mail with attachments, we have sent the above e-mail to our ISP, then a minute or so later we received it back, as shown in Fig. 7.20 on the next page.

Note that the received e-mail shows the graphics (.jpg) file open at the bottom of the Preview pane, but there is no indication of any other attachments. To find out how many attachments were included with the received e-mail, left-click the Clip icon to reveal all of them in a drop-down menu list, also shown on the next page.

Fig. 7.20 A Received E-mail with Attachments.

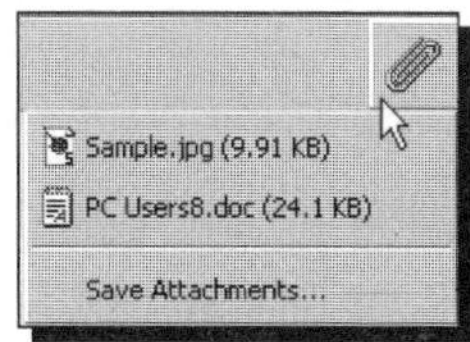

To view or save an attachment file, left-click its entry on the list. This opens the Warning box shown in Fig. 7.21 below.

Each file can be saved to disc or opened in situ. All attachments to an e-mail can also be saved by selecting the **Save Attachments** command from the above drop-down menu.

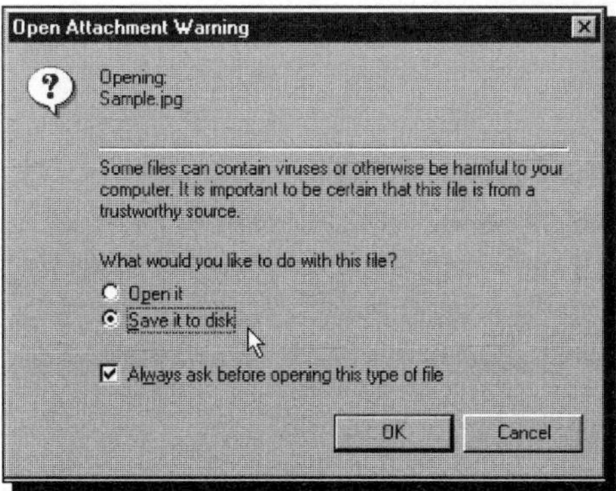

Fig. 7.21 The Open Attachment Warning Window.

Replying to a Message

When you receive an e-mail message that you want to reply to, Outlook Express makes it very easy to do. The reply address and the new message subject fields are both added automatically for you. Also, by default, the original message is quoted in the reply window for you to edit as required.

With the message you want to reply to still open, click the Reply to Sender Toolbar icon to open the New Message window and the message you are replying to will, by default, be placed under the insertion point.

With long messages, you should not leave all of the original text in your reply. This can be bad practice, which rapidly makes new messages very large and time consuming to download. You should usually edit the quoted text, so that it is obvious what you are referring to. A few lines may be enough.

Removing Deleted Messages

Whenever you delete a message it is actually moved to the Deleted Items folder. If ignored, this folder gets bigger and bigger over time, so you need to check it frequently and manually re-delete messages you are sure you will not need again.

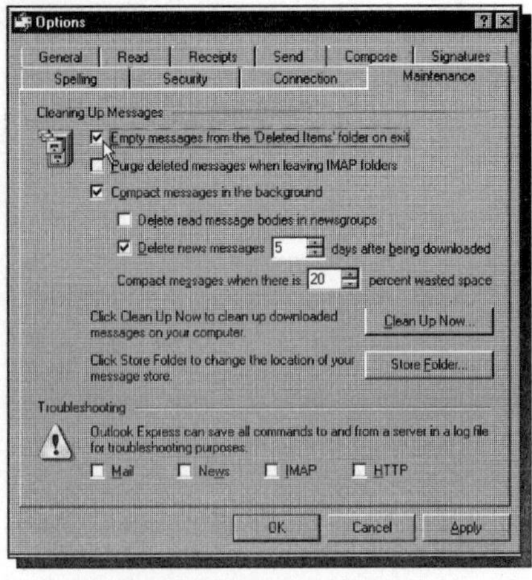

Fig. 7.22 Cleaning up Messages.

If you are confident that you will not need this safety net, you can opt to **Empty messages from the 'Deleted Items' folder on exit** in Maintenance tab settings of the **Tools**, **Options** box, opened from the Main window, as shown in Fig. 7.22.

Organising your Messages

Perhaps most of the e-mail messages you get will have no 'long term' value and will be simply deleted once you have dealt with them. Some however you may well need to keep for future reference. After a few weeks it can be surprising how many of these messages can accumulate. If you don't do something with them they seem to take over and slow the whole process down. That is the reason for the Folders List.

As we saw earlier you can open and close new folders in this area, and can move and copy messages from one folder into another.

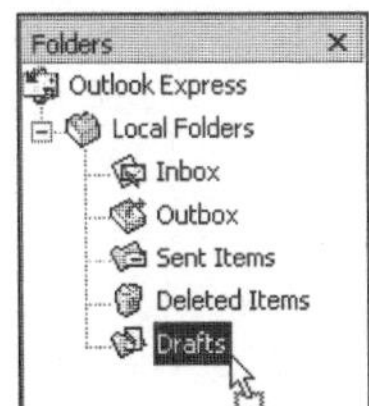

To move a message, you just select its header line in the Message List and with the left mouse button depressed 'drag' it to the folder in the Folders List, as shown to the left. When you release the mouse button, the message will be moved to that folder.

The copy procedure is very much the same, except you must also have the <Ctrl> key depressed when you release the mouse button. You can tell which operation is taking place by looking at the mouse pointer. It will show a '+' when copying, as on the right.

The System Folders

Outlook Express has five folders which it always keeps intact and will not let you delete. Some of these we have met already.

The ***Inbox*** holds all incoming messages. You should delete or move messages from this folder as soon as you have read them.

The ***Outbox*** holds messages that have been prepared but not yet transmitted. As soon as the messages are sent they are automatically removed to the ***Sent Items*** folder. You can then decide whether to 'file' your copies of these messages, or whether to delete them. As we saw on the last page, any messages you do delete are placed in the ***Deleted Items*** folder as a safety feature.

The last system folder is the ***Drafts*** folder, which does not seem to be mentioned at all in Microsoft's program information. If you close a message without sending it, Outlook Express will ask you to save it in this folder. We also use the Drafts folder to store our message pro-formas and unfinished messages that will need more work before they can be sent.

Spell Checking

Many of the e-mail messages we receive seem to be full of errors and spelling mistakes. Some people do not seem to read their work before clicking the 'Send' button. With Outlook Express this should be a thing of the past, as the program is linked to the spell checker that comes with other Microsoft programs. If you do not have any of these, the option will be greyed out, meaning that it is not available.

To try it out, prepare a message in the New Message window, but make an obvious spelling mistake, maybe like ours below. Pressing the Spelling Toolbar button, the **F7** function key, or using the **Tools, Spelling** menu command, reveals the drop-down sub-menu shown below in Fig. 7.23.

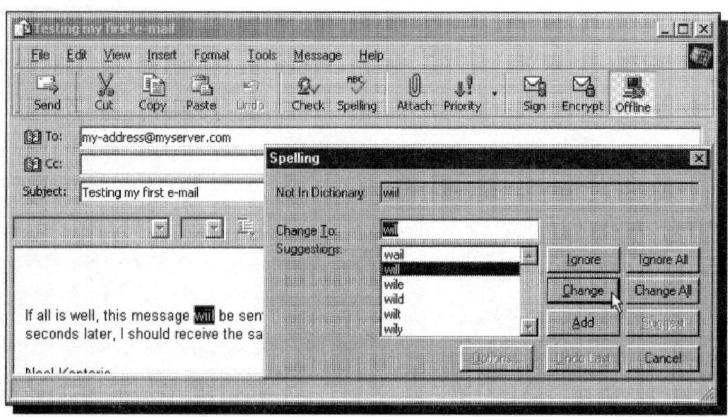

Fig. 7.23 Using the Spell Checker.

Any words not recognised by the checker will be flagged up as shown. If you are happy with the word just click one of the **Ignore** buttons, if not, you can type a correction in the **Change To:** field, or accept one of the **Suggestions:**, and then click the **Change** button. With us the **Options** button always seemed 'greyed out', but you can get some control over the spell checker on the settings sheet opened from the main Outlook Express menu with the **Tools**, **Options** command, and then clicking the Spelling tab.

The available options, as shown in Fig. 7.24, are self explanatory so we will not dwell on them. If you want every message to be checked before it is sent, make sure you select the **Always check spelling before sending** option.

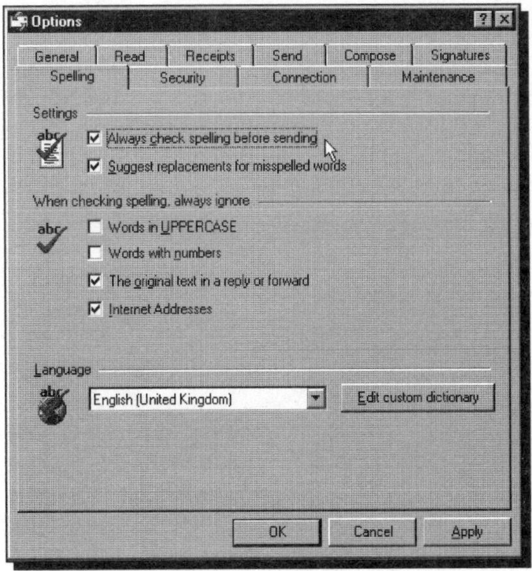

Fig. 7.24 The Options Spelling Dialogue Box.

In the above dialogue box, you could also choose to have the Spell Checker ignore **Words with numbers**, if you so wished, before clicking the **Apply** button.

Connection at Start-up

While you are looking at the program settings, open the **Tools**, **Options**, Connection tabbed sheet, shown in Fig. 7.25

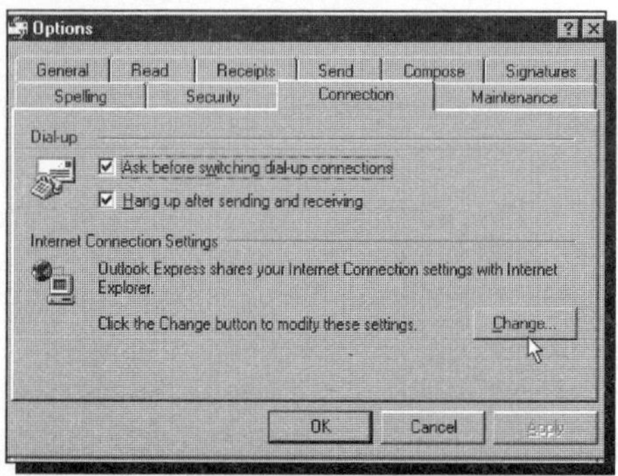

Fig. 7.25 The Options Connection Dialogue Box.

This gives you some control of what happens when you open Outlook Express, depending on your connection settings for Internet Explorer. If you have a modem connection to the Internet, it can be annoying when a program goes into dial-up mode unexpectedly. To look at these settings, click the **Change** button which displays the dialogue box below.

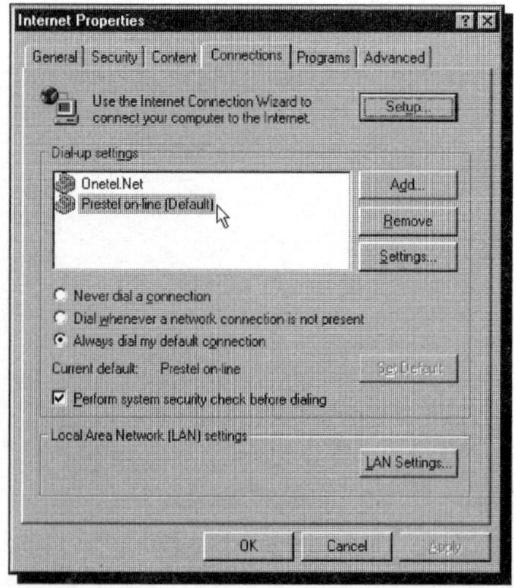

Fig. 7.26 The Internet Properties Dialogue Box.

Next, select the **Never dial a connection** option so that you only 'go on line' (as long as you have not chosen to **Work Offline** from the **File** menu option), when you click the Send/Recv toolbar icon shown here. If you have more than one Internet connection, the down arrow to the right of the icon lets you select which one to use.

If, on the other hand, you have a permanent Internet connection, you might like to deselect the **Never dial a connection** option.

Printing your Messages

It was originally thought by some, that computers would lead to the paperless office. That has certainly not proved to be correct. It seems that however good our electronic communication media becomes most people want to see the results printed on paper. As far as books are concerned, long may that last!

Outlook Express 5 lets you print e-mail messages to paper, but it does not give you any control over the page settings it uses. You can, however, alter the font size of your printed output as it depends on the font size you set for viewing your messages. As shown here, you have five 'relative' size options available from the **View**, **Text Size** menu command.

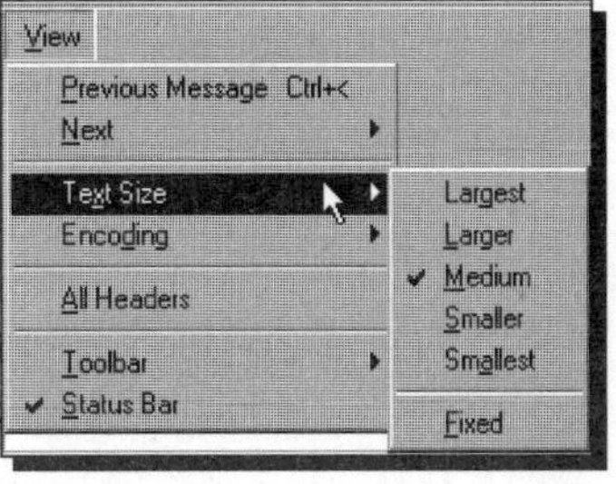

When you are ready to print a message in the Read Message window, use the <Ctrl+P> key combination, or the **File**, **Print** menu command, to open the Print dialogue box shown in Fig. 7.27 on the next page.

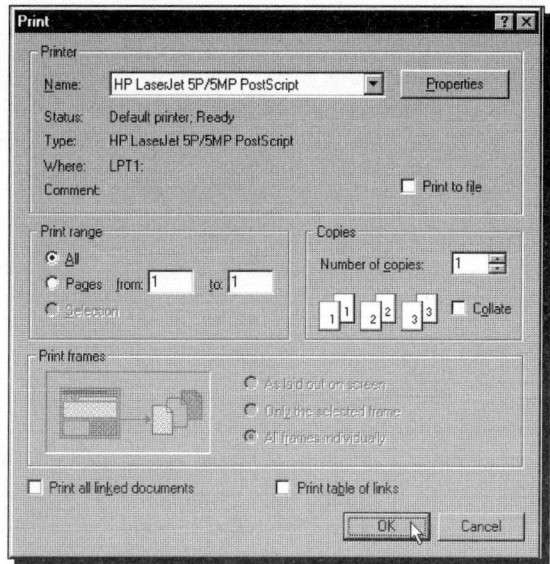

Fig. 7.27 The Print Dialogue Box.

Make sure the correct printer, **Page range**, and **Number of copies** you want are selected, then click **OK**. You can also start the printing procedure by clicking the Print Toolbar icon shown here.

If the message has Web page links on it, there are two useful features at the bottom of the Print dialogue box shown above. These are:

- The **Print all linked documents** option, which when checked not only prints the message, but also all the Web pages linked to it.

- The **Print table of links** option, which when when checked, gives a hard copy listing of the URL addresses of all the links present in the page.

Outlook Express Help

Outlook Express has a built-in Help system, which is accessed with the **Help**, **Contents and Index** menu command, or the **F1** function key. These open a Windows type Help window, as shown below.

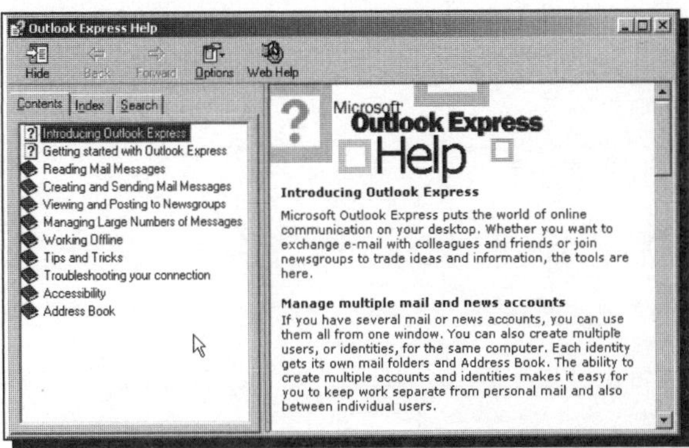

Fig. 7.28 The Outlook Express Help System.

We strongly recommend that you work your way through all the items listed in the **Contents** tabbed section. Clicking on a closed book icon will open it and display a listing of its contents. Double-clicking on a list item will then open a window with a few lines of Help information.

Another way of browsing the Help system is to click the **Index** tab and work your way through the alphabetic listing. The **Search** tab, on the other hand, opens a search facility you can use by typing your query in the **Type in the keyword to find** text field and clicking the **List Topics** button, then selecting one of the topics found and clicking **Display** to open Help information on it.

The Help provided by Microsoft with Outlook Express 5, is a big improvement over some earlier versions of the program, and it is well worth spending some time getting to grips with it. If you are connected to the Internet, the Web Help icon accesses the Support Online from Microsoft Technical Support, which can give more specific help with the program.

The Address Book

E-mail addresses are often quite complicated and not at all easy to remember. With Outlook Express there is a very useful Address Book built in and accessed by clicking the menu icon with the same name. Below, we show part of an example.

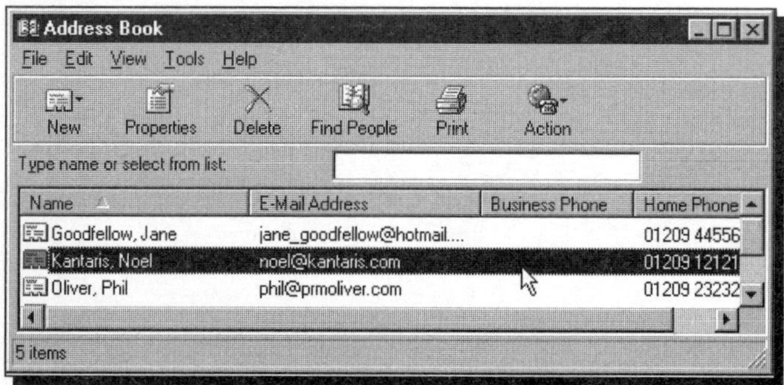

Fig. 7.29 The Address Book Screen.

Once in the Address Book, you can manually add a person's full details and e-mail address, in the Properties box that opens when you click the New Toolbar icon and select **New Contact**, as shown here. Selecting **New Group** from this drop-down menu lets you create a grouping of e-mail addresses, you can then send mail to everyone in the group with one operation.

To send a new message to anyone listed in your Address Book, open a New Message window and use the **Tools**, **Select Recipients** command, or click on any of the To, Cc, or Bcc icons shown here on the left.

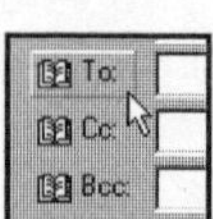

In the Select Recipients box which is opened (Fig. 7.30), you can select a person's name and click either the **To:->** button to place it in the **To:** field of your message, the **Cc->** button to place it in the **Cc:** field, or the **Bcc->**button to place it in the **Bcc:** field.

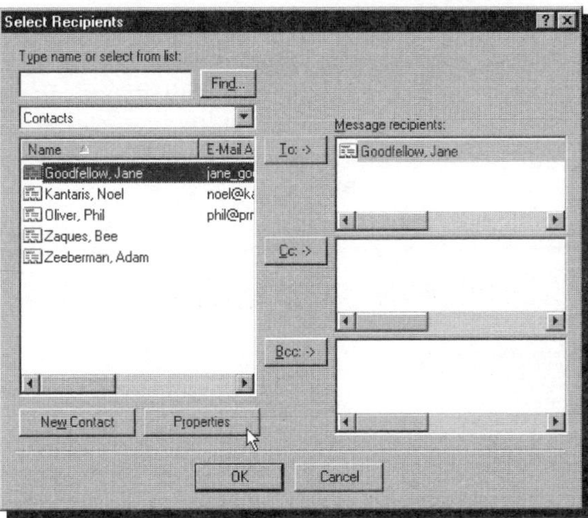

Fig. 7.30 The Select Recipients Screen.

The **New Contact** button lets you add details for a new person to the Address Book, and the **Properties** button lets you edit an existing entry, as shown below.

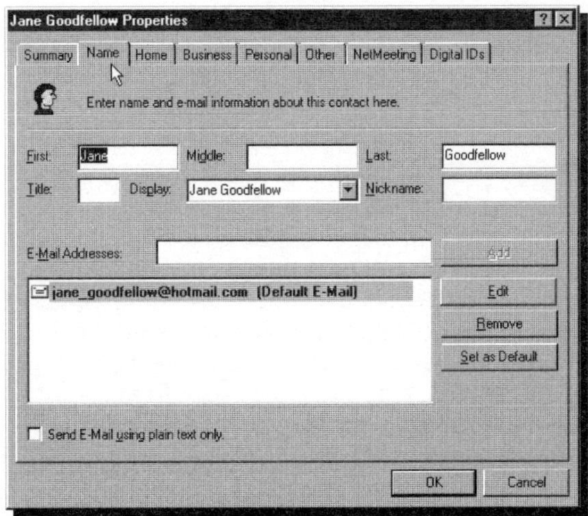

Fig. 7.31 A Recipient's Properties Screen.

Address Book Help

We will leave it to you to find your way round this very comprehensive facility. Don't forget that it has its own Help system that you can use with the **Help**, **Contents and Index** menu command. An example section is shown open below.

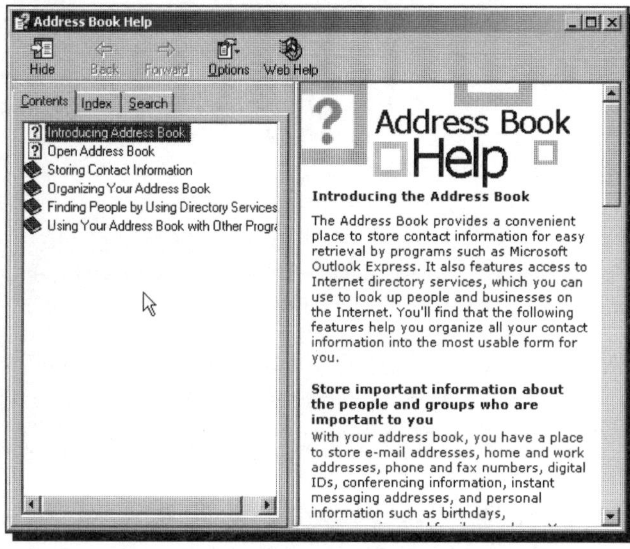

Fig. 7.32 The Address Book Help System.

In this chapter of the book, we have tried to cover sufficient information on Outlook Express, so that you can get on with the job of sending and receiving e-mail effectively, being one of the most used activities on the Internet. If, however, you want to know more about this subject, such as using News groups, or would like to learn how to use the Internet Explorer (also supplied with Windows Me) to surf the Net, then may we suggest you have a look at our books *Internet Explorer 5 explained* (BP488), and *E-mail and News with Outlook Express* (BP464), also published by Bernard Babani (publishing) Ltd.

8

Controlling Multimedia

Windows Me has a multitude of 'hidden' features built into it to improve the PC's multimedia performance, which is simply the ability to play sound and images (both still and moving) through a computer, usually from a CD-ROM or DVD disc. These new multimedia features lead to a big improvement in both video and audio speed, quality, and ease of use.

Whether all the features described in the next few pages work on your PC will depend on your system. Most of them require at least a CD-ROM player, a sound card and speakers, to be fitted and correctly set up. Other options require additional hardware. For example, to use the Web TV you need a TV tuner card, to use portable digital devices you need a CompactFlash or SmartMedia reader and media, while to use the Windows Movie Maker you need a fast modem, a good quality microphone and a video capture device.

The Windows Media Player 7

The Windows Media Player can be activated by either clicking its icon on the Quick Launch Toolbar, or selecting it from the **Start**, **Programs**, **Accessories**, **Entertainment** cascade menu, as shown in Fig. 8.1 below.

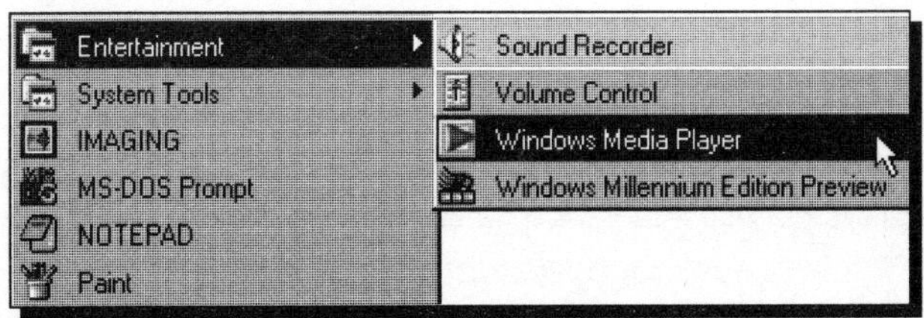

Fig. 8.1 The Entertainment Menu.

Either of these actions displays the screen in Fig. 8.2 with the Media Player in Compact Mode at the top left corner of your screen, and an additional large button at the bottom right of the screen, as shown.

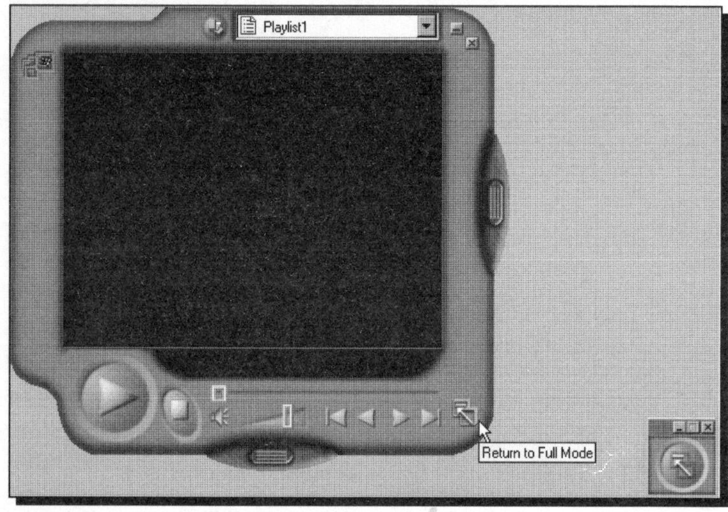

Fig. 8.2 The Windows Media Player.

Clicking the button on the screen image of the Media Player (the one pointed to), displays the Media Player in Full Mode. This can also be achieved by clicking the large button at the bottom right of the screen to reveal a menu with several choices, as shown below. From here you can **Return to Full Mode**, **Select a New Skin**, **Open** a folder on your computer or the network you might be connected to, so that you can load an appropriate media file, or use the **Open URL** option to search the Internet or Intranet for a media file.

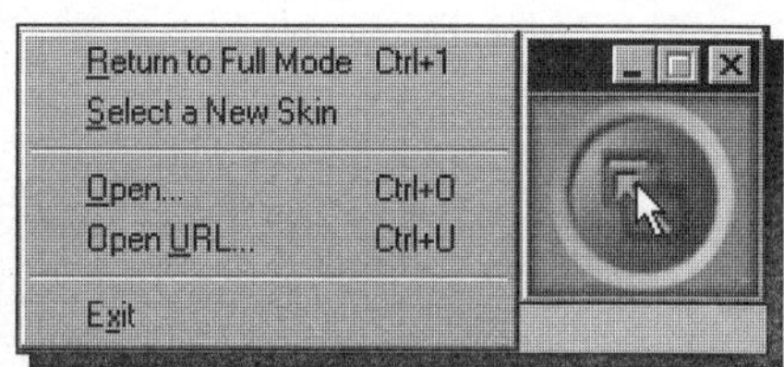

On the next page, we first show the Media Player in Compact Mode playing an audio file, but with its hidden options displayed (Fig. 8.3), then the same thing, but in Full Mode (Fig. 8.4).

Fig. 8.3 The Media Player Playing an Audio File in Compact Mode.

To reveal or hide details of a playing media file, click on the oval handles at the end of the extensions on the above screen.

Fig. 8.4 The Media Player Playing an Audio File in Full Mode.

Note the options displayed on the left of the Media Player when in Full Mode (see Fig. 8.4). What these options offer when you activate them are:

Watch a currently playing file. When playing music you can select an 'Ambience'.

Find the latest music, movie trailers, and news updates on the Internet.

Copy CD music to your computer's hard disc.

Create play lists and manage media.

Set radio station pre-sets.

Transfer files to a portable device.

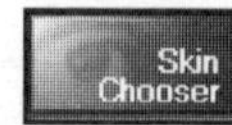

Customise the player.

Watching a Currently Playing Media File

Figures 8.3 and 8.4 show what you see when the Media Player is playing an audio file. You can select a different audio file by using the **File, Open** command, to choose a file stored on your computer, or use the **File, Open URL** command (also shown to the left), to browse your network or access the Internet for an audio or video file which can then be added to your library.

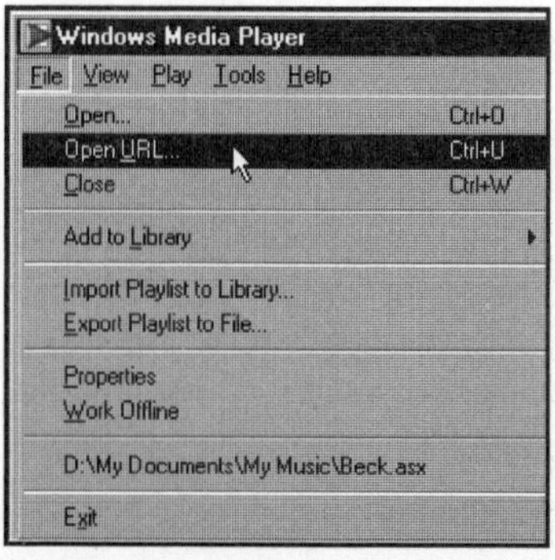

Using the Media Guide

This option requires you to be connected to the Internet before you can use it. Having connected, click the option to display a screen similar to the following:

Fig. 8.5 Using the Media Guide.

From here you can find entertainment (both audio and video) and information. We suggest you play a bit with this option to find out what is available.

Using the CD Audio Option

Use this option to copy music from a CD to your computer's hard disc, or get information about the CD from the Internet (provided you are already connected to it before activating the option).

Placing a CD in your computer's CD-ROM drive automatically loads the Media Player, then starts playing the music on it and displays the Now Playing screen (see Fig. 8.4). Selecting the **CD Audio** option displays a screen, the top half of which is shown in Fig 8.6 on the next page.

At the top of the screen you will find three radio buttons, the first to **Copy Music**, the second to **Get Names**, and the third to give you **Album Details**. Of these, the second and third require you to be already connected to the Internet.

Fig. 8.6 The CD Audio Option Screen.

Clicking the **Get Names** radio button displays the screen in Fig. 8.7 which asks you for the Artist's name.

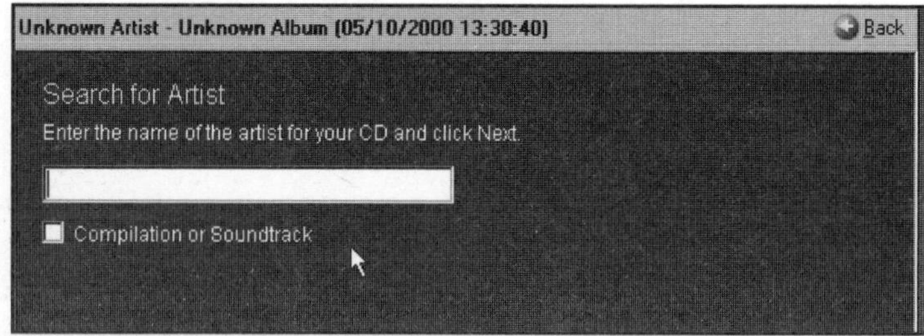

Fig. 8.7 The Search for Artist Screen.

Since quite a sizeable portion of our CD collection is classical music, searching by Artist or Title of CD is not much use! The option works well for modern music, though we found the information on the site's database not complete. Perhaps some of our taste in music is not modern enough!

The Media Library

The first time you use this option, the Media Player searches your system for media files and then displays the screen in Fig. 8.8 below.

Fig. 8.8 The Media Library Screen with Video All Clips Selected.

As you can see, both Audio and Video files are searched for and a tree-like structure is displayed in a separate pane. Selecting **Video, All Clips** displays the appropriate files on the right pane of the screen, as shown above. Double-clicking on one of these files starts playing the chosen clip and the Media Player reverts to the Now Playing screen, as shown in Fig. 8.9 overleaf. To see this in full screen, use the **View, Full Screen** menu command. To exit the full screen mode press <Esc>.

Obviously, it will be highly unlikely if what is available on our system is to be found on your PC, although one or two media files might be the same as they are installed by Windows Me. It is worth spending some time examining the Media Library structure because you can use it to manage and organise your music collection and video files and create custom playlists.

Fig. 8.9 Playing a Video Clip.

The radio buttons at the top of the Media Library screen, shown below magnified, can help you to organise your playlist. Most of these are self-explanatory, except for the last four which have the following functions.

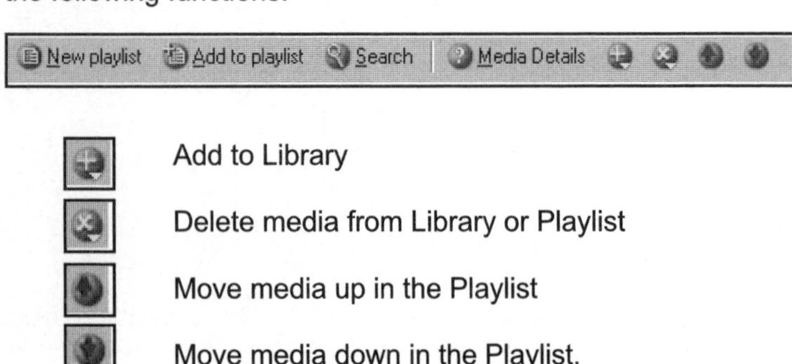

Add to Library

Delete media from Library or Playlist

Move media up in the Playlist

Move media down in the Playlist.

Finally, note that you can change the brightness, contrast, hue, and saturation of the playing video.

Using the Radio Tuner

The Radio Tuner option has to be a winner. You can have immediate access to over 3,000 Internet-radio stations from all over the world that use the Microsoft Windows Media format. The screen in Fig. 8.10 displays information on the radio station we selected to try the Media Player. It actually works extremely well, so watch out; you could be amassing a sizeable telephone bill!

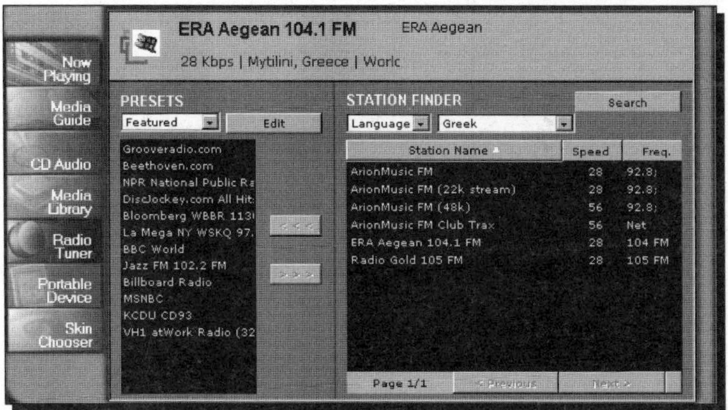

Fig. 8.10 Listening to a Radio Station.

To use the Radio Tuner, you must first connect to the Internet before you select the option. Having done so, two panels are displayed, as shown above. On the left panel, a list of preselected stations is displayed, while on the right panel and under the **Station Finder** caption you can use the first of two text boxes to find a station by Format, Band, Language, Location, etc. To do so, simply click the down-arrow of the first text box, as shown to the left, and select one of the options from the drop-down menu. Having selected, say Language, the second text box can then be used to make an appropriate choice, as shown here to the right.

Next, the Media Player displays all the available radio stations on the Internet that meet your requirements. Alternatively, you could click the **Search** button to display the Advanced Station Search facility, shown here to the left, which allows you to find a radio station by combining several criteria, such as Band, Format, Language, etc. All you need to do now is learn some of the listed languages!

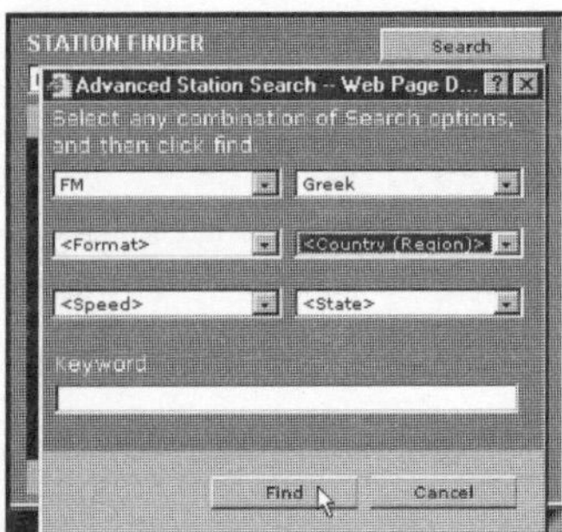

Transferring Files to a Portable Device

You can use the **Portable Device** option to transfer music from your PC to palm-size PCs, Smart Media, Iomega Jaz and Zip drives, CompactFlash cards, or the next generation of portable music devices. Selecting this option, displays the screen shown in Fig. 8.11.

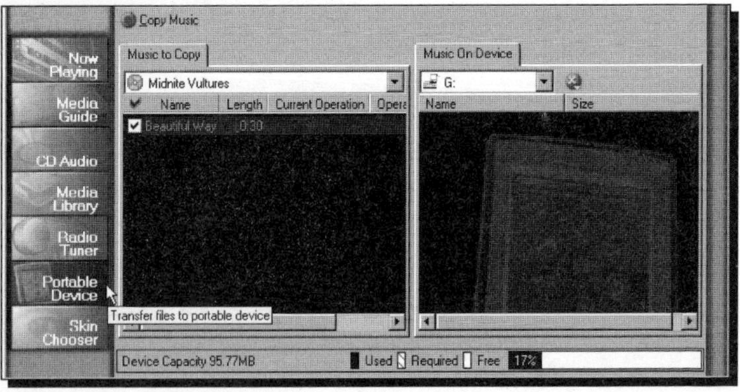

Fig. 8.11 Using the Portable Device Option.

First select in the left panel the music you want to copy to your portable device, then click the **Copy Music** radio button located at the top of the screen. That is all it takes, provided you have the right equipment for the operation.

Customising the Media Player

You can customise the looks of your Media Player by selecting one of several predefined looks. What we have shown so far has been the Default Media Player look. Clicking on the **Skin Chooser** button, displays a list of several choices. In the screen below, we show what the WinME option looks like. As you select each option from the list on the left panel, a preview of that option appears on the right panel.

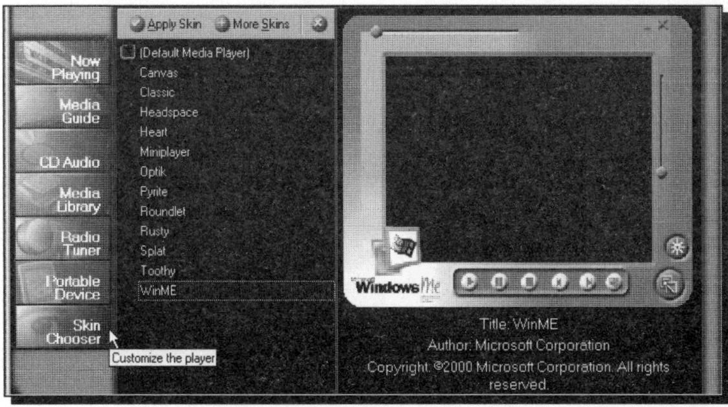

Fig. 8.12 A different Media Player Skin.

To select a different skin for your Media player, select it from the list, then click the **Apply Skin** radio button located at the top of the screen. You can use the other two radio buttons to either download more skins from the Internet, or delete a selected skin from the list.

Which skin you use for your Media Player is a matter of personal preference. However, we found that only the Default, Classic and WinME skins gave a sufficiently large display area for watching a video clip in comfort. Furthermore, with the first two of these, you can use the **View, Full Screen** menu command for maximum screen size viewing (to return to normal size press the <Esc> key). The other skins are fun to look at, but impractical for viewing video clips. The choice, of course, is yours!

The Sound Recorder

To record a sound, use the Sound Recorder from the Entertainment group, but apart from a sound card and speakers you will also need a microphone connected to your computer. You can use the Sound Recorder not only to record, mix, play, and edit sounds, but also link sounds to or insert sounds into a document.

To start using the Sound Recorder to record audio, make sure you have an audio input device, then use the **File, New** command and press the 'Record' button pointed to below. When you finish recording, click the Stop button (the one next to the Record button), rewind the recorded music on the Sound Recorder and use the **File, Save As** command to save your recording to a **.wav** file with an appropriate name.

Fig. 8.13 The Sound Recorder.

To play a recorder file, use the **File, Open** command, select a file and press the 'Play' button.

We have also found this accessory very useful for playing existing **.wav** sound files, and also for editing them. The Wav sub-folder of Windows/Help/Tour/Audio folder contains several such files. Use the **Effects** menu to 'play around' with the sound, and the **Edit** menu to insert and mix other sound files into the loaded one. If you have to save such experimental files, do make sure you save them under a name different from the ones in the Wav folder, otherwise you might be spoiling the audio files of the Windows Me Tour.

For more information on how to edit audio files, link sounds to, or insert sounds into a document, have a look at the extensive Help topics of the Sound Recorder. In the end, the only way to learn is to experiment, so good luck and have fun!

Managing your Photos

You can have a look at the 'Preview Facility', which lets you preview photos and images and also turn them into a slide show, by double-clicking on the My Pictures sub-folder that Windows Me has placed in the My Documents folder during installation, as shown below in Fig. 8.14.

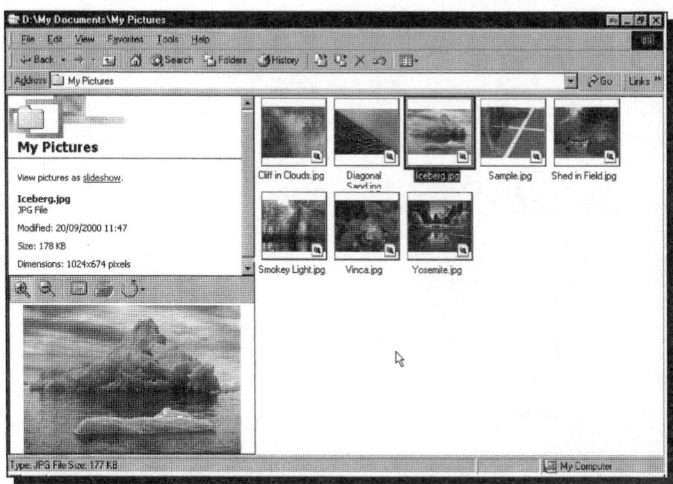

Fig. 8.14 The Image Preview Facility.

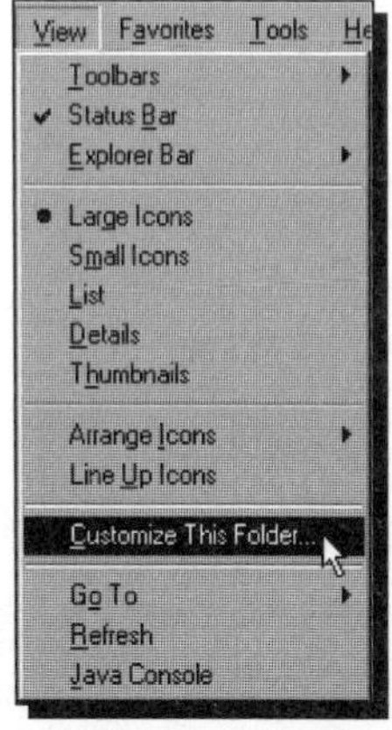

To turn on the Image Preview on a folder other than the My Pictures folder, double-click the My Computer icon on your desktop, locate and double-click on the folder in question, and use the **View, Customize This Folder** menu command, as shown here to the left.

This starts the Welcome to the Customize This Folder Wizard. As usual, clicking the **Next** button displays the next Wizard screen, until you reach the final screen which asks you to click the **Finish** button.

Below we show the second and third screens of the Customize This Folder Wizard with the options we selected.

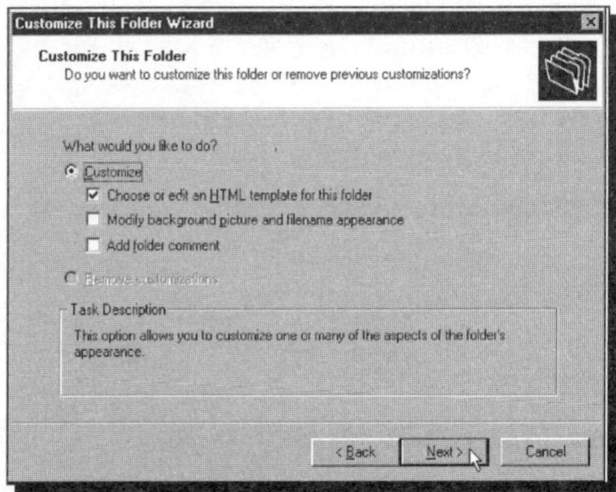

Fig. 8.15 The Second Screen of the Customize This Folder Wizard.

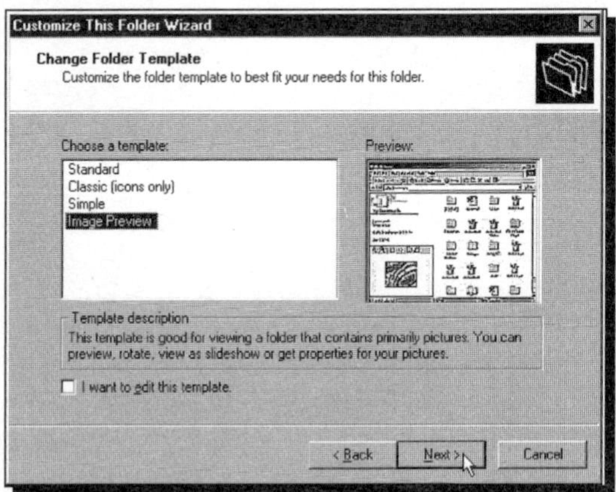

Fig. 8.16 The Third Screen of the Customize This Folder Wizard.

Note: For the Image Preview window to appear, the 'Web Content' must be enabled in the General tab of the Folder Options in the Control Panel (see Fig. 2.6, page 21).

Finally if you also want the ability to view the pictures in such a folder as thumbnails, use the **View, Thumbnails** command. Next, click the slideshow link and sit back and enjoy!

The Windows Movie Maker

The Movie Maker is new to Windows Me. You can now edit and rearrange your home-made video cam movies, make a shorter version of them, add a still picture and voice over, and either post them to your Web site for all to see, or send them as an attachment to an e-mail to your favourite people.

The Windows Movie Maker can be found in the **Programs, Accessories** folder. Left-clicking its icon, shown here to the left, starts the program and displays a screen similar to the one in Fig. 8.17.

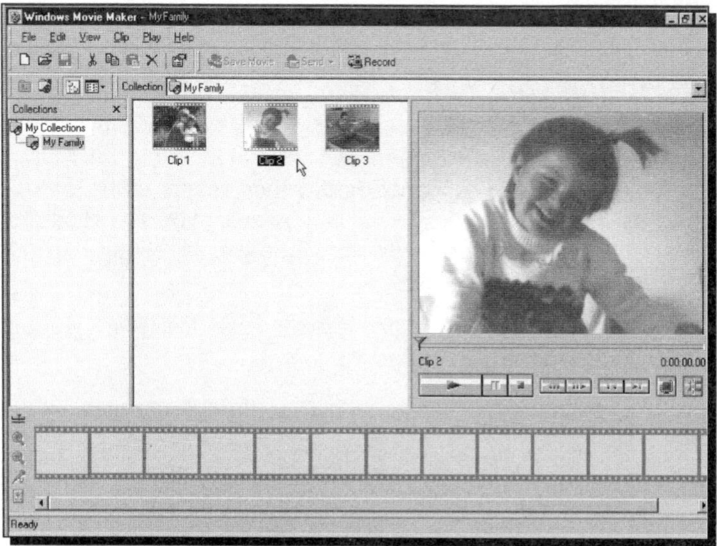

Fig. 8.17 The Windows Movie Maker Screen.

The displayed screen is divided into three panes, with the left pane showing the folder holding your video collection. Windows Me automatically created during installation a sub-folder within My Documents, named My Videos, and placed within this folder any video films that it might have found on your computer. In our case one of our collections is the My Family folder, shown open with three segments, called clips, of the video film showing in the middle pane.

Selecting each clip of the video displays that clip in the right pane of the Movie Maker screen, as shown in Fig. 8.17. Each selected segment can then be played by clicking the 'Play' button to be found below the display area.

At the top of the Movie Maker screen there is the usual selection of menu options and Toolbar icons, while at the bottom of the screen is the 'Workspace' area. It is here that you assemble your movie, which can be viewed either as a 'timeline' (focuses on timing) or 'storyboard' (focuses on sequencing) view. In the timeline view, you can synchronise video clips with audio clips or create fading transitions between clips with the help of a number of tools that appear at the far left of the Workspace area.

Recording your Film

You can use the Windows Movie Maker to record from a variety of sources, such as a camcorder, television, radio, or CD. As far as audio sound is concerned, most sound cards can be used as they support audio in. If, however, you are recording from a camcorder or the television, then you will require a video capture card or equivalent.

To record using the Movie Maker, use the **File, Record** menu command, which opens the following dialogue box.

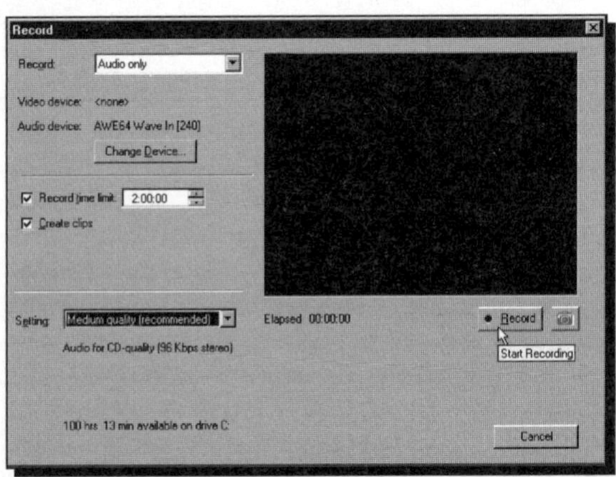

Fig. 8.18 The Record Screen of the Movie Maker.

On this dialogue box you can specify the maximum time of the recording, the device you will be recording from, and whether you will be recording video only, audio only, or both - if you are recording from a camera, don't forget to switch it to playback before starting to record. Next, when you are ready, click the **Record** button on the dialogue box of Fig. 8.18.

By default, your recording will be broken up into manageable chunks of clips. These are the ones shown in Fig. 8.17, and you can monitor what is being recorded, as shown in Fig. 8.19 below.

Fig. 8.19 Monitoring what you Record.

You can stop recording at any time by clicking the **Stop** button, or you can let it run through the specified time. When recording has finished, you will be asked for a filename under which to save your newly created Windows Media File. The file format for this type of media has a 300:1 compression ratio, which means you can store up to 23 hours of video on 1 GB of disc space. So now is the time to upgrade your hard disc!

Editing Video Clips

Video clips can be edited at will, and can be rearranged to produce the final film sequence. To rearrange the sequence of your creation, drag the clips in the sequence you want them to appear in your final film onto the Workspace area. You can even add a voice-over by selecting the **Record Narration** menu command.

A clip can be edited by trimming it, splitting it, or joining it. To trim a clip, start playing it, and when the point is reached where you want to trim it, use the **Clip, Set Start Trim Point** menu command. When you reach the end point of the trim, use the **Clip, Set End Trim Point** command. If you change your mind, use the **Clip, Clear Trim Point**. An alternative method is to use the trim handles in Timeline view and move them to where you want to cut the clip.

To split a clip, play the clip, and when you reach the desired point, use the **Clip, Split** command. The original clip is then split into two chunks that can be dragged independently onto the workspace area. To join clips together into one long one, select the first, press the <Shift> key down, then click on the last one and use the **Clip, Combine** command.

In Fig. 8.20, we display a selected film sequence together with an imported audio file while the movie is actually playing. The audio file was incorporated into our collection using the **File, Import** command, and choosing a file from My Music folder. You can also import a title clip that you created in Paint.

To save your creation on your hard disc, use the **File, Save Project** menu command. This allows you to return to it later for further editing, or additions. To save such edited work with another name, so that you can retain the original, use the **File, Save Project As** command.

Finally, you might like to include 'transitions' between clips so that you do not have abrupt changes from one clip to the other. To do this, switch to Timeline view, select the rightmost of the two clips you are creating a transition between, and drag it slightly so that it overlaps the left clip. The shaded area indicates the length of the overlap.

Fig. 8.20 The Final Movie Assembly while Playing.

Finally, when you are satisfied that no more edits will be required, save the movie using the **File, Save Movie** menu command. This displays the dialogue box shown to the left, in which you can specify the quality settings which will affect its size on the disc.

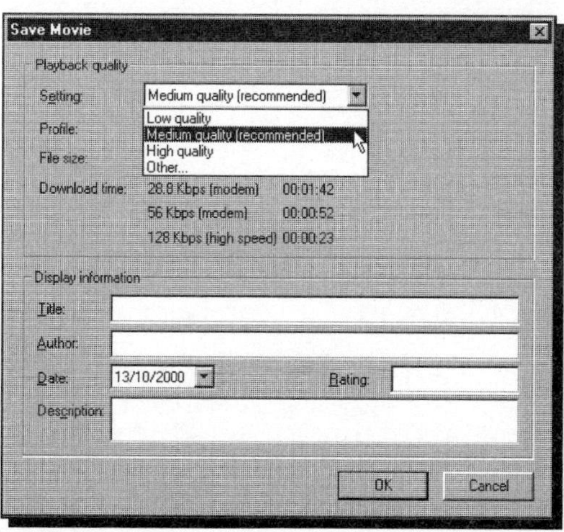

Playing and Sending your Movie

Having created your movie, you can either play it, using the Windows Media Player, as shown in Fig. 8.21 below, or send it as an e-mail to a friend.

Fig. 8.21 Playing a Saved Movie in the Media Player.

Sending a Movie as an E-mail Attachment

Having saved a movie, you can send it to a friend as an attachment to an e-mail. The easiest way of doing this is by starting your e-mail program then attaching the saved movie file to it (see Chapter 7, page 125). The movie file is to be found in the My Videos folder with the **.wmv** file extension.

If you were to use the **File, Send Movie To, E-mail** command, Movie Maker will re-save your work, but this time in a temporary folder, then ask you which e-mail program you would like to use! Microsoft is trying to make the process easy for you, but at the expense of repeating a procedure you have already gone through!

9

Other Communications Utilities

Home Networking

Windows Me allows you to easily connect two or more computers at home or in a small business, so that they can share files, printers, modems, and connection to the Internet. Even better, the Home Networking Wizard guides you through the procedure and makes the whole process of networking painless. However, before we activate the Home Networking Wizard, we need to discuss what hardware you require for making such connections.

Hardware Requirements for Networking

Apart from having two or more computers, the following additional hardware is essential:

- Network Adapters - otherwise known as Network cards which have to be plugged into one of the slots (PCI or ISA slot) inside your computer, or for more modern computers a USB connection at the back of your computer.
- Network Media - this includes the cables or other methods used to connect the computers together.
- Internet Connection - this is optional, but can provide access to the Internet for all the networked computers by sharing one Internet connection. The hardware for this could be an ordinary or wireless modem, or a broad-band cable modem, an ISDN or DSL connection.

In addition to the above hardware, at least one computer should be running Windows Me, while the rest can be running under Windows 95/98.

To start the Home Networking Wizard select it from the **Start**, **Programs, Accessories, Communications** sub-menu. Alternatively, start My Computer and click the My Network Places link shown in Fig. 9.1.

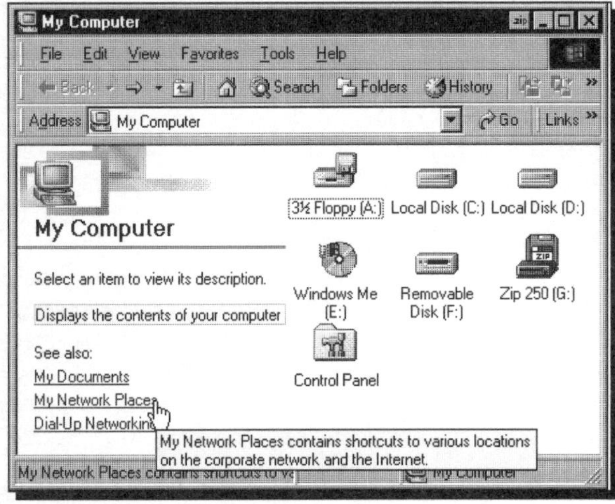

Fig. 9.1 The My Networking Places Link in My Computer.

This opens the following screen with the three application icons. Next, double-click the Home Networking Wizard icon.

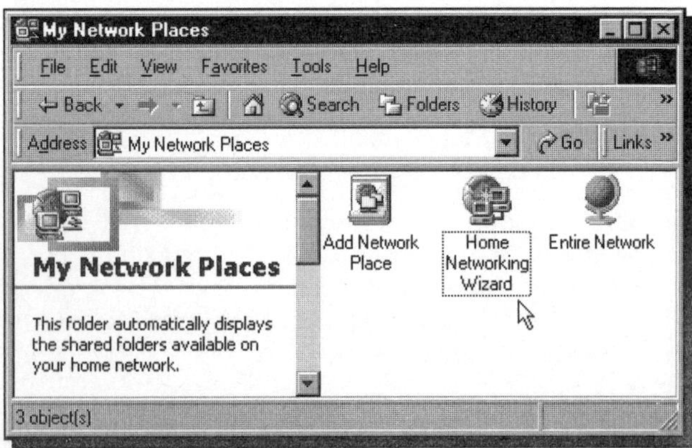

Fig. 9.2 The My Networking Wizard Icon.

Either action will display the screen shown in Fig. 9.3 below.

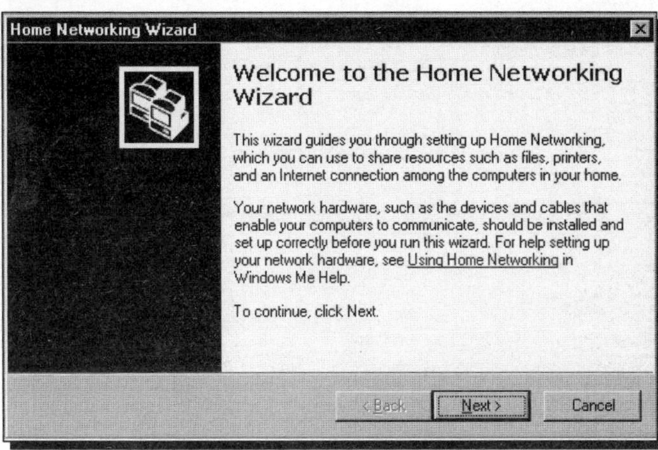

Fig. 9.3 The Opening Screen of the Home Networking Wizard.

Assuming that your Network Adapters are installed and that the computers are appropriately connected, clicking **Next** displays the screen in Fig. 9.4. If, you have not installed or connected your Network Adapters, Windows Me will detect this and the Wizard will tell you so.

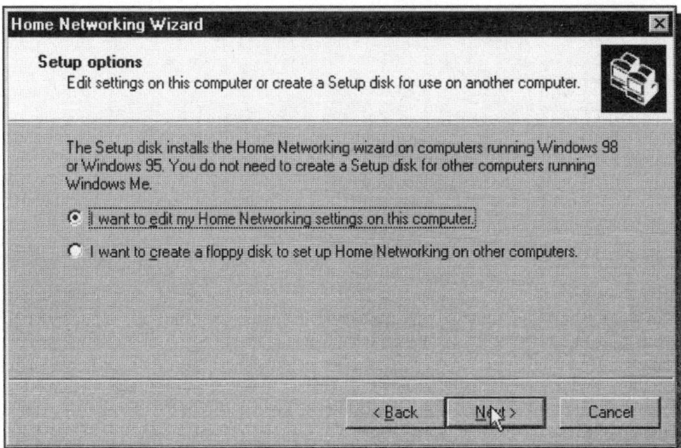

Fig. 9.4 The Second Screen of the Home Networking Wizard.

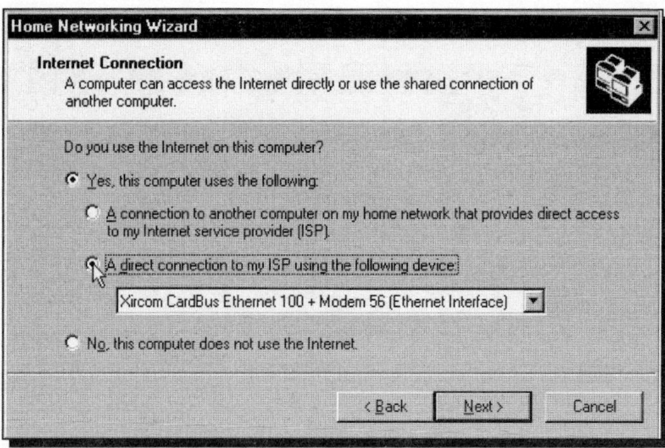

Fig. 9.5 The Third Screen of the Home Networking Wizard.

If the computer you are working on is the one connected to the Internet, click the **A direct connection to my ISP...** radio button and specify the type of connection on the next screen, shown in Fig. 9.6.

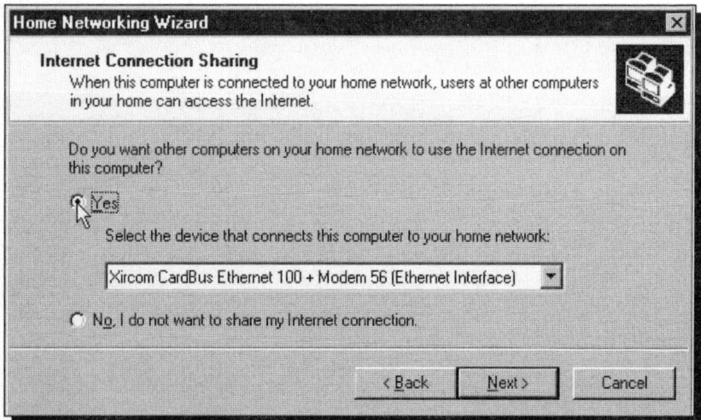

Fig. 9.6 The Fourth Screen of the Home Networking Wizard.

On the fifth Wizard screen, you give your computer a unique name and specify the group it belongs to (you can use the default name for this), while on the sixth Wizard screen you specify how you want to share your files, as shown in Fig. 9.7.

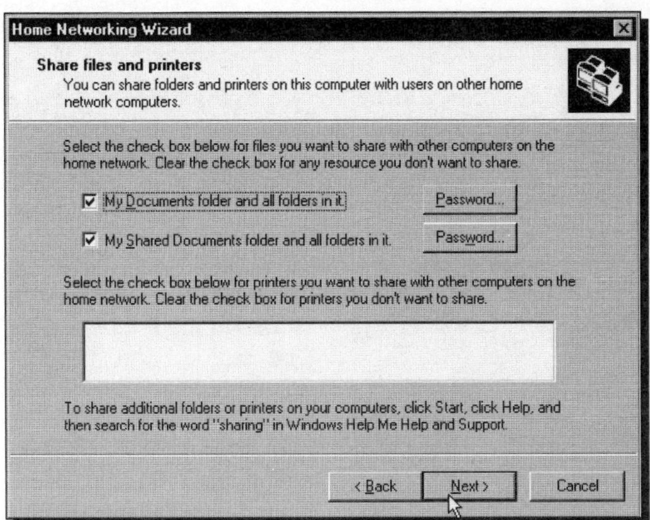

Fig. 9.7 The Sixth Screen of the Home Networking Wizard.

It is up to you if you want to share the whole of the My Documents folder or My Shared Documents folder only. For greater flexibility, you also have the choice of Password protecting these folders. In addition, if a printer was connected to the computer you are working with, it would have been detected and you could share that one as well.

The next Wizard screen asks you whether you would like to create a Home Networking Setup Disc which can then be used on the other computers on the network, particularly those running Windows 95/98, so that you can run the Home Network Wizard on them. If you do have such computers on the network, follow the instruction on the screen to complete the installation.

If the other computers on the network are to use your Internet connection, then their versions of Internet Explorer will have to be reconfigured. From each such PC, run the Internet Connection Wizard from the **Control Panel** by double-clicking the Internet Options icon, selecting the Connections tab and clicking the **Setup** button. Then select the **I want to set up my connection manually...** option on the first screen of the Wizard.

The Phone Dialer

If you have the facility to connect a normal telephone to your modem, you should be able to use the Phone Dialer to easily dial and log all your calls. The program can be found in the **Programs, Accessories, Communications** sub-group of the **Start** menu.

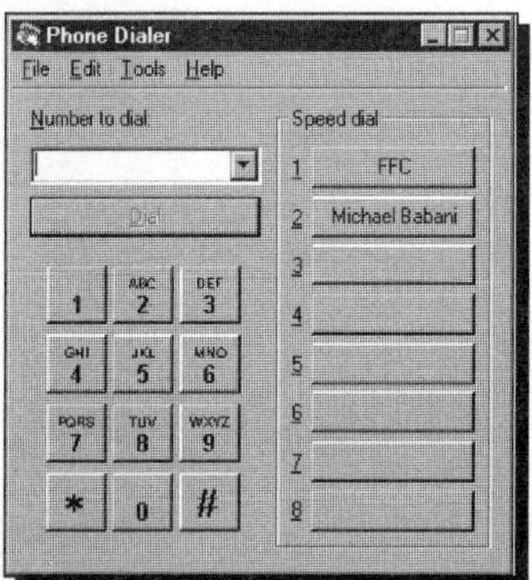

To make a call, simply enter the number in the text box, shown to the left, and click the **Dial** button. The down arrow will open a list of most recently used numbers. To enter numbers into the 'Speed dial' option buttons, use the **Edit, Speed Dial** menu command, click one of the 8 buttons, type its name and then the required number, as shown below left.

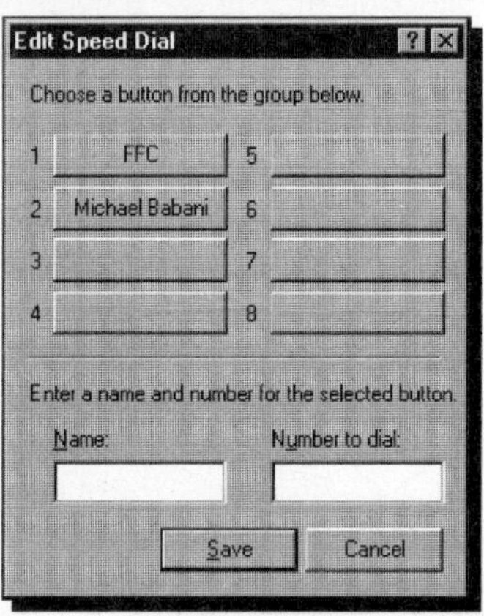

When the 'Speed dial' facility is set up, you just click one of the buttons to dial its number. To see a log of calls made or calls received, use the **Tools, Show Log** command to display the Call Log screen shown below. This gives you the name of the person you called (obscured in our example), the date, time and duration of the call.

HyperTerminal

The HyperTerminal utility also allows you to connect your computer to other computers in different locations via a modem, so that you can interchange information. You could, for example, search a library catalogue, or browse through the offerings of a bulletin board.

However, before you can connect to an outside service, you need to know their communications settings. For example, you need to know the settings for 'maximum speed', 'data bits', 'stop bits', and 'parity', though most of these can be safely assumed to be the same as the default values offered by HyperTerminal. Finally, before you can make the connection, you might need your credit card and to know a password or two, as these services are not free.

Starting HyperTerminal

To start HyperTerminal, click the **Start** button, and point to **Programs**, **Accessories**, **Communications**. This opens the sub-menu shown to the left. As you can see, it gives access to several communications services, such as Dial-Up Networking, Direct Cable Connection, and some others that we have discussed already.

You can also make additional connections to the Internet, or change an existing one with the help of the Internet Connection Wizard. NetMeeting allows you to connect to other users on the Internet or your local network.

Left-clicking the HyperTerminal menu option displays the Copyright screen, shown to the left, and a few seconds later starts HyperTerminal itself.

Every time you access HyperTerminal, a colourful window, shown to the left, is opened to help you make a new connection. Every call connection in HyperTerminal can be named and saved with an icon, so that in future it is very easy to recall the same number.

After typing in a connection name, click the **OK** button which opens the Connect To window, in which you enter the phone number of the site you want to connect to. Make sure the modem is correctly selected and press **OK** again to display the Connect window. To use the default modem settings, just click the **Dial** button to attempt a connection.

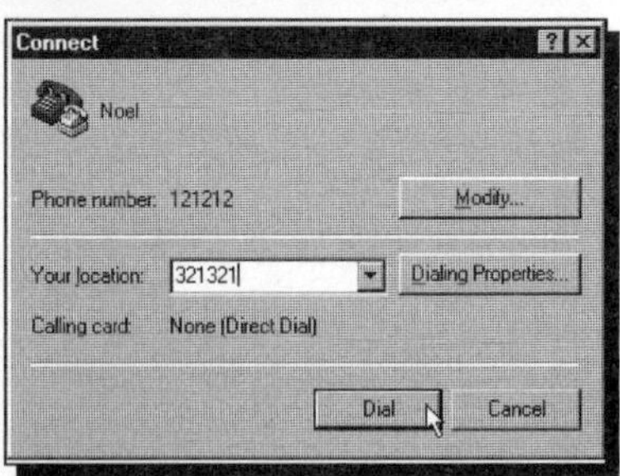

To call the same number again in the future, use the HyperTerminal **File, Open** command to display the Open dialogue box, where all the saved connections are to be found (Noel & Phil in our example below).

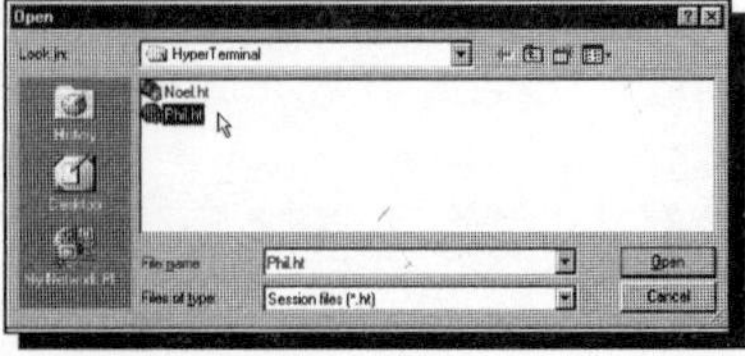

For more information about how to use HyperTerminal, click its Help menu and browse through the 'Contents'.

Specifying Communications Settings

If you have trouble getting through, you may need to fine tune the settings. Any time a call is 'open' in the HyperTerminal window, as shown in Fig. 9.8, click on the **Cancel** button of the Connect window, then use the **File**, **Properties** menu command to change call settings, or if necessary, to **Configure** the modem so that it speaks the same 'language' as the remote system.

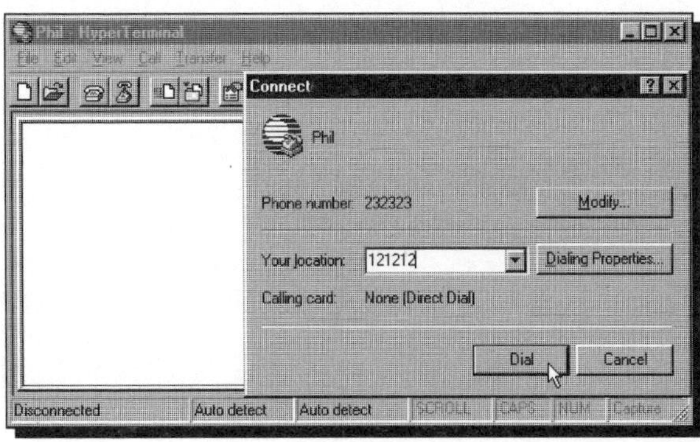

Fig. 9.8 Opening a HyperTerminal Connection.

This opens the tabbed Properties dialogue box shown in Fig. 9.9. Normally, you will find that the default parameters in this are the ones you want to use. However, in case you need to change them, we list on the next page some alternatives and their usage.

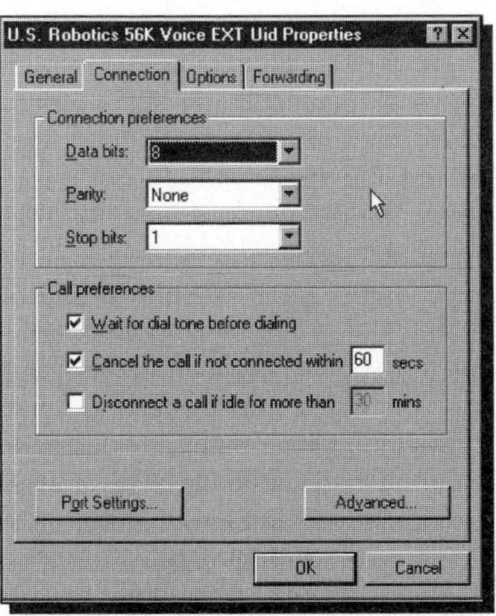

Fig. 9.9 The HyperTerminal Properties Dialogue Box.

Option	*Result*
Port speed	Specifies the transmission, or baud, rate at which your PC communicates with your modem. Typically most serial modem connections support 115.2 Kbps, which is set during installation of the modem.
Data bits	Specifies the number of data bits (binary digits) that each data packet, sent or received, contains. Most online services use '8' data bits, although a few use '7'.
Parity	Allows you to specify how the receiving computer verifies the accuracy of the data you are sending. Typically this is 'None', as most connections these days use more sophisticated error checking techniques.
Stop bits	Specifies the time between transmitted characters. This is nearly always set to '1'.
Modulation	Allows you to specify what modulation HyperTerminal should use so as to be compatible with the modem signals of the computer you are trying to connect. Most modems fall within the 'Standard' type, but if you have trouble connecting, try switching to a non-standard modulation type.

Setting Terminal Preferences

The terminal type used by the destination site will determine the terminal type which should be used for a connection. HyperTerminal supports several common types, but in most cases the **Auto detect** option will sort this out automatically.

To make a manual selection, click the Settings tab of the Properties sheet, as shown on the next page, with the **Emulation** list open. Select the correct terminal option and then click the **Terminal Setup** button to set its preferences.

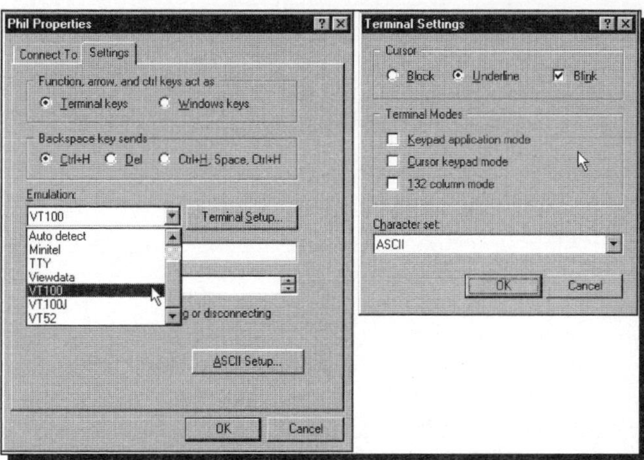

Fig. 9.10 The Properties Settings Emulation List.

File Transfer Protocols

Before you can send or receive files, use the HyperTerminal's **Transfer** command to specify the transfer protocol in either the **Send**, or **Receive** operation. The type of files you send or receive will be either binary or text files.

Text files: are normally prepared with a text editor, such as WordPad or Notepad, and saved in unformatted ASCII with only a few formatting codes such as carriage returns and linefeeds. Use the Settings tab on the Properties dialogue box and press the **ASCII Setup** button to display a sheet on which you can specify the transmission parameters for this type of file.

Binary files: are normally program or picture files which contain characters from both the ASCII and the extended ASCII character sets.

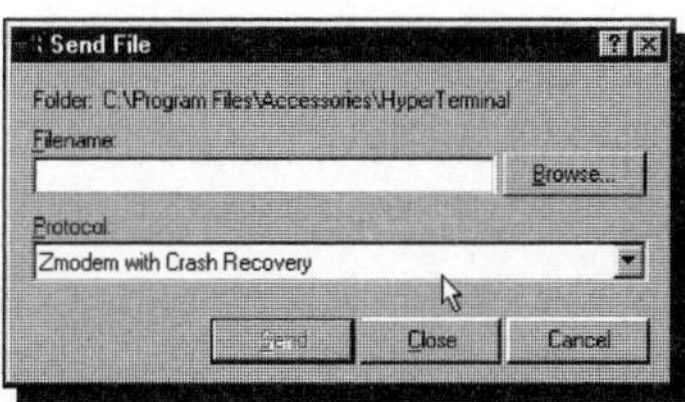

HyperTerminal supports many of the most popular protocols; which one to use depends on the receiving site. Use ZModem whenever possible as it gives the fastest transfer rates and remembers its place if your transmission is interrupted.

Towards the Mobile Office

Several of Windows Me's features are geared to making life a little easier for those who use computers on the move.

Dial-Up Networking

With Dial-Up Networking, you can access shared information on another computer, even if your computer is not connected to the network. To do this you must dial directly to the network server, which controls the resources of the network. If you have a computer at home, you can dial in to your office network server and connect to your work computer. Obviously, both your computer at home and the network server at work must have modems installed.

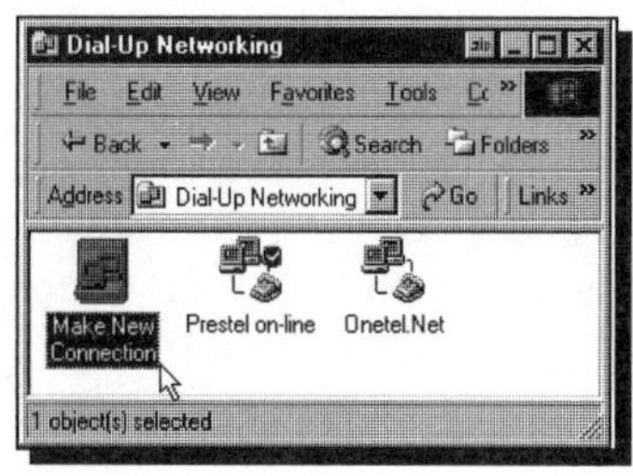

The easiest way of starting Dial-Up Networking is to double-click the My Computer icon and then click the Dial-Up Networking link to open the dialogue box shown here to the right. The program can also be found in the **Programs, Accessories, Communications** subgroup of the **Start** menu.

Double-clicking the Make New Connection icon, starts the New Connection process, as shown in Fig. 9.11 on the next page. Having selected the appropriate connection for you, click the **Next** button to proceed with the set-up, and eventually, you will be asked to give a name to your newly created connection.

Next time you open the Dial-up Networking utility, you will find that an extra icon has been added in its window. To connect to the newly created service, double-click its icon, enter a password and click the **Connect** button.

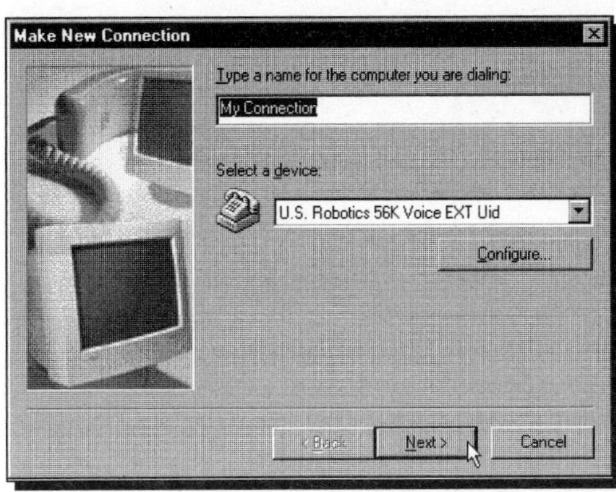

Fig. 9.11 The Network Connection Wizard.

Using a Briefcase

You can use the Briefcase feature to keep your copies of files updated when you work on them away from your PC. The two main uses are if you work with a mobile when away from the office, or if you transport files home in the evening on removable discs to work on your own PC. Sooner or later, you end up with the situation that the two sets of files are different and you don't know which one to use.

Windows Me automatically places the My Briefcase icon on your desktop. To use My Briefcase with a mobile, you connect both computers and drag the files from their folders on your main computer to the My Briefcase folder icon on your mobile. When you next return to the office, after working on the files, reconnect to your main computer, open the Briefcase and click **Update All** in the **Briefcase** menu to automatically update the files on your main computer with the modified ones in your Briefcase. Sounds a little complicated, but it's not really.

To use a Briefcase with a removable disc, you first move the Briefcase icon onto the disc, then you drag the files you want to take home, from your main computer to the Briefcase icon on it.

Take the disc home and burn the midnight oil, using the files from the Briefcase. No need to copy them anywhere, but obviously make sure you save your work back to the Briefcase, before packing it in.

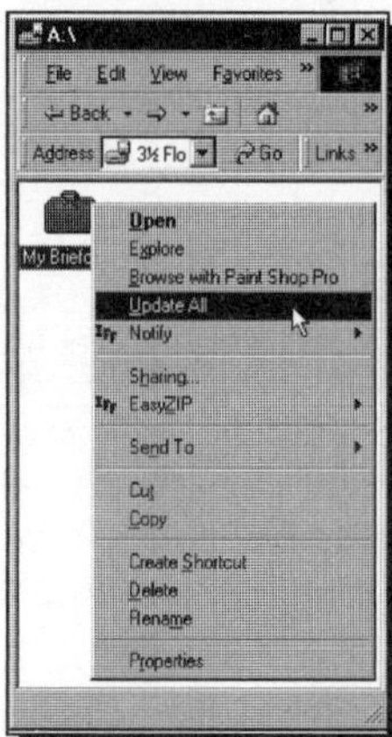

When back in the office, open your disc, right-click on the Briefcase icon and select **Update All**, as shown above. Now to the clever bit. The window below will open, listing any files that have been amended. In our case, there was only one file. If you are happy with the suggested course of action in this window, click the **Update** button.

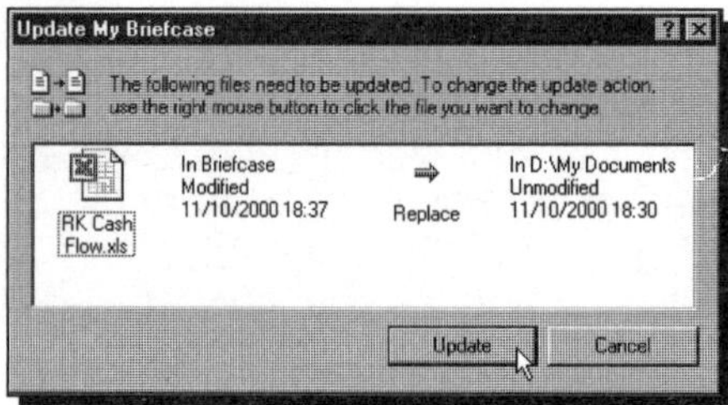

Fig. 9.12 The Update Briefcase Dialogue.

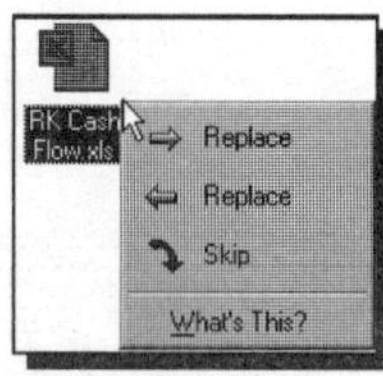

If not, you can right-click a file name and change the action, as shown to the left. The **What's This** option gives you some help, if you need it.

NOTE: It is essential that you close the Briefcase located on a removable disc, before you actually remove the disc from your PC. This is to ensure that the Briefcase database is updated, otherwise you will be in danger of losing data. If you are careless here, Windows tries to warn you with a message. Do not ignore this!

10

System Tools

Windows Me, as you would expect, comes equipped with a full range of system utility programs so that you can maintain your PC's set-up as easily as possible. By default, access to all these tools is from the **Start** menu, using the **Programs, Accessories, System Tools** route which opens the cascade menu options shown below.

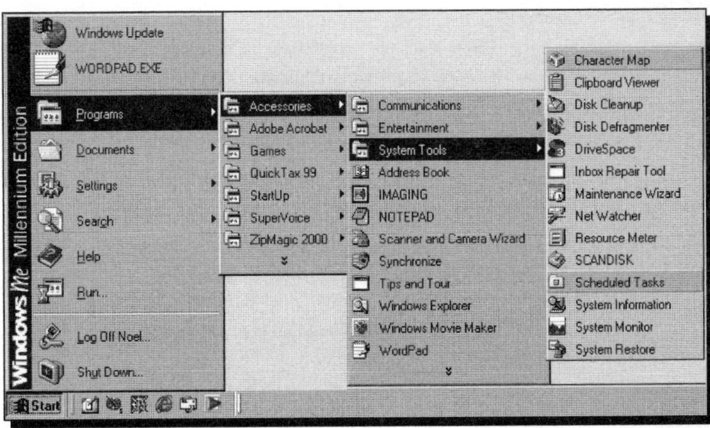

Fig. 10.1 The Cascade System Tools Menu.

We have already come across two of the **System Tools** sub-menu options; the **Clipboard Viewer** utility was discussed in Chapter 5 (page 75), while the **Character Map** utility was discussed in Chapter 6 (page 96). Of the remaining options, the **System Information** is the easiest to examine. This option loads the **Microsoft Help and Support** program, and offers a number of choices, such as System Summary, Hardware Resources, etc., each one of which will be different for you from that of our system. Therefore, we leave it to you to examine the information of your own system.

System Problem Prevention

In the past, backing up both your system set-up and data files from hard disc to another storage medium, was essential. With Windows Me, you have a threefold protection against System corruption. These are: System File Protection, Automatic Update, and System Restore, all of which will be discussed shortly. So now, all you have to look after is your data. After all, hard discs can 'crash' (though not as often these days as they used to) and your PC could be stolen, or lost in a fire, or flood. Any of these events would cause a serious data loss, unless you had a copy of it all, and stored it safely.

System File Protection

Windows applications sometimes can, and do, overwrite important System files which, in the past, could render your system unusable. Windows Me protects such System files by automatically restoring them to their original version, if any changes have been attempted by an application program.

Automatic Update

Windows Me can update automatically any System files, if these become available, from Microsoft's Web site. To be sure that your system is configured to do this, use the **Start, Settings, Control Panel** command and double-click the **Automatic Updates** icon. This opens the dialogue box shown in Fig. 10.2 in which you should select the **Notify me before downloading any updates...** option.

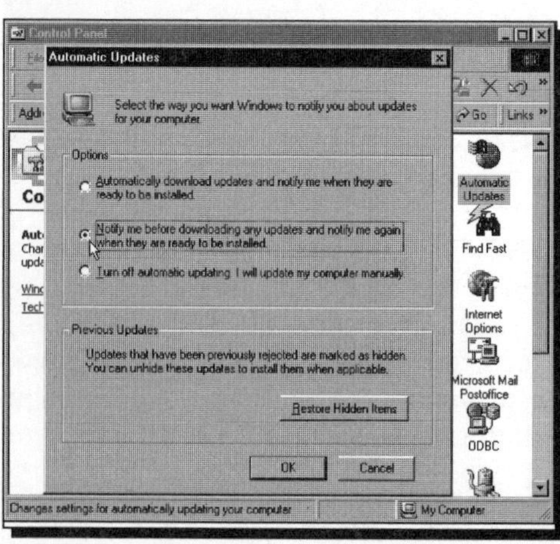

Fig. 10.2 The Automatic Update Dialogue box.

To start the Update process, use the **Start**, **Windows Update** command. After connecting to the Internet through your Internet Service Provider (ISP), you will be connected automatically to the Microsoft's Web site, as shown below.

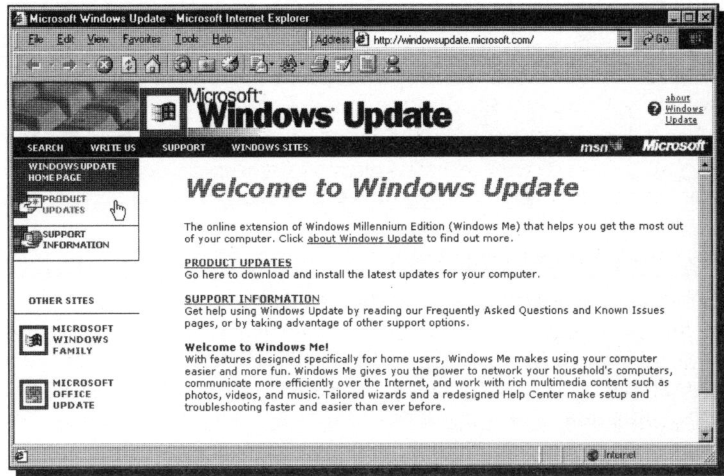

Fig. 10.3 Connecting to Microsoft's Update Home Page.

If automatic connection fails, it might be because you have selected to either work Offline, or have more than one ISP, in which case you must select one from the **Start, Settings, Dial-Up Networking** list.

Next left-click the 'PRODUCT UPDATES' link, to get an appropriate list of Critical Updates for your system, together with other lists, such as Picks of the Month, etc. However, in order to be able to download program patches to your system, the Windows Update program needs to have information relating to your system configuration. Such information is apparently not passed on to Microsoft. Once this is done, you can select which software to download, if any. In our case, the screen shown in Fig. 10.4 on the next page was displayed.

Be careful you don't go overboard with your selection of downloads ... think of your telephone bill. What is suggested above is a critical update download of just over 1.5 MB.

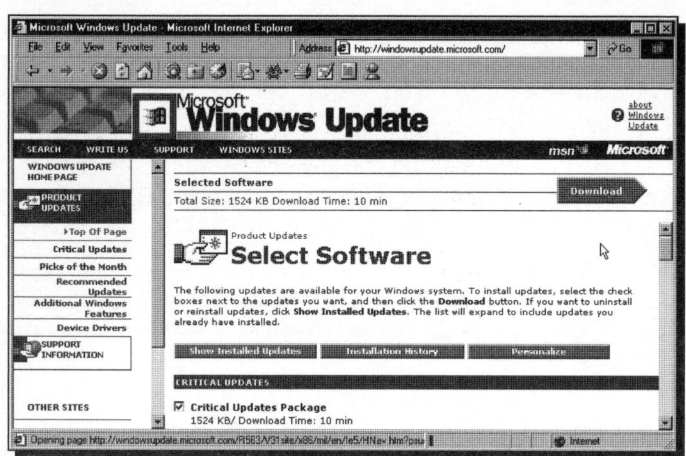

Fig. 10.4 Recommended Critical Updates for Downloading.

Once you have completed your selection, click the DOWNLOAD button to see a Download Checklist. Although the total time for the download is shown as 10 minutes, this depends on a lot of factors, one of which is the speed of data transfer in your particular connection. So don't be surprised if it takes twice as long as the stated time. We suggest that you download only from the list of Critical Updates. Selecting downloads from the other lists should be confined to only those you really need, and then only to one at a time. The reason for this is that should you find it takes too long to complete a given transfer, cancelling it will exit the **Setup** program and you will lose all the files already transferred before you issued the cancel command.

On successful completion of program downloads, the Windows **Setup** program installs the new patches and or programs to your system automatically, after which, you can either go back to browse Microsoft's site, or you can disconnect from the Internet. Just to find out how intelligent the Windows Update program is, we reconnected an hour or so later, and this time we found that the program patch and the other programs we downloaded earlier were not on the offered lists. In other words, this facility works very well indeed, and gives novices the sense of being in charge of their Windows installation.

System Restore

If things go really wrong, System Restore can be used to return your PC to the last date it was working perfectly. Every time you start to install a new program, Windows Me takes a snapshot of your system prior to starting the new installation. Alternatively, you can force Windows to take a snapshot any time you choose.

To examine the System Restore utility, use the **Start, Programs, Accessories, System Tools** and click on its icon, shown here, which displays the following screen.

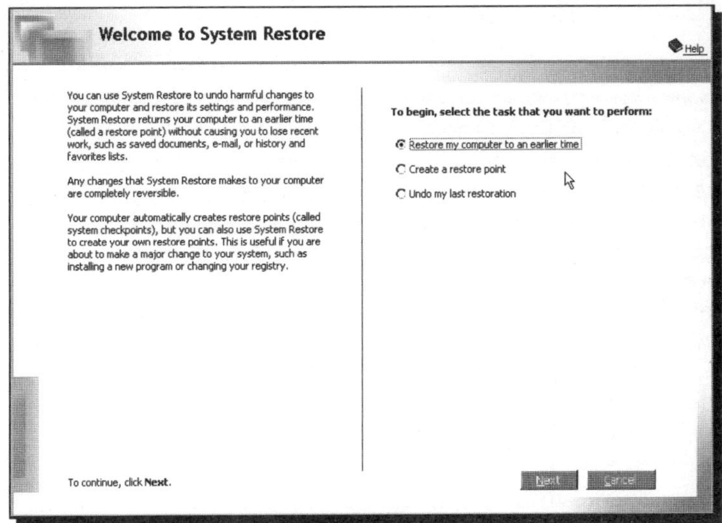

Fig. 10.5 The Welcome to System Restore Screen.

As you can see, from this screen you can select to Restore your computer to an earlier date, create a Restore point, or Undo the last restoration. To demonstrate further what happens, we chose the **Restore my computer to an earlier time** option, then clicked the **Next** button. This displays a further screen, as shown in Fig. 10.6 on the next page.

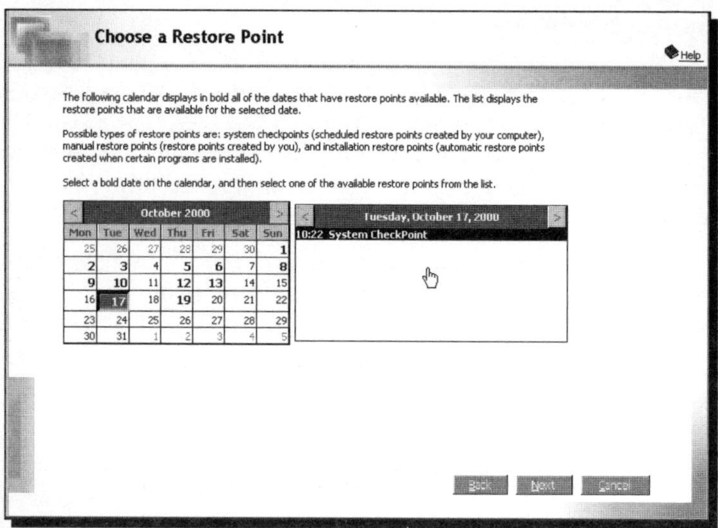

Fig. 10.6 Selecting a System Restore Point.

The dates shown in bold in the calendar are Restore points created by Windows Me. The three possible types of Restore points are:

- System Restore points created by your computer
- Manual Restore points created by you
- Restore points automatically created prior to installing certain programs.

If you select to create a Manual Restore point, Windows Me asks you to give a description of this Restore point so that you can identify it easily at a later stage, as shown below.

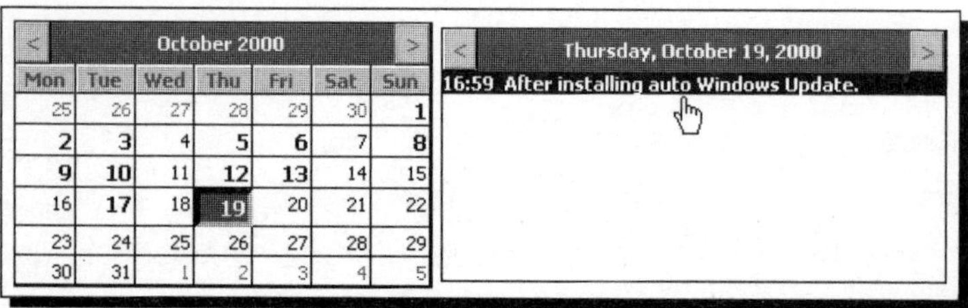

Disc Cleanup

You can run Disk Cleanup to help you free up space on your hard drive. The first thing that Disk Cleanup does after activation, is to ask you to select the drive you want to cleanup, as shown here. It then scans the specified drive, and then lists temporary files, Internet cache files, and unnecessary program files that you can safely delete, as shown in Fig. 10.7.

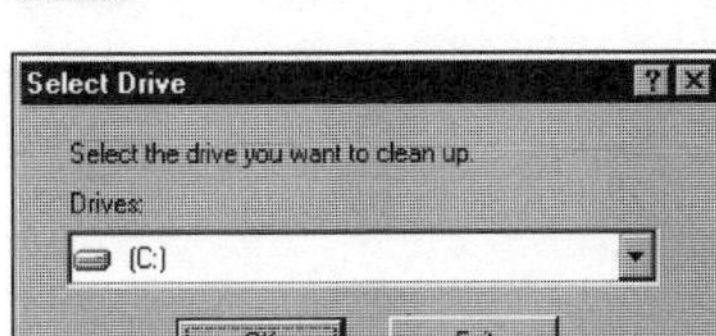

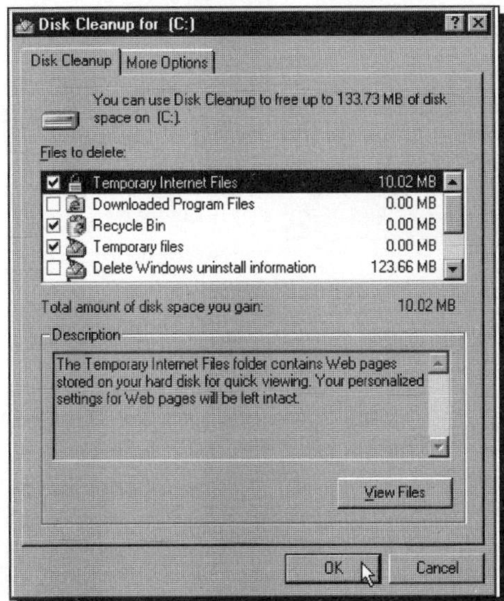

Fig. 10.7 Files Found by Cleanup.

As you can see, in our case, we could free 10.02 MB of disc space by simply deleting the Temporary Internet Files (Web pages stored on your hard disc for quick viewing), and 123.66 MB by deleting the Windows uninstall information. The More Options tab allows you to remove Windows components and installed programs that you do not use any more.

Defragmenting your Hard Discs

The Disk Defragmenter optimises a hard disc by rearranging the data on it to eliminate unused spaces, which speeds up access to the disc by Windows operations. You don't need to exit a running application before starting the Disk Defragmenter. Choose which drive to defragment in the Select Drive box, shown here, and you can defragment it in the background while working by minimising the utility onto the Task bar. On the other hand, you can watch the process of the operation, or display it in minimal status.

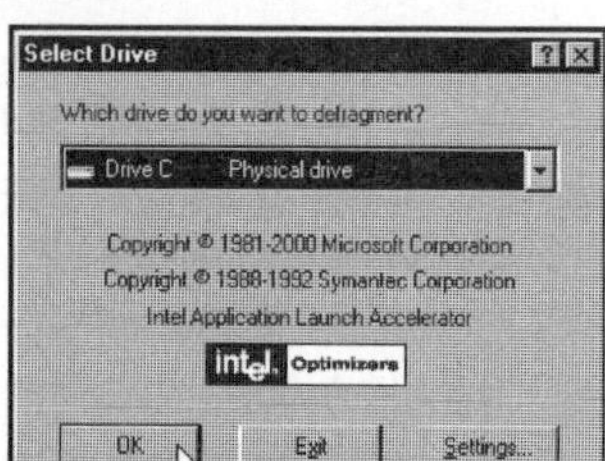

For example, having selected a drive and pressed the **OK** button, defragmenting starts and the result is shown on a compact dialogue box, as shown to the left.

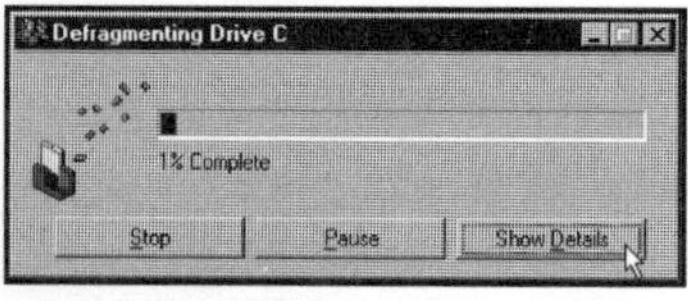

Pressing the **Show Details** button, opens up a very colourful screen, as shown in Fig. 10.8 below.

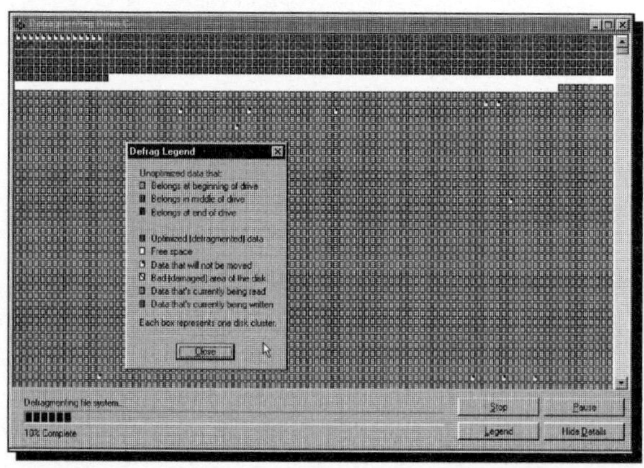

Fig. 10.8 The Disk Defragmenter Screen.

Scanning a Hard Disc for Errors

Windows Me incorporates a utility that can check the integrity of your hard disc, and if it finds any errors, it can attempt to repair them. You might have to start this utility because an error was found on your hard disc while attempting to defragment it, in which case the box shown here will be displayed. If, on the other hand, you would like to periodically check the integrity of your hard disc, start the utility yourself by clicking its icon in the **System Tools** folder. Either action displays the following dialogue box.

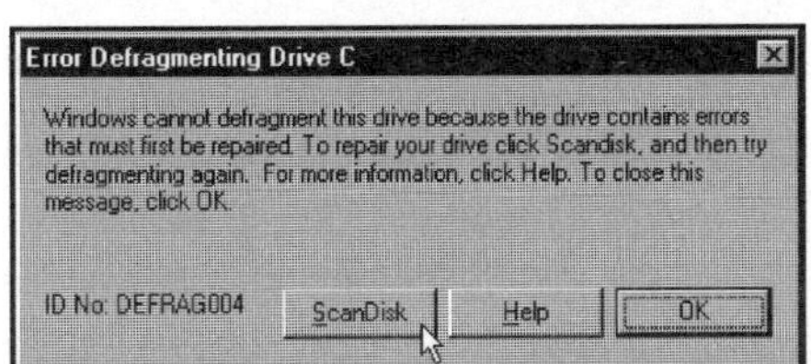

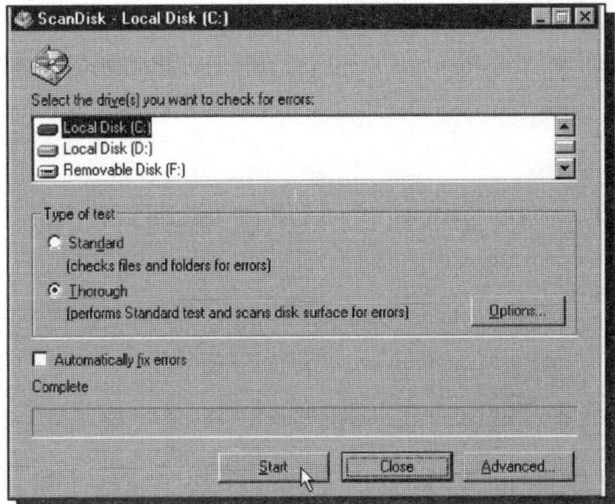

Fig. 10.9 The Disk Properties Screen.

As you can see, you can select from two types of test: **Standard**, or **Thorough**. If errors have been detected by the Defragment utility, then you will do well to choose the **Thorough** test, make yourself a cup of coffee and sit back for the next hour or so. However, before you can start scanning your selected drive for errors, all running programs and applications on that drive must be closed.

Scheduled Tasks

The **Scheduled Tasks** option allows you to carry out several housekeeping tasks, such as disc cleanup, checking for disc errors, or defragmenting your data, at times convenient to you. Starting the Scheduled Tasks utility, found in the **Accessories, System Tools** folder, the icon of which is shown here, opens the window of Fig. 10.10 below.

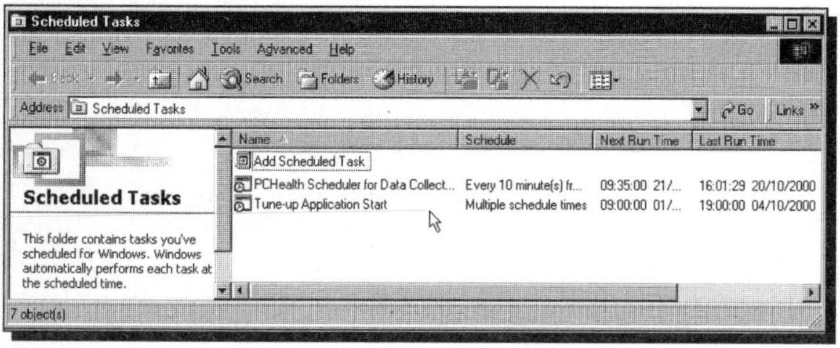

Fig. 10.10 The Scheduled Tasks Window.

On here, double-click the **Add Scheduled Task** icon to start the Wizard. Clicking **Next** on the first Wizard screen displays:

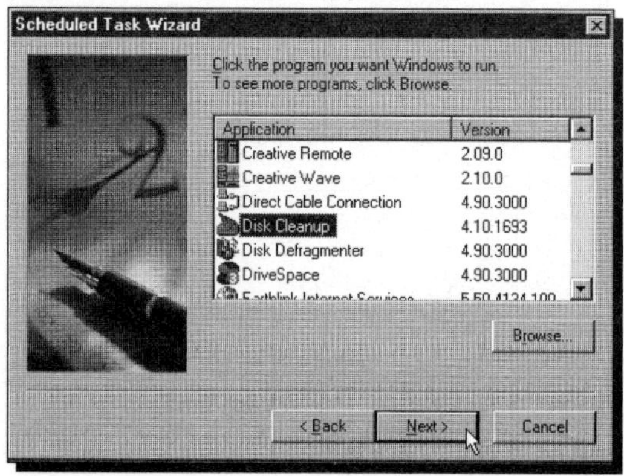

Fig. 10.11 The Second Scheduled Task Wizard.

On this screen shown in Fig. 10.11, select the task to be Scheduled then click the **Next** button to display:

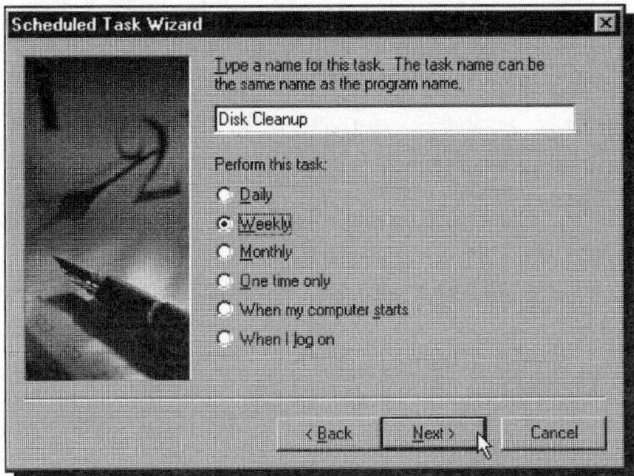

Fig. 10.12 The Third Scheduled Task Wizard Screen.

On this screen (Fig. 10.12) you are asked to specify the frequency at which you would like the selected task to be performed (we selected weekly in our example). Having done so, press the **Next** button to display the fourth Wizard screen, shown below.

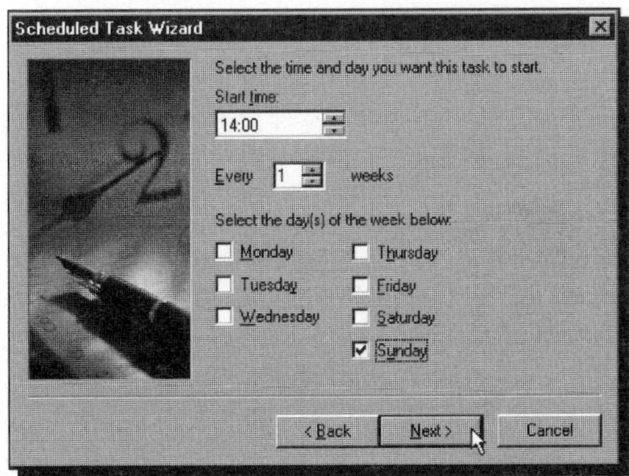

Fig. 10.13 The Fourth Scheduled Task Wizard Screen.

Here you are asked to specify when you want the selected task to be carried out. Obviously, your computer must be switched on in order to perform such scheduled tasks, so it's up to you to choose a convenient time. Having done so, press the **Next** button to display the fifth Wizard screen, shown below.

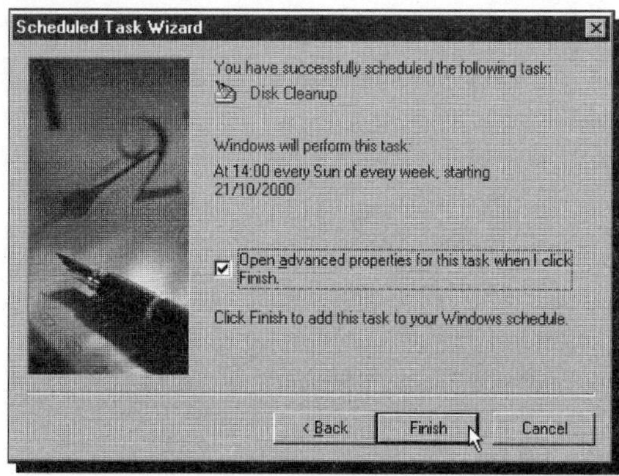

Fig. 10.14 The Fifth Scheduled Task Wizard Screen.

If you check the **Open advanced properties for this task...** box, then click **Finish**, displays the Disk Cleanup dialogue box.

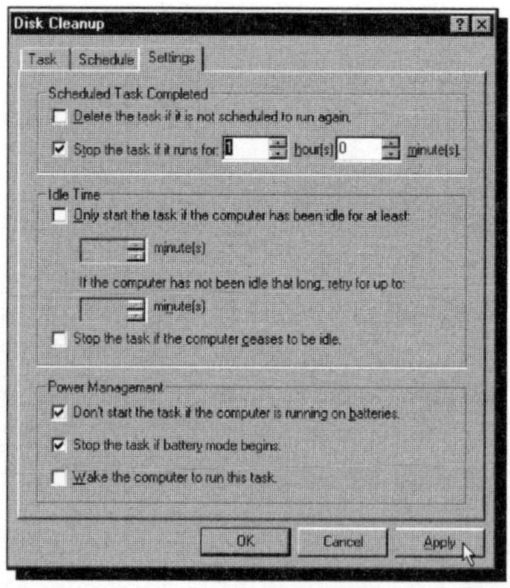

Fig. 10.15 The Disk Cleanup Dialogue Box.

What we show in Fig. 10.15 is the Settings screen of the Disk Cleanup dialogue box, where we changed the period the task is allowed to run for to 1 hour from its default setting of 72 hours! Finally, clicking the **Apply** button followed by the **OK** button, enters the created task in the scheduled task list, as shown below.

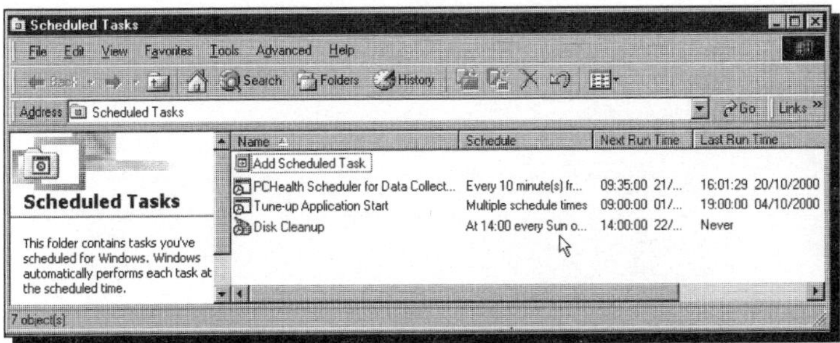

Fig. 10.16 The New Scheduled Tasks Window.

To return to the Disk Cleanup Properties dialogue box of any listed scheduled task, right-click it and select **Properties** from the drop-down menu shown to the left. To remove an unwanted scheduled task from the list, right-click it and select **Delete** from the drop-down menu. Selecting **Run**, executes the task immediately.

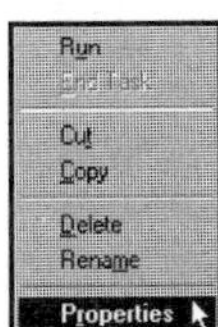

It is a good idea to perform such tasks regularly, but make sure that

(a) your computer is switched on at the selected times, and

(b) you are not inconvenienced by your time selection.

It is, of course assumed that your PC's clock is showing the same time as your watch, otherwise you might get some unexpected surprises!

DriveSpace 3

Windows Me does not use DriveSpace 3 to compress drives, but allows you to use the utility to access information or allocate disc space on compressed drives, and to decompress floppy discs, which were compressed by a previous version of Windows.

To start DriveSpace 3, click its icon in the **System Tools** folder, shown here, which displays the following dialogue box.

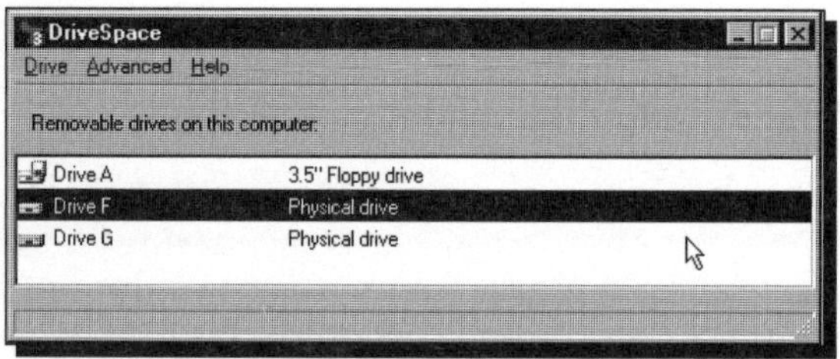

Fig. 10.17 The Disk Properties Screen.

As you can see, only the removable drives attached to our computer are listed here, which emphasises the fact that you cannot use DriveSpace on the system's hard drives.

To use a compressed external drive disc or a compressed floppy disc you need to first mount it. This can be done by first selecting the drive that contains the compressed volume file you want to mount, then using the **Advanced**, **Mount** menu option as shown here to the left.

Other options on the **Advanced** menu can be used to carry out the following functions:

- **Unmount** a mounted compressed volume file.
- **Delete** a compressed drive, which unmounts the drive and deletes the compressed volume file on it.
- **Settings** which allows you to automatically mount compressed discs that you insert in a drive.

Power Saving Management

You can automatically put your computer into hibernation or standby, provided your computer is set up by the manufacturer to support these options. If your computer is connected to a network, network policy settings may prevent you from completing these tasks.

Hibernation and Standby Modes

When your computer is put into hibernation mode, everything in the computer memory is saved on your hard disc, and your computer is switched off. When you turn the computer back on, all programs and documents that were open when you turned the computer off are restored on the desktop.

To initiate hibernation, activate the **Control Panel** and click on the **Power Options** icon shown here. Then, in the displayed Power Options Properties dialogue box, click the Hibernate tab. If the Hibernate tab is unavailable, as shown below, then this is because your computer does not support this feature. At least that is the reason given in Microsoft's Help and Support utility.

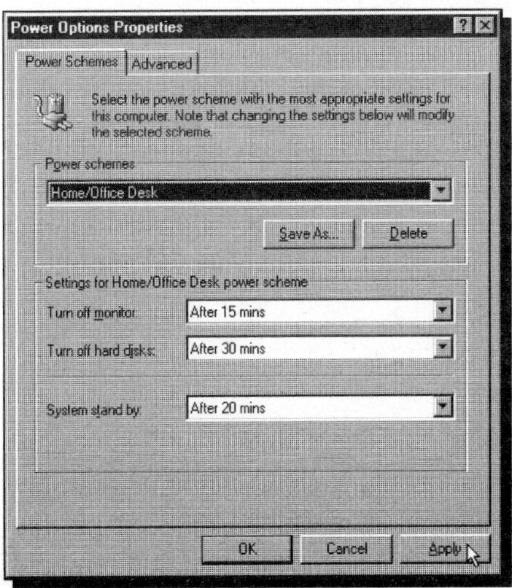

Fig. 10.18 The Power Options Properties Screen.

However, this very computer that Windows Me says is unable to use the Hibernate mode, can also run under Windows 2000 (using the dual-boot capability) and for that Operating System the Hibernate tab is present and the mode can be activated! So, obviously something is wrong here, and we don't think it is the computer. Perhaps the fact that we upgraded to Windows Me from Windows 98 instead of making a clean (new) installation has something to do with it.

When your computer is put into standby mode, information in the computer memory is not saved to your hard disc. You must save all your work before putting your computer into standby mode, because if there is an interruption in power, all information in the computer's memory will be lost.

To initiate standby mode, click the Power Schemes tab shown in Fig. 10.18. Power schemes let you select from 'Home/Office desktop', 'Laptop', or 'Always on'. These affect the settings below, which tell the system when to turn off the monitor and hard drive to go into Standby - you can change the default figures, if you like. This feature will save valuable battery life on a laptop, but on one of our desktops we found it would not let us run any program that was not loaded when Standby was first activated, including the autorun feature of the CD-ROM drive!

Compressing Folders and Files

Compressing folders and files allows you to greatly increase the storage capacity of your discs with no extra hardware cost. To activate the option, select the folder in which you want to create a compressed folder, then use the **File, New** menu command, and select the **Compressed Folder** option from the drop-down menu.

Note: If you are running the program ZipMagic 2000, you must disable it because it interferes with the Compressed Folder utility. In fact, you will not even see the Compressed Folder option on the drop-down menu. Previous versions of ZipMagic must be uninstalled - unloading the program is not enough.

To illustrate the procedure of creating a compressed folder and storing compressed files into it, we created a folder in **My Documents**, as shown below, and renamed it **WinMe**.

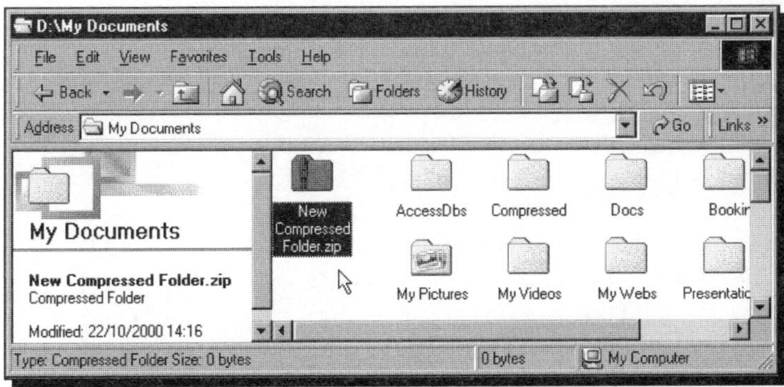

Fig. 10.19 Creating a New Compressed Folder.

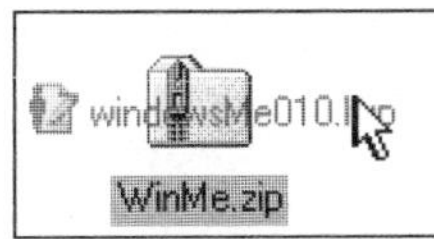

We then dragged the word processor file of the current chapter of this book with all its screen dumps to the newly renamed folder, as shown here, which displayed the following box.

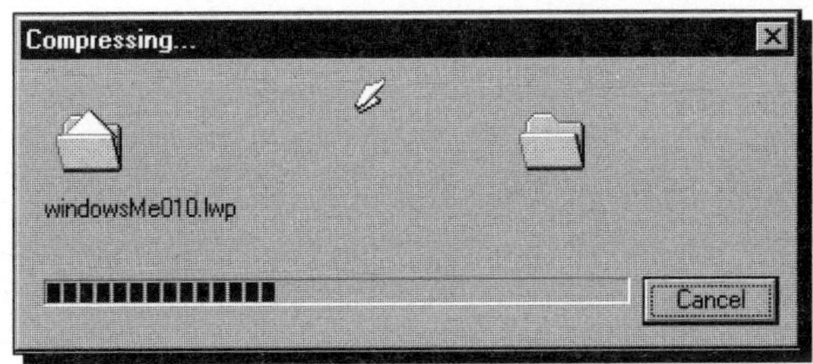

Fig. 10.20 Compressing a File Dragged into a Compressed Folder.

You can send other files and folders into the compressed folder by dragging them onto it. Selected files are then compressed one at time before they are moved into the folder, while the contents of the dragged folders are also compressed.

To find out the size of the file before and after compression, double-click the compressed folder, right-click the file and select **Properties** from the drop-down menu to display the following:

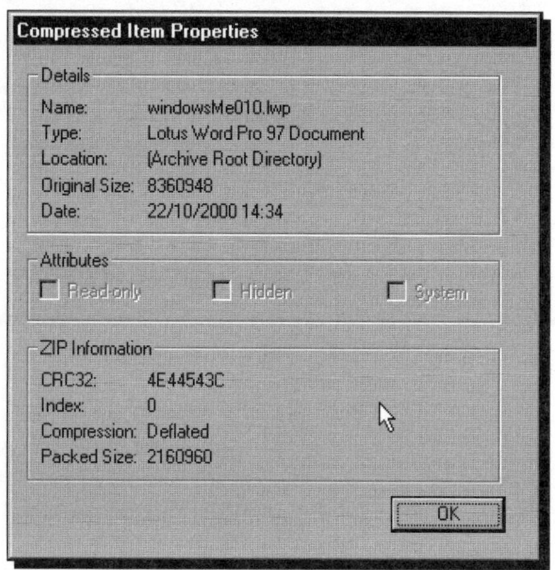

Fig. 10.21 Compressing File Properties.

Note that the original file size is displayed as 8.36 MB, while its packed size as 2.16 MB. This is quite a large compression ratio and worth while exploiting.

You can open files and programs in a compressed folder by double-clicking them. If a program requires **.dll** or data files to run, then those files must first be extracted. To extract a file or folder from a compressed folder, simply drag it to its new location. To extract all files and folders within a compressed folder, right-click the folder and select **Extract All**. In the Extract Wizard you can specify where you want these files and folders to be extracted to. When you extract a file or folder it leaves a copy of it in the compressed folder. To remove files and folders from a compressed folder you must delete them.

11

Using DOS Programs

If you are an experienced PC user, you may well prefer to do much of your work by entering instructions at the DOS command line, or prompt. Windows Me still lets you do this.

For this book we have assumed that if you want to use this method of working you will already be familiar with DOS commands, switches, filters and batch files, configuration files, etc. If not, we suggest you use the methods described in earlier chapters. All the available DOS commands can be found in the COMMAND sub-directory of the WINDOWS directory, and they all support the Windows Me 32-bit features.

Before we go on with our discussion of how to run DOS programs, you might like to know that the **autoexec.bat** and **config.sys** files, if found by Windows Me as a result of upgrading from previous versions of Windows, are retained, archived and hidden as they are deemed to be protected system files. Deleting or renaming them has no effect whatsoever, because they are resurrected by Windows Me automatically next time you reboot your computer.

Windows Me does not require these two configuration files at all, with the result that it takes a few seconds longer to start Windows than it should. The reason for this is that all the information contained in those two files (loading necessary drivers for use by your peripherals into memory) are executed first, then Windows scans your system using its Plug and Play facility, discovers what peripherals are connected to your system and reloads all the drivers again!

The only way to remove such files from your system is to uninstall Windows Me, return to your previous version of Windows, delete the two files, and reinstall Windows Me. Hardly worth it!

The MS-DOS Window

You can action any DOS commands you like in the MS-DOS

window. To do this, use the **Start, Programs, Accessories** command, and click on the MS-DOS Prompt icon, to open the following MS-DOS window.

Fig. 11.1 The MS-DOS Prompt Screen.

To view the toolbar, if it is not showing, click the MS-DOS icon in the title bar to open the command menu, and then click the **Toolbar** toggle option.

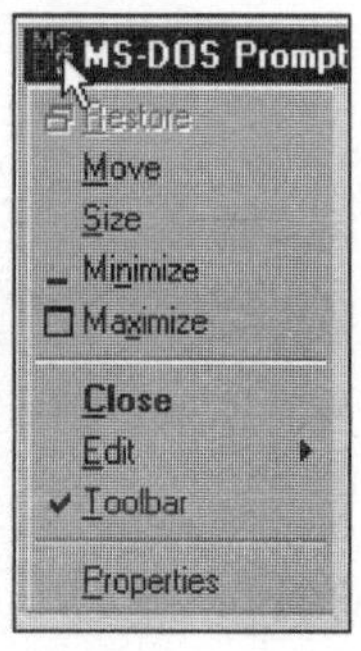

To switch between a window and full screen, click the Full screen toolbar icon shown to the right. The <Alt+Enter> key combination also toggles between these two modes.

To quit the MS-DOS window and return to normal Windows Me operation, click the **x** (close) button of a window, or type **exit** at the command prompt.

Using the Toolbar

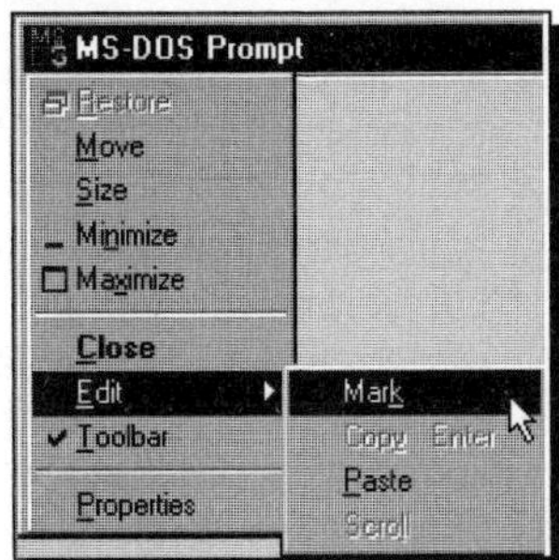

The toolbar (see Fig. 11.2) is a very useful feature of an MS-DOS window. You can mark text and copy it to the Windows clipboard, or paste from the clipboard. You can also carry out these functions from the Command menu, by selecting **Edit**, **Mark**, **Edit**, **Copy**, or **Edit**, **Paste**, as shown here.

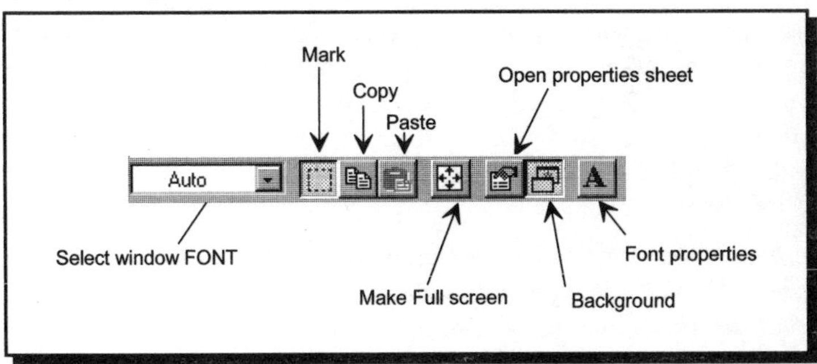

Fig. 11.2 The MS-DOS Window Toolbar.

Using the Run Window

With Windows Me, just as in Windows 95/98, the easiest way to issue a single DOS command, that involves running a program, is in the **Run** window, shown here, opened from the **Start** menu. Its big advantage is that all previous commands are remembered. Clicking the down arrow, opens a small 'database' of your most used commands, including path and file names. To action a command, select it and click **OK**.

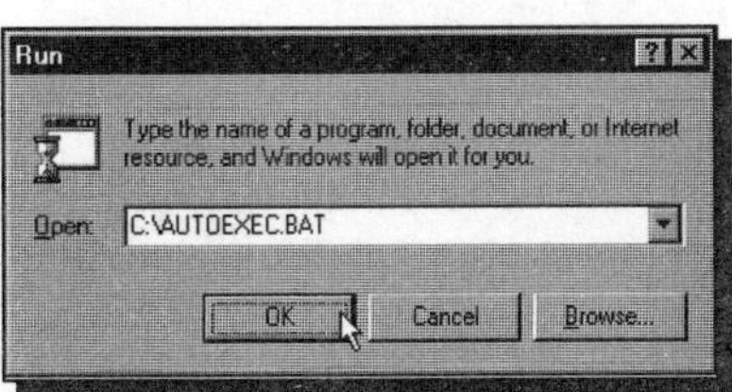

The MS-DOS Editor

Windows Me includes the **Edit** text editor, to be found in the \WINDOWS\COMMAND subdirectory, as shown here. Users of MS-DOS will find the editor very familiar, but the version provided in Windows Me, as well as Windows 95/98 has several improvements over earlier versions of the program. **Edit** is now smaller and faster, and you can open up to nine files at the same time, split the screen between two files, and easily copy and paste information between them. Furthermore, you can open files as large as 4MB; and you can open filenames and navigate through the directory structure just as you can in the rest of Windows.

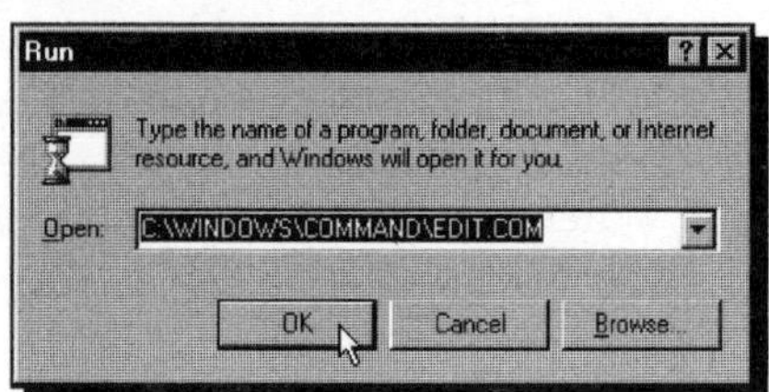

The editor is opened, as one would expect from its name, by typing **Edit** at the command prompt. The screen below shows the **File** drop-down sub-menu.

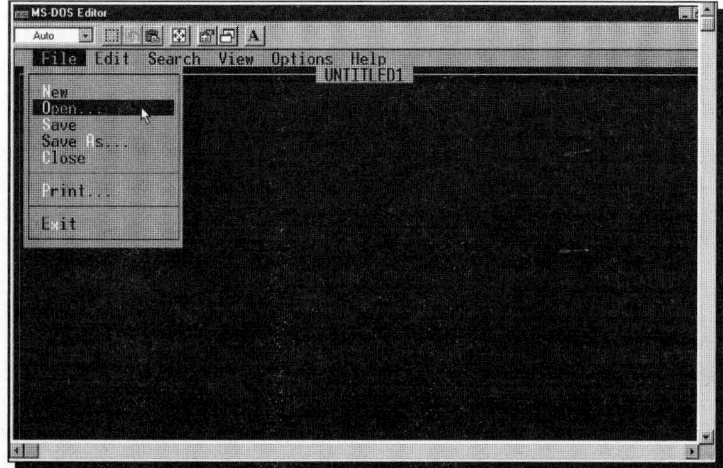

Fig. 11.3 The MS-DOS Editor Screen.

Selecting the **Open** sub-menu command, displays a list of folders and files, as shown in Fig. 11.4 below.

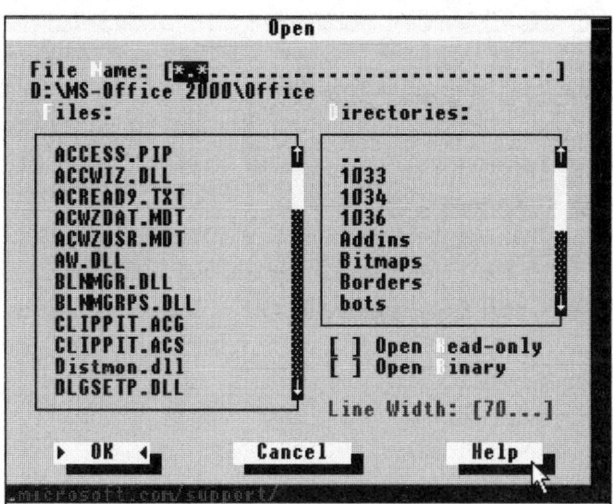

Fig. 11.4 The Open Dialogue Box of Edit.

We will leave it up to you to explore the MS-DOS editor. To help you on your way, clicking the **Help** key, or pressing the **F1** function key while the **Open** dialogue box is displayed, brings up the following help screen.

Fig. 11.5 The Open Dialogue Box Help Screen of Edit.

In fact, no matter what you are doing, while using the MS-DOS editor pressing the **F1** function key will open a context sensitive help screen with a list of relevant information such as cursor movement, editing, and function commands, as well as some shortcut keys that you might need to know about.

Long Filenames in DOS

Be careful when using MS-DOS Prompt to copy or rename files with long names (they can be up to 254 characters). Unlike the My Compter or Explorer utilities which can deal with long names, MS-DOS will use the first 6 letters of your long file name, then place a tilde (~) sign followed by a number. So, if you had long names such as 'Letter to John', 'Letter to Paul', etc., you will end up with 'Letter~1', 'Letter~2', etc., which is not much use to you as it defeats the whole idea of long names. Apart from long names, MS-DOS should be able to deal with everything else you would like it to do.

You can get help with DOS commands by typing the command followed by a space and the characters '/?', as follows:

```
copy /?
```

Wildcard Characters

You are probably aware of the two Wildcard characters, * and ?. When used in a command line, * can be substituted for any number of characters in a filename mask, and ? for just a single character. Thus ***.exe**, means all files with the extension of **exe**, and ***.e??** means all files with a 3 character extension beginning with **e**.

The use of the * wildcard was extended in Windows 95 and 98, to make it more powerful when used with long filenames. You can use more than one * in a name mask. The following is legal in Windows:

```
Del *Jan*
```

This command would delete all the files in the current directory with 'Jan' anywhere in their name, and is not case sensitive. So be aware!

12

Glossary of Terms

ActiveX	A set of technologies that enables software components to interact with one another in a networked environment, regardless of the language in which the components were created.
Add-in	A mini-program which runs in conjunction with another and enhances its functionality.
Address	A unique number or name that identifies a specific computer or user on a network.
Anonymous FTP	Anonymous FTP allows you to connect to a remote computer and transfer public files back to your local computer without the need to have a user ID and password.
Application	Software (program) designed to carry out a certain activity, such as word processing, or data management.
Applet	A program that can be downloaded over a network and launched on the user's computer.
Archie	Archie is an Internet service that allows you to locate files that can be downloaded via FTP.

ASP	Active Server Page. File format used for dynamic Web pages that get their data from a server based database.
Association	An identification of a filename extension to a program. This lets Windows open the program when its files are selected.
ASCII	A binary code representation of a character set. The name stands for 'American Standard Code for Information Interchange'.
Authoring	The process of creating web documents or software.
Autoexec.bat	A file that contains commands which are automatically executed on boot-up.
AVI	Audio Video Interleaved. A Windows multimedia file format for sound and moving pictures.
Backbone	The main transmission lines of the Internet, running at over 45Mbps.
Backup	To make a back-up copy of a file or a disc for safekeeping.
Bandwidth	The range of transmission frequencies a network can use. The greater the bandwidth the more information that can be transferred over a network.
Banner	An advertising graphic shown on a Web page.
BASIC	Beginner's All-purpose Symbolic Instruction Code - a high-level programming language.

Batch file	A file that contains commands which are automatically executed when the file is run.
BBS	Bulletin Board System, a computer equipped with software and telecoms links that allow it to act as an information host for remote computer systems.
Beta test	A test of software that is still under development, by people actually using the software.
Bitmap	A technique for managing the image displayed on a computer screen.
Bookmark	A marker inserted at a specific point in a document to which the user may wish to return for later reference.
Boot up	To start your computer by switching it on, which initiates a self test of its Random Access Memory (RAM), then loads the necessary system files.
Browse	A button in some Windows dialogue boxes that lets you view a list of files and folders before you make a selection.
Browser	A program, like the Internet Explorer, that lets you view Web pages.
Bug	An error in coding or logic that causes a program to malfunction.
Button	A graphic element in a dialogue box or toolbar that performs a specified function.
Cache	An area of memory, or disc space, reserved for data, which speeds up downloading.

Card	A removable printed-circuit board that is plugged into a computer expansion slot.
CD-ROM	Compact Disc - Read Only Memory; an optical disc which information may be read from but not written to.
CGI	Common Gateway Interface - a convention for servers to communicate with local applications and allow users to provide information to scripts attached to web pages, usually through forms.
Cgi-bin	The most common name of a directory on a web server in which CGI programs are stored.
Chart	A graphical view of data that is used to visually display trends, patterns, and comparisons.
Click	To press and release a mouse button once without moving the mouse.
Client	A computer that has access to services over a computer network. The computer providing the services is a server.
Client application	A Windows application that can accept linked, or embedded, objects.
Clipboard	A temporary storage area of memory, where text and graphics are stored with the Windows cut and copy actions.
Command	An instruction given to a computer to carry out a particular action.
Compressed file	One that is compacted to save server space and reduce transfer times.

	Typical file extensions for compressed files include .zip (DOS/Windows) and .tar (UNIX).
Configuration	A general purpose term referring to the way you have your computer set up.
Config.sys	A file that contains commands which configure your system on boot-up.
Controls	Objects on a form, report, or data access page that display data, perform actions, or are used for decoration.
Cookies	Files stored on your hard drive by your Web browser that hold information for it to use.
CPU	The Central Processing Unit; the main chip that executes all instructions entered into a computer.
Cyberspace	Originated by William Gibson in his novel 'Neuromancer', now used to describe the Internet and the other computer networks.
Data access page	A Web page, created by Access, that has a connection to a database; you can view, add, edit, and manipulate the data in this page.
Database	A collection of data related to a particular topic or purpose.
DBMS	Database management system - A software interface between the database and the user.
Dial-up Connection	A popular form of Net connection for the home user, over standard telephone lines.

Direct Connection	A permanent connection between your computer system and the Internet.
Default	The command, device or option automatically chosen.
Desktop	The Windows screen working background, on which you place icons, folders, etc.
Device driver	A special file that must be loaded into memory for Windows to be able to address a specific procedure or hardware device.
Device name	A logical name used by DOS to identify a device, such as LPT1 or COM1 for the parallel or serial printer.
Dialogue box	A window displayed on the screen to allow the user to enter information.
Directory	An area on disc where information relating to a group of files is kept. Also known as a folder.
Disc	A device on which you can store programs and data.
Disconnect	To detach a drive, port or computer from a shared device, or to break an Internet connection.
Document	A file produced by an application program. When used in reference to the Web, a document is any file containing text, media or hyperlinks that can be transferred from an HTTP server to a browser.
Domain	A group of devices, servers and computers on a network.
Domain Name	The name of an Internet site, for example www.microsoft.com, which

	allows you to reference Internet sites without knowing their true numerical address.
DOS	Disc Operating System. A collection of small specialised programs that allow interaction between user and computer.
Double-click	To quickly press and release a mouse button twice.
Download	To transfer to your computer a file, or data, from another computer.
DPI	Dots Per Inch - a resolution standard for laser printers.
Drag	To move an object on the screen by pressing and holding down the left mouse button while moving the mouse.
Drive name	The letter followed by a colon which identifies a floppy or hard disc drive.
DSL	Digital Subscriber Line - a broad-band connection to the Internet through existing copper telephone wires.
EISA	Extended Industry Standard Architecture, for construction of PCs with the Intel 32-bit microprocessor.
Embedded object	Information in a document that is 'copied' from its source application. Selecting the object opens the creating application from within the document.
Engine	Software used by search services.
E-mail	Electronic Mail - A system that allows computer users to send and receive messages electronically.

Ethernet	A very common method of networking computers in a LAN.
FAQ	Frequently Asked Questions - A common feature on the Internet, FAQs are files of answers to commonly asked questions.
FAT	The File Allocation Table. An area on disc where information is kept on which part of the disc a file is located.
File extension	The suffix following the period in a filename. Windows uses this to identify the source application program. For example .mdb indicates an Access file.
Filename	The name given to a file. In Windows 95 and above this can be up to 256 characters long.
Filter	A set of criteria that is applied to data to show a subset of the data.
Firewall	Security measures designed to protect a networked system from unauthorised access.
Floppy disc	A removable disc on which information can be stored magnetically.
Folder	An area used to store a group of files, usually with a common link.
Font	A graphic design representing a set of characters, numbers and symbols.
Freeware	Software that is available for downloading and unlimited use without charge.

FTP	File Transfer Protocol. The procedure for connecting to a remote computer and transferring files.
Function key	One of the series of 10 or 12 keys marked with the letter F and a numeral, used for specific operations.
Gateway	A computer system that allows otherwise incompatible networks to communicate with each other.
GIF	Graphics Interchange Format, a common standard for images on the Web.
Graphic	A picture or illustration, also called an image. Formats include GIF, JPEG, BMP, PCX, and TIFF.
Graphics card	A device that controls the display on the monitor and other allied functions.
GUI	A Graphic User Interface, such as Windows Me, the software front-end meant to provide an attractive and easy to use interface.
Hard copy	Output on paper.
Hard disc	A device built into the computer for holding programs and data.
Hardware	The equipment that makes up a computer system, excluding the programs or software.
Help	A Windows system that gives you instructions and additional information on using a program.
Helper application	A program allowing you to view multimedia files that your web browser cannot handle internally.

Hit	A single request from a web browser for a single item from a web server.
Home page	The document displayed when you first open your Web browser, or the first document you come to at a Web site.
Host	Computer connected directly to the Internet that provides services to other local and/or remote computers.
Hotlist	A list of frequently used Web locations and URL addresses.
HTML	HyperText Markup Language, the format used in documents on the Web.
HTML editor	Authoring tool which assists with the creation of HTML pages.
HTTP	HyperText Transport Protocol, the system used to link and transfer hypertext documents on the Web.
Hyperlink	A segment of text, or an image, that refers to another document on the Web, an Intranet or your PC.
Hypermedia	Hypertext extended to include linked multimedia.
Hypertext	A system that allows documents to be cross-linked so that the reader can explore related links, or documents, by clicking on a highlighted symbol.
Icon	A small graphic image that represents a function or object. Clicking on an icon produces an action.
ICS	Internet Connection Sharing.
Image	See graphic.

Insertion point	A flashing bar that shows where typed text will be entered into a document.
Interface	A device that allows you to connect a computer to its peripherals.
Internet	The global system of computer networks.
Intranet	A private network inside an organisation using the same kind of software as the Internet.
ISA	Industry Standard Architecture; a standard for internal PC connections.
ISDN	Integrated Services Digital Network, a telecom standard using digital transmission technology to support voice, video and data communications applications over regular telephone lines.
IP	Internet Protocol - The rules that provide basic Internet functions.
IP Address	Internet Protocol Address - every computer on the Internet has a unique identifying number.
ISP	Internet Service Provider - A company that offers access to the Internet.
Java	An object-oriented programming language created by Sun Microsystems for developing applications and applets that are capable of running on any computer, regardless of the operating system.
JPEG / JPG	Joint Photographic Experts Group, a popular cross-platform format for image files. JPEG is best suited for true colour original images.

Kilobyte	(KB); 1024 bytes of information or storage space.
LAN	Local Area Network - High-speed, privately-owned network covering a limited geographical area, such as an office or a building.
Laptop	A portable computer small enough to sit on your lap.
LCD	Liquid Crystal Display.
Links	The hypertext connections between Web pages.
Linux	A version of the UNIX operating system for PCs which incorporates a Graphical User Interface (GUI) similar to that of Microsoft Windows.
Local	A resource that is located on your computer, not linked to it over a network.
Location	An Internet address.
Log on	To gain access to a network.
MCI	Media Control Interface - a standard for files and multimedia devices.
Megabyte	(MB); 1024 kilobytes of information or storage space.
Megahertz	(MHz); Speed of processor in millions of cycles per second.
Memory	Part of computer consisting of storage elements organised into addressable locations that can hold data and instructions.
Menu	A list of available options in an application.

Menu bar	The horizontal bar that lists the names of menus.
MIDI	Musical Instrument Digital Interface - enables devices to transmit and receive sound and music messages.
MIME	Multipurpose Internet Mail Extensions, a messaging standard that allows Internet users to exchange e-mail messages enhanced with graphics, video and voice.
MIPS	Million Instructions Per Second; measures speed of a system.
Modem	Short for Modulator-demodulator. An electronic device that lets computers communicate electronically.
Monitor	The display device connected to your PC, also called a screen.
Mouse	A device used to manipulate a pointer around your display and activate processes by pressing buttons.
MPEG	Motion Picture Experts Group - a video file format offering excellent quality in a relatively small file.
MS-DOS	Microsoft's implementation of the Disc Operating System for PCs.
Multimedia	The use of photographs, music and sound and movie images in a presentation.
Multitasking	Performing more than one operation at the same time.
Network	Two or more computers connected together to share resources.
Network server	Central computer which stores files for several linked computers.

Node	Any single computer connected to a network.
ODBC	Open DataBase Connectivity - A standard protocol for accessing information in a SQL database server.
OLE	Object Linking and Embedding - A technology for transferring and sharing information among software applications.
Online	Having access to the Internet.
On-line Service	Services such as America On-line and CompuServe that provide content to subscribers and usually connections to the Internet.
Operating system	Software that runs a computer.
Page	An HTML document, or Web site.
Password	A unique character string used to gain access to a network, program, or mailbox.
PATH	The location of a file in the directory tree.
PCI	Peripheral Component Interconnect - a type of slot in your computer which accepts similar type peripheral cards.
Peripheral	Any device attached to a PC.
Perl	A popular language for programming CGI applications.
PIF file	Program information file - gives information to Windows about an MS-DOS application.
Pixel	A picture element on screen; the smallest element that can be

	independently assigned colour and intensity.
Plug-and-play	Hardware which can be plugged into a PC and be used immediately without configuration.
POP	Post Office Protocol - a method of storing and returning e-mail.
Port	The place where information goes into or out of a computer, e.g. a modem might be connected to the serial port.
Posix	The specification for a look-alike UNIX operating system drawn by the American National Standards Institute (ANSI). Linux is an independent Posix implementation.
PPP	Point-to-Point Protocol - One of two methods (see SLIP) for using special software to establish a temporary direct connection to the Internet over regular phone lines.
Print queue	A list of print jobs waiting to be sent to a printer.
Program	A set of instructions which cause a computer to perform tasks.
Protocol	A set of rules or standards that define how computers communicate with each other.
Query	The set of keywords and operators sent by a user to a search engine, or a database search request.
Queue	A list of e-mail messages waiting to be sent over the Internet.

RAM	Random Access Memory. The computer's volatile memory. Data held in it is lost when power is switched off.
Real mode	MS-DOS mode, typically used to run programs, such as MS-DOS games, that will not run under Windows.
Resource	A directory, or printer, that can be shared over a network.
Robot	A Web agent that visits sites, by requesting documents from them, for the purposes of indexing for search engines. Also known as Wanderers, Crawlers, or Spiders.
ROM	Read Only Memory. A PC's non-volatile memory. Data is written into this memory at manufacture and is not affected by power loss.
Scroll bar	A bar that appears at the right side or bottom edge of a window.
Search	Submit a query to a search engine.
Search engine	A program that helps users find information across the Internet.
Serial interface	An interface that transfers data as individual bits.
Server	A computer system that manages and delivers information for client computers.
Shared resource	Any device, program or file that is available to network users.
Shareware	Software that is available on public networks and bulletin boards. Users are expected to pay a nominal amount to the software developer.

Signature file	An ASCII text file, maintained within e-mail programs, that contains text for your signature.
Site	A place on the Internet. Every Web page has a location where it resides which is called its site.
SLIP	Serial Line Internet Protocol, a method of Internet connection that enables computers to use phone lines and a modem to connect to the Internet without having to connect to a host.
SMTP	Simple Mail Transfer Protocol - a protocol dictating how e-mail messages are exchanged over the Internet.
Socket	An endpoint for sending and receiving data between computers.
Software	The programs and instructions that control your PC.
Spamming	Sending the same message to a large number of mailing lists or newsgroups. Also to overload a Web page with excessive keywords in an attempt to get a better search ranking.
Spider	See robot.
Spooler	Software which handles transfer of information to a store to be used by a peripheral device.
SQL	Structured Query Language, used with relational databases.
SSL	Secure Sockets Layer, the standard transmission security protocol

	developed by Netscape, which has been put into the public domain.
Subscribe	To become a member of.
Surfing	The process of looking around the Internet.
SVGA	Super Video Graphics Array; it has all the VGA modes but with 256, or more, colours.
Swap file	An area of your hard disc used to store temporary operating files, also known as virtual memory.
Sysop	System Operator - A person responsible for the physical operations of a computer system or network resource.
System disc	A disc containing files to enable a PC to start up.
TCP/IP	Transmission Control Protocol/ Internet Protocol, combined protocols that perform the transfer of data between two computers. TCP monitors and ensures the correct transfer of data. IP receives the data, breaks it up into packets, and sends it to a network within the Internet.
Telnet	A program which allows people to remotely use computers across networks.
Text file	An unformatted file of text characters saved in ASCII format.
Thread	An ongoing message-based conversation on a single subject.
TIFF	Tag Image File Format - a popular graphic image file format.

Tool	Software program used to support Web site creation and management.
Toolbar	A bar containing icons giving quick access to commands.
Toggle	To turn an action on and off with the same switch.
TrueType fonts	Fonts that can be scaled to any size and print as they show on the screen.
UNIX	Multitasking, multi-user computer operating system that is run by many computer servers on networks.
Upload/Download	The process of transferring files between computers. Files are uploaded from your computer to another and downloaded from another computer to your own.
URL	Uniform Resource Locator, the addressing system used on the Web, containing information about the method of access, the server to be accessed and the path of the file to be accessed.
USB	Universal Serial Bus - an external bus standard that enables data transfer rates of 12 Mbps.
Usenet	Informal network of computers that allow the posting and reading of messages in newsgroups that focus on specific topics.
User ID	The unique identifier, usually used in conjunction with a password, which identifies you on a computer.
Virtual Reality	Simulations of real or imaginary worlds, rendered on a flat

	two-dimensional screen but appearing three-dimensional.
Virus	A malicious program, downloaded from a web site or disc, designed to wipe out information on your computer.
W3C	The World Wide Web Consortium that is steering standards development for the Web.
WAIS	Wide Area Information Server, a Net-wide system for looking up specific information in Internet databases.
WAV	Waveform Audio (.wav) - a common audio file format for DOS/Windows computers.
Web	A network of hypertext-based multimedia information servers. Browsers are used to view any information on the Web.
Web Page	An HTML document that is accessible on the Web.
Webmaster	One whose job it is to manage a web site.
WINSOCK	A Microsoft Windows file that provides the interface to TCP/IP services.
Wizard	A Microsoft tool that asks you questions and then creates an object depending on your answers.

Index

Companion Discs

COMPANION DISCS are available for most computer books written by the same author(s) and published by BERNARD BABANI (publishing) LTD, as listed at the front of this book (except for those marked with an asterisk). These books contain many pages of file/program listings.

There is no Companion Disc for this book.

To obtain companion discs for other books, fill in the order form below, or a copy of it, enclose a cheque (payable to **P.R.M. Oliver**) or a postal order, and send it to the address given below. **Make sure you fill in your name and address** and specify the book number and title in your order.

Book No.	Book Name	Unit Price	Total Price
BP		£3.50	
BP		£3.50	
BP		£3.50	
Name		Sub-total	£............
Address		P & P (@ 45p/disc)	£............
		Total Due	£............
Send to: P.R.M. Oliver, CSM, Pool, Redruth, Cornwall, TR15 3SE			

PLEASE NOTE

The author(s) are fully responsible for providing this Companion Disc service. The publishers of this book accept no responsibility for the supply, quality, or magnetic contents of the disc, or in respect of any damage, or injury that might be suffered or caused by its use.